WITHDRAWN
WRIGHT STATE UNIVERSITY LIBRARIES

T5-AFB-343

Higher Education across the Circumpolar North

Higher Education across the Circumpolar North
A Circle of Learning

Edited by

Douglas C. Nord
Professor of Political Science
Center for International Education
Wright State University
Ohio

and

Geoffrey R. Weller
Professor of International Studies
University of Northern British Columbia

LA
2277.5
.H55
2002

Editorial matter and selection © Douglas C. Nord and the estate of
Geoffrey R. Weller 2002
Chapters 1–11 © Palgrave Publishers Ltd 2002

All rights reserved. No reproduction, copy or transmission of this
publication may be made without written permission.

No paragraph of this publication may be reproduced, copied or
transmitted save with written permission or in accordance with the
provisions of the Copyright, Designs and Patents Act 1988, or under the
terms of any licence permitting limited copying issued by the Copyright
Licensing Agency, 90 Tottenham Court Road, London W1T 4LP.

Any person who does any unauthorised act in relation to this publication
may be liable to criminal prosecution and civil claims for damages.

The authors have asserted their rights to be identified as the authors of
this work in accordance with the Copyright, Designs and Patents Act
1988.

First published 2002 by
PALGRAVE MACMILLAN
Houndmills, Basingstoke, Hampshire RG21 6XS and
175 Fifth Avenue, New York, N. Y. 10010
Companies and representatives throughout the world

PALGRAVE MACMILLAN is the global academic imprint of the
palgrave Macmillan division of St. Martin's Press, LLC and of Palgrave
Macmillan Ltd. Macmillan® is a registered trademark in the United
States, United Kingdom and other countries. Palgrave is a registered
trademark in the European Union and other countries.

ISBN 0–333–91783–9

This book is printed on paper suitable for recycling and made from fully
managed and sustained forest sources.

A catalog record for this book is available from the Library of congress.

Library of Congress Cataloging-in-Publication Data

Higher education across the circumpolar north: a circle of learning /
edited by Douglas C. Nord and Geoffrey R. Weller.

    p. cm.
  Includes bibliographical references and index.
  ISBN 0–333–91783–9

    1. Universities and colleges—Arctic regions—Evaluation.
2. Education, Higher—Aims and objectives—Arctic regions.
I. Nord, Douglas C. (Douglas Charles), 1952- II. Weller, Geoffrey R.

LA2277.5 .H55 2002
378—dc21

                                  2001058086

10 9 8 7 6 5 4 3 2 1
11 10 09 08 07 06 05 04 03 02

Printed and bound in Great Britain by
Antony Rowe Ltd, Chippenham and Eastbourne

For Jean

Contents

Acknowledgements

Surprisingly, the inspiration for this book did not emerge from a snow-covered northern landscape. Instead, the idea developed from a brief spring visit to the central California coast in 1998. It arose from a conversation that four northern scholars (Kjell Lundmark, Doug Nord, Esko Riepula and Geoffrey Weller) had during the Northern Studies Section of the Western Regional Studies Association's meeting of that year. The four wondered aloud why so few residents and scholars of the North were conversant regarding the establishment of new universities in the region. In an effort to overcome this profound lack of awareness, it was decided to launch a comparative study of university development in the circumpolar north.

Geoffrey Weller and I contacted knowledgeable researchers from around the circumpolar north and asked them to investigate the growth of post-secondary institutions in the northern areas of their country or region. The two of us gratefully received nine contributions from scholars in Canada, the United States, the Nordic countries, Russia and Japan. We proceeded to craft these into the volume which follows. Geoff continued to help with the review and editing processes right up to his unexpected death in the summer of 2000. He was a true guiding light and inspiration for this project.

I took up the task of finishing the volume from that point. I have been sustained in the effort by the memory of Geoff's friendship. My thanks go as well to the authors of the various chapters of the book who gave me their encouragement and support as the volume made its slow progress from draft to final copy. Many thanks for your patience. I want to acknowledge, as well, the several members of the Circumpolar Universities Association who provided me with good counsel and advice throughout the course of this project.

My thanks go, as well, to Betty Jolie, who expertly typed the first drafts of the book, and to Ruth Willats, who helped with the final editing process.

Lastly, a special note of thanks goes Geoff's family and my own. Without their continued support and encouragement this project would never have been finished.

Douglas C. Nord
February 2002

List of Contributors

Shigeo Aramata is President of Kushiro Public University of Economics, Japan.

Peter Arbo is an Assistant Professor in the Department of Planning and Community Studies, University of Tromsø, Norway.

Ingi Runar Edvardsson is an Associate Professor in Management Studies at the University of Akureyri, Iceland.

Narve Fulsås is a Professor of History at the University of Tromsø, Norway.

Thorsteinn Gunnarsson is the Rector of the University of Akureyri, Iceland.

Diddy M. Hitchins is a Professor of Political Science and Director of the Canadian Studies Program at the University of Alaska, Anchorage, Alaska, USA.

Per Langgård is Prorector of the University of Greenland.

Kjell Lundmark is a Professor of Political Science at the University of Umeå, Sweden.

Douglas C. Nord is Professor of Political Science at Wright State University, USA. He was the Founding Dean of Management and Administration at The University of Northern British Columbia, Canada.

Esko Riepula is the Rector of the University of Lapland, Finland.

Nicolai Toivonen is Vice-Rector of Petrozavodsk State University, Republic of Karelia, Russia.

Victor Vasiliev is the Rector of Petrozavodsk State University, Republic of Karelia, Russia.

Geoffrey R. Weller was Professor of International Studies at the University of Northern British Columbia (UNBC), British Columbia, Canada. He was the Founding President and Vice-Chancellor of UNBC.

1
Introduction

Geoffrey R. Weller

The purpose of this book is to analyse the role of the new circumpolar universities in northern development. Many universities have been built in the circumpolar north since the end of the Second World War, most of them since 1960. This volume analyses and compares the reasons for their founding, the roles of each of them, their development and current status, the impact that they have had on access to education, and the impact that they have had on the economic, social, cultural and political development of their respective northern regions.

Since the end of the Second World War there has been an increase in interest in the circumpolar north. In part this has been because during the Cold War the circumpolar north became a major strategic area, as a consequence of which it became relatively heavily militarised. In part it has been because of the steady movement of industry and population northwards in a relentless search for natural resources. It has also been partly because since the end of the Cold War there has been increasing international cooperation among the nations of the circumpolar north as indicated by the formation of organisations such as the Arctic Council, the Barents Council and the Inuit Circumpolar Conference.

The circumpolar north is a term that developed because of the need for a concept that would encompass both the arctic and subarctic regions of the northern hemisphere. There is no truly common agreement on just what areas are included in the circumpolar north so it should be noted that this volume uses an essentially political definition of the region. That is, it includes those areas that the circumpolar northern states themselves define as northern. The circumpolar northern nations are here taken to be Finland, Sweden, Norway, Iceland, Greenland, Canada, the United States, Russia and Japan. The entire land area of Iceland and Greenland is within the circumpolar north. In Canada the north is taken

1

to be the three northern territories, the Yukon, the Northwest Territories and Nunavut, along with those parts of some provinces that those provinces themselves take to be northern and for which most have some kind of special administrative unit. Finland defines its northern region as the two northern provinces of Oulu and Lapland. Sweden defines its north as the five northern counties of Norbotten, Västerbotten, Jamtland, Västernorrland and Gävleborg. Norway defines its north as the three northern counties of Nordland, Troms and Finnmark. In the United States, Alaska is regarded as part of the circumpolar north. The Russian north is extensive and includes both the European north of Russia and Siberia. Hokkaido in Japan is not usually regarded as part of the circumpolar north because of its relatively southern location but it has many physical, human and economic characteristics that are similar to the subarctic parts of the circumpolar north and has numerous contact with the circumpolar northern region.

The land areas included in the circumpolar north are huge. Northern Russia covers some 10 million square kilometres, northern Canada about 7 million, Greenland 2.2 million, Alaska 1.5 million, northern Scandinavia 375,000 and Iceland 103,000. To put these figures in a comparative perspective, just the northern part of British Columbia, which is served by the University of Northern British Columbia, is roughly the size of France. There is a wide variation in the geology of the circumpolar north, however much of it is comprised of shield areas, namely the Canadian Shield in North America (Greenland being largely an extension of this) and the Baltic Shield and the Anaba Shield in Europe and Siberia. These formations are rich in minerals, which is a major reason for the northward movement of population in recent decades. However, such formations are not suitable for agriculture. The climate of the circumpolar north is very variable, with some of the coastal areas being surprisingly warm. By and large however the region has long cold winters and short cool summers.

The populations of the various parts of the circumpolar north are small and everywhere constitute only tiny percentages of the total of the various nations of which they are a part. Northern Russia and Hokkaido have about six million people each, northern Canada and northern Scandinavia approximately one million each, and Alaska about 340,000. Iceland has a population of just over 200,000 and Greenland a population of 50,000. Most of these populations are very variegated, both racially and ethnically. They are divided between indigenous and non-indigenous peoples, with the proportions varying considerably from one part of the circumpolar north to another. The indigenous peoples are made up of a very wide variety of different peoples, often with many peoples being represented in one country. The non-indigenous populations in northern North America and northern Russia are also very variegated ethnically. The population of the circumpolar north is mostly widely scattered in widely dispersed pockets with very few major cities to be found outside the Russian north and Hokkaido. Most of the non-indigenous peoples live at resource development sites or transportation hubs, and there is no widely spread population pattern the equivalent of an agricultural area. In some places the non-indigenous population is relatively transient, largely because of the boom-and-bust cycle of the resource sector. The indigenous population tends to be located in small – often very small – and relatively remote communities; some are still semi-nomadic.

In most parts of the circumpolar north two economies exist side by side. One of them is the resource economy of mining, forestry, hydro-electric power generation, and oil and gas exploration and development. Most of the larger cities and towns in the circumpolar north are associated with this economy, or with government services, as is most of the non-indigenous population. The other is the traditional economy of hunting, fishing, trapping and reindeer herding. This economy is associated with the smaller and more remote communities and the indigenous populations. The economy of the north is nowhere a fully integrated regional one and few places are very diversified economically as there is little manufacturing or agriculture in the circumpolar north. Transportation systems reveal the nature of the resource economy, namely that it is based upon extraction for use elsewhere, because they are good for bulk exports to southern centres, but are relatively poor for almost all other purposes.

Much of the politics of the circumpolar north is characterised by the activities of various groups with a sense of grievance and varying degrees of alienation. The non-indigenous populations often regard themselves and their hinterland regions as being exploited by their respective southern metropolitan centres with little thought being given by those centres to balanced economic development, the provision of services equivalent to those available in the south or proper environmental protection. The indigenous populations usually feel alienated for much the same reasons, but with the added political dimension of a desire for increased self-government.

Most of the universities that are located in the circumpolar north are of relatively recent origin. Only the University of Alaska, a few of the Siberian universities (notably Irkutsk State University) and a few on Hokkaido (notably Hokkaido University) were established before the

Second World War. The great majority of them are of post-war, and indeed post-1960, origin. The dates of their founding to some degree reflect the timing and location of population movements into the circumpolar north. The two basic reasons for establishing them were to accord northerners more equitable access to university education and to assist in the economic, social and cultural development of their respective regions. Some were located in the north as part and parcel of regional economic development plans; others came about as a consequence of much local pressure; and some as a combination of the two. Most of the circumpolar universities began as very small ones. However, some have grown to be quite large and to have had a significant impact on their regions. Those that have grown to be quite large, such as the University of Umeå and the University of Oulu, and to have had a large impact have often been the ones that have not remained dependent on their region's population from which to draw their students but have managed to draw students from southern regions to the north. Those that have grown larger and have had the most regional impact tend to be those established mainly for regional development purposes rather than those established mainly for regional access purposes. The former tended to have a wider range of programmes from the outset, including in some instances professional schools such as medicine, dentistry and engineering.

The wave of university building in the circumpolar north now seems to be over. This may well reflect that the economic future of the circumpolar north is increasingly uncertain. With the end of the Cold War its strategic importance has waned. With the steady decline in prices for natural resources the terms of trade are increasing unfavourable to resource development. Also resource development is constrained by the discovery of similar resources in less climatically severe regions closer to major markets, by environmental constraints on resource development, and the uncertainty created by the land and other claims made by the indigenous peoples around the circumpolar north. The economic situation in some parts of the circumpolar north has become severe and populations are static or declining, rapidly in some places, in absolute terms. The only new northern university now being contemplated is the University of the Arctic. This is intended to be a 'university without walls' operated cooperatively by all member nations of the Arctic Council and operating largely in the interests of the indigenous peoples of the circumpolar north. The Circumpolar Universities Association presented a proposal for a University of the Arctic to the Senior Arctic Officials (SAOs) at the meeting of the Arctic Council held in March 1997. This resulted in the creation of an ad hoc task force, which reported back to the Arctic Council in October of the same year. An Interim Council was established and planning is currently proceeding on proposals for a structure and governance system and for a course structure – in particular for a Bachelor of Circumpolar Studies. However, at the time of writing the likelihood of the actual establishment and operations of this new university is uncertain.

The core of the book consists of chapters that analyse the nature of the university or universities in several of the nations of the circumpolar north. In some nations there is only one university (Greenland and Iceland), in others there are two in the north (Finland and Sweden) and in others there are several in the north (Canada, Alaska, Russia and Japan). Each of the chapters covers much the same themes, thus enabling the reader to make comparisons between countries.

It should be noted that each of the authors has a detailed knowledge of their respective northern regions and of the universities within them. Five of the authors are, or have been, the vice-chancellors of one of the circumpolar universities. All the other authors have held senior positions within circumpolar universities and have had long familiarity with them. Also, all of the authors are, or have been, active and prominent in higher education and northern studies organisations and activities.

Each of the chapters provides the reader with some understanding of the particular northern region being discussed and how the nature of that region affects the university or universities located within it. The size of the region covered by the northern universities (or university) and the size and the nature of the population being served (e.g. ethnic or racial mix) are indicated. There is also a brief description of the nature of the regional economy and society, and some social status indicators are provided (e.g. education and health).

Each chapter provides the reader with a basic, and brief, understanding of the nature of the higher educational system and the place of the northern universities (or university) within that system. The level of government responsible for universities is indicated. The waves of university building over the centuries (where applicable) are noted, along with the place of the northern universities within those waves. The relative importance and reputation of the northern universities are then noted, by indicating their percentage of the total number of students enrolled nationally and by using other relevant statistics. The manner of the funding of universities is noted, particularly any special funding received by the northern universities.

Each chapter discusses the founding of the particular new university under consideration. The author indicates whether or not local pressure of state planning, or some combination of the two, was the primary reason for the establishment of the northern universities. The original objectives of the universities are described, in part by reference to the original mandates and missions. It is noted whether or not any particular national model (e.g. German, British or American) was followed. The original range of programmes, number of students, amount of research conducted and other such matters are detailed. The manner of the hiring of the initial faculty members and staff will also be described. So also will any special features of campus planning and campus construction. The authors note specific problems, such as whether or not the universities were expected to have a single campus or multiple sites throughout their region.

The longest section in each of the chapters is that on the impact of the universities. The authors were asked to place emphasis on four aspects of their impact: first, the impact on access to university education by northern residents; second, the impact on local and regional economic development; third, the impact on professional training, that is, on the availability of educated professionals such as doctors, dentists, nurses and social workers; and fourth, the impact on the social and cultural development of the region. In this connection the authors were asked to try to compare how the universities themselves regard their impact, and how the regional residents, regional groups and the government regard their impact.

Each author was also asked to have a clear conclusion to their chapter that would briefly assess whether or not the original expectations for the universites were met, that gave an assessment of the overall impact of the northern universities in their region and that mentioned what they thought the likely future was for the universities in their part of the circumpolar north. The final chapter is a comparative one which draws conclusions from the experiences of all of the circumpolar universities discussed in the book.

Reference

CUA (Circumpolar Universities Association) (1998) *With Shared Voices: Launching the University of the Arctic* (University of Lapland, Rovaniemi, Finland).

2
Universities in Northern Finland
Esko Riepula

Northern Finland

Northern Finland lies on the northern periphery of Europe, where the northernmost border of the European Union meets the northwestern edge of the Russian Federation. It is also the region where Finland shares a border with Norway and Sweden. Northern Finland comprises the country's two northernmost provinces of Lapland and Oulu, with a total area accounting for half of the entire country.

Characteristics of the region are its sparse population, long distances and natural conditions which are harsher than those found in the southern parts of the country. Thanks to the Gulf Stream, however, virtually the entire region supports agriculture. The population density is clearly lower than that in the rest of the country, and the population of 645,000 accounts for only 12.8 per cent of the national total.

Due to its considerable size, northern Finland itself is far from uniform in character. Vast in extent (100,000 square kilometres), but with a sparse population (two inhabitants per square kilometre), the province is on the periphery of a region that is itself peripheral. Similarly Kainuu, in the eastern part of the province of Oulu, is a peripheral area that is characterised by a sparsely populated area that is heavily dependent upon traditional forms of livelihood (agriculture, forestry and reindeer husbandry). Most of the large-scale industry in northern Finland is concentrated along the coast of the Gulf of Bothnia, in Oulu and the Kemi-Tornio district. Together with its Swedish counterpart, the Finnish coast forms what is called the Bothnian Crescent, a region that features the bulk of the industry to be found in the northern parts of the countries.

Northern Finland's diversity can be seen in the region's many robust local cultures. The most distinctive such culture in Lapland is that of the

7

Saami people, who also live in the northern parts of Norway, Sweden and Russia. The Saami in Finland number some 4,000–5,000. The Saami populations in Norway and Sweden are appreciably greater, while that of Russia is somewhat smaller.

Until the Second World War, northern Finland was an isolated region. The degree of economic integration was low and the area functioned largely as a source of raw material for the forest industry; the wood processing there was low. The livelihoods supported were principally based on the natural economy (agriculture and reindeer husbandry) and the bulk of the population lived in rural areas; urbanisation was low. The population of northern Finland grew steadily, but, with few jobs in industry, the region was unable to support everyone; the result was a wave of emigration to industrialised communities in southern Finland or, far more frequently, to the United States and Canada. Nearly 50,000 people emigrated to North America between 1870 and 1914 (Kero, 1974: 230–2).

During the Second World War, the situation in Lapland changed as some 200,000 German troops (transit troops) moved into the region for three years. While the war brought with it an internationalisation of sorts and stemmed emigration, the number of lives lost in the conflict was every bit as great as the earlier decline in population due to emigration. Compounding this loss was the destruction in 1944 by the retreating German troops of virtually all the buildings, transportation and communications in the region. For example, 90 per cent of the city of Rovaniemi and some 50 per cent of the province of Lapland was destroyed (Ursin, 1980: 383).

The period following the war brought sweeping changes to northern Finland with the rebuilding of Lapland and the increase in economic integration. Previously, little more than a store of raw materials for the forest industry, the north became an important national source of energy. Its large reserves of hydroelectric power were needed to rebuild industry lost in the war and to turn out the products required as part of the war reparations to the Soviet Union.

In fact, vigorous industrialisation began immediately after the war, a development that encompassed the construction not only of hydroelectric power stations but wood-processing, metallurgical and fertiliser plants. Transportation, communications and other regional infrastructure were improved at the same time. All in all, there was plenty of work to offer those returning to the region from the war. This intense development, coupled with a baby boom, led to rapid growth of the population of northern Finland, this increase being some 30 per cent of the entire region between 1945 and 1960 and even greater (35 per cent) in Lapland.

The population of Lapland increased through 1963, when it reached 212,000. At present the population is approximately 200,000.

By the time the baby boom age groups had grown up in the 1960s and 1970s the reconstruction of Lapland and the industrialisation projects in northern Finland had been largely completed. This, along with the rationalisation of agriculture and forestry which was taking place at the time, brought about a drastic change in the structure of the regional economy and sparked another wave of emigration, with Sweden the principal destination this time. Swedish industry needed large inputs of new labour and that is precisely what northern Finland had to offer.

A free labour market was created in the Nordic countries (Denmark, Sweden, Norway, Finland and Iceland) in 1954. Workers no longer had to have permits to take a job in another Nordic country. Initially, the free labour market did not bring about major changes in the mobility of labour, but the period between 1964 and 1975 saw a veritable rush from Finland to Sweden, with nearly half a million Finns seeking work there (Central Statistical Office, 1970–80). Almost half of this number (40 per cent) were from one of the country's three northernmost provinces (Lapland, Oulu and Vaasa), which meant nothing short of a population drain as far as northern Finland was concerned. Although some of those who emigrated returned in the late 1970s and in the 1980s, the wave of emigration has had a lasting effect on the population of the region.

This wave of emigration was followed by a period of steady economic development, which lasted through the early 1990s. Then, the country was hit by the worst recession since the 1930s. Northern Finland, too, has had a price to pay. While the economy has begun to recover, emigration has again accelerated, this time in the direction of the capital, Helsinki, and other economic centres in the southern part of the country.

Thus, in the twentieth century three waves of emigration affected the population in northern Finland: emigration to the United States in the early 1900s, emigration to Sweden in the 1960s and 1970s, and emigration to southern Finland in the late 1990s. Underlying all three waves was a dramatic social change in the structure of the regional economy and in the people's sources of livelihood. Outdated structures have proved unable to support an increasing population. Among the positive developments, one can cite the period of reconstruction following the Second World War and the high birth rate at that time, which persisted into the 1990s. On balance, in proportion to the population of the country as a whole, the population of northern Finland remained essentially the same throughout the twentieth century.

Today, northern Finland is fully integrated economically with the rest of Finland and the European Union. The Bothnian coast is a robust industrial area with growing electronics and communications industries alongside forestry and metal-working. In addition to the industrial coast, business life in the region is marked by a strong service sector, particularly in Lapland, where tourism is playing an increasingly significant role. Despite these burgeoning livelihoods, both primary production (agriculture, forestry and reindeer husbandry) and the public sector still occupy a crucial position in the economic life of the region. Because these sectors are the ones which are most seriously affected by structural change, the changes now sweeping the region have sparked emigration from sparsely populated regions to economic centres within northern Finland (Oulu and Rovaniemi) as well as to the capital region and the other centres in the south.

The economic recession at the beginning of the 1990s brought record unemployment to Finland, with nearly 20 per cent of the labour force out of work. The figure was even higher in the north. While unemployment has gradually declined nationally (it is currently [2001] 11 per cent), this positive development has been comparatively slow in northern Finland. The average unemployment rate in the region is still over 20 per cent, and even exceeds 30 per cent in some areas. At the same time, economic growth in the country as a whole has been very robust (over 6 per cent in 1997). People are abandoning the worst-hit areas and foresaking occupations in decline in favour of locations and jobs that promise growth, initiating a trend of uneven regional development in many ways.

In order to stem the decline, the Finnish government established a working group in 1997 which drafted long-term measures for developing northern Finland and for realising the potential of high-level know-how in the region. Part of the group's mission was to diversify the use of natural resources in the region and promote the implementation of high technology. The goal of these efforts is to direct the ongoing changes in livelihoods and business in northern Finland in a way that will reduce structural unemployment. The working group submitted its recommendations in 1998 (Northern Finland Working Group, 1998). Its proposals were based on increasing the know-how of people in the region through the development of research and education and of know-how and policy networks related to these activities. Clearly the region's universities, the University of Oulu and the University of Lapland, and its five polytechnics will have a crucial role to play in these developments.

The Finnish system of higher education

As recently as 1996, the Finnish system of higher education consisted solely of university-level instruction and research. That year marked the establishment of the first permanent polytechnics alongside the more traditional universities. The function of the polytechnics is to provide non-academic higher education.

Finland has twenty universities: ten are multidisciplinary; six comprise a single discipline (technology or business administration universities); and four are schools of the arts (music, theatre, industrial design and fine arts). Nearly half these institutions (eight) are located in and around Helsinki, with the remainder situated in nine different communities. Northern Finland is home to two of these universities, the University of Oulu and the University of Lapland. The latter is located in the city of Rovaniemi.

The development of the university system in Finland can be divided into three phases. The first period lasted from 1640 to the 1950s and can be referred to as old elitism. The second was the period of state control, which can be subdivided into two periods, the first from 1958 to 1970 and the second from 1974 to 1990. The third period, new elitism, extends from 1990 to the present.

During the period of old elitism, university teaching was strongly concentrated, first in Turku and then, in the 1800s, in Helsinki and, some 100 years later (at the beginning of the 1900s), in both. Finland's first university, the Academy of Turku, was founded upon the order of the Swedish ruler in 1640, primarily to provide education to public officials. The Academy operated in Turku until the Great Fire of 1812. As Finland had been annexed to Russia shortly before that date (1809), the university was not rebuilt in Turku but in Helsinki, where it would be closer to the Russian capital of St. Petersburg and further from Stockholm, the capital of the former ruling state. In Helsinki the university was called Emperor Alexander University until Finland declared its independence in 1917. Since that time it has been known as the University of Helsinki. In the first half of the twentieth century, a number of new Finnish- and Swedish-speaking universities were founded in Helsinki and Turku, and by the early 1950s a total of eight universities were operating in the two cities.

In addition to this regional concentration of universities, the old elitism was characterised by the fact that university students came from the upper social classes and that university graduates enjoyed very high social status. In this way, the social position of the universities remained high and they were highly respected. The universities largely educated senior civil servants, and their graduates held all the key positions in society. Above all, the societal function of the universities was to maintain and solidify what was a class-based social order.

As the industrial and economic structure of the country improved, pressure increased to extend higher education to other regions. Initiatives had been taken at the beginning of the 1900s to establish universities in both eastern and northern Finland, but to no avail. At the end of the 1950s, the efforts of the people in northern Finland finally bore fruit: the University of Oulu was founded in 1958 and began operating one year later. This marked the beginning of a state-controlled, decentralised, higher education policy which lasted throughout the next two decades.

The first phase of state-controlled higher education policy can be placed between the mid-1950s and the early 1970s, but it was at its strongest in the latter half of the 1960s. It was manifest in the founding of new universities in eastern and central Finland and in the vigorous legislative development of higher education and research through the reorganisation of the Finnish Academy and the Universities Development Act. The Act set quantitative goals for the year 1981 for the number of students who were to enter different fields of study as well as for the resources needed to cover the expanding activities. Significantly, the government and Parliament committed themselves in the legislation to a five-year plan to develop higher education by increasing the resources it required in the annual state budgets. Later, the law was extended, with a revision of its objectives and a number of its provisions ensuring resources for universities are, in fact, still in force today.

A variety of factors can be identified which underpinned this strong policy of development. First, knowledge and research were becoming increasingly important factors of production in society. The more far-sighted politicians perceived the importance of this more readily and more clearly than those within the universities. Second, international comparisons showed that, with its antiquated structure, Finland was falling behind other European countries in the development of higher education. Of particular significance were the Robbins Committee proposals for the development of the British university system. The Committee's suggestions sparked discussion and prompted comparisons concerning the extent of higher education in Finland, where it had not been the custom to deal with such issues in the political arena at all. Third, Finland needed university graduates not only to expand industry and production but also to administer the country's new systems of social services, which were being developed in health care, social security and education at the time. Through decisions at the state level, Finland was moulding itself into a modern welfare society whose public services urgently needed more academically trained labour. In fact, academic unemployment was unknown in Finland well into the late 1980s. Fourth, a university education, and the research that forms an integral part of it, were increasingly seen as a resource contributing to regional development. For this reason an expanded system of higher education was seen as part of a policy geared towards more stable regional development and one means for implementing this policy. Whereas under the old elitism universities sought to preserve and reinforce the social status quo, universities were now seen as ensuring social change and bringing about desired social and regional outcomes. They were pivotal institutions for building the welfare state, and their principal mission was to train staff for what was a continually expanding public sector.

The second period in the state control period occurred between 1974 and 1990, a time when the Finnish university system was expanded and rounded out to rectify shortcomings remaining after the first period. The regional significance of new facilities and new disciplines was stressed even more than before, a conviction fuelled by the positive experiences on record of a decentralised, regional network of universities.

In keeping with its aims, the state-controlled higher education policy effected a dramatic rise in the number of students at the end of the 1960s. However, this did not lead to large-scale admissions to university, because every discipline selected students using a grade-point system, and the new universities were established to accommodate the increasing cohorts of students. The increase in the number of students nationally led to a student body from more diverse social backgrounds and to a decline in the status of university students. Universities also came closer to society. People came to expect them to have an impact regionally and socially, and gradually the institutions began to see such an impact as a measure of their success.

The recession which hit at the beginning of the 1990s did not leave Finnish higher education unscathed. State budget cuts affected the universities every bit as much as they did other facets of public administration. Between 1993 and 1995 total expenditures for higher education were cut by 20 per cent relative to the 1992 levels. The cutbacks sent a wave of disquiet through the universities and prompted an assessment of existing structures and operations.

It was no surprise that the decentralised structure of higher education became a political target. The recession proved to be an opening for the forces which had opposed such a development from its inception and preferred to see higher education and research concentrated in the capital region and other large centres.

The economic difficulties led to a war of everyone against everyone else (*bellum omnium contra omnes*). However, when the national political leadership took a clear position in support of a decentralised, regional network of universities, cost efficiency was sought not by reducing the network but by the structural development of all the universities. This meant taking a closer look at the division of labour among the institutions, eliminating overlapping activities and running a tighter ship with more clearly defined objectives. The policy decisions did much to calm the situation, and the university system has been developed in keeping with these structural decisions in recent years.

However, the recession left deeper scars on Finnish academic and higher education policies. Under state control, voices could be heard – inspired by international trends – that called for a concentration of resources in units of excellence in research and for specialisation of universities in line with this expertise. Efforts were made to limit the universities' share of higher education by expanding the polytechnics and emphasising the universities' role in research over their role in education. Ideas like these even led people to speak – if not quite officially – of setting as the national goal for this policy the winning of a second Nobel science prize for Finland!

In order to ensure a more transparent and equitable funding, the university funding system has been revised and is now based on results, that is, the number of Masters and PhD degrees completed. The full impact of this system is yet to be seen, but it is the larger universities that have voiced the sharpest criticism so far, for they tend to emphasise research over education more than the smaller institutions do.

Since Finland joined the European Union at the beginning of 1995, the funding of regional development policy has taken place increasingly through EU structural funds. This opens wholly new opportunities for universities located in the target areas (northern and eastern Finland) accustomed as they are to collaborating with regional authorities in development work.

What we see, then, is a dual picture of the Finnish university system. On the one hand, it embraces large institutions, chiefly in and around the capital, which are oriented towards the elitist unit-of-excellence policy. On the other hand, it encompasses smaller and medium-sized universities – most of them outside the capital region – that strive to achieve a regional impact.

Like their predecessors under the old elitism, the proponents of the new elitism seek to restrict the social background and experience criteria of those admitted to the university system and, thereby, to enhance their social status. The goal is to make the universities once again the servants of the upper class, of those who wield the commercial and economic power. Under the new elitism, students, and the entire university, are principally interested in the economic gains to be made in commercial markets. They are no longer concerned with maintaining or strengthening the social order; and they are even less interested in bringing about social development more generally through measures that increase equality and improve social services, as was the case during the period of state control. On the other hand, one might anticipate that the forces of social change in Finland will come from the universities, which still place priority on regional and social impact and continue to follow the policies of the state-controlled period in their work.

It is difficult to speculate how strong a foothold the new elitism will ultimately gain in Finland. Ideologically, it has unmistakable connections to neoliberalist trends and new public management policy. The vitality of these ideas – which seem already to be fading – depends upon how far down the road of new elitism Finland goes.

Founding the northernmost universities in Finland

The founding of the University of Oulu

To the best of our knowledge, the first attempt to found the University of Oulu was made in 1905. The idea did not catch on at the time, but it was not forgotten either and came up from time to time throughout the early decades of the twentieth century. In fact, a university society was established in Oulu in 1919 to promote the cause of founding a university there (Julka, 1983: 14 and 36).

It was not until the 1950s, however, that the idea got as far as a state committee. In 1957, a bill calling for the founding of the University of Oulu was introduced by the government. The driving force was a powerful campaign-turned-popular movement in northern Finland calling for a university of its own. Yet, it was no easy matter to get the bill brought before Parliament and passed, for the plan was vigorously opposed by the existing universities at the time and by the people of southern Finland in general. Much of the bill's success can, in fact, be attributed to the fact that the Minister of Education (Saalasti) and President Kekkonen were both from northern Finland and personally supported the legislation. The University of Oulu Act was finally passed in May 1958. The founding of the University of Oulu owes much to regional initiative and lobbying, although the plan was ultimately carried out throught the state planning apparatus. Without efforts at the local level, the plan never would have got off the ground, nor would state bodies have carried it through without regional pressure.

The new university opened in 1959 in temporary facilities with a relatively small number of students. It was not until later that the university buildings were planned – a phase that took many years. In fact only now – four decades later – is the last phase of construction, which includes the main university building, being completed. Even without its own buildings, the university expanded rapidly and has operated in dozens of different locations around the city.

The original plans for the University of Oulu called for a far more modest institution than we see today. The university was to have concentrated on the exploitation of natural resources, peat land and forest research, construction technology and the social sciences. In the bill concerning the university, the Finnish government widened the scope of activity for the institution to: three Faculties – Philosophy, Technology and Medicine – the Research Institute for Northern Finland and a teacher training institute. Thus from the very outset, the university had a decided emphasis on basic and applied natural sciences.

The arguments in favour of founding the university centred on the need to improve social conditions in northern Finland. One of the most acute problems at the time was a shortage of doctors, but engineers, teachers and university graduates were also needed in increasing numbers. From the very beginning, the impact of the university was greatest in health care. In 1959 there was one doctor for every 1,450 people in Finland as a whole, but only one doctor for every 3,850 people in Oulu province and one for every 3,450 in Lapland. By 1995 the situation had changed fundamentally, with one doctor for every 324 people nationally and one doctor for every 310 people in Oulu province and for every 520 in Lapland (Rantakallio, 1996). Clearly, this would have been impossible without a university in the area. Along with its contribution to health care, the University of Oulu has had a significant impact on changing the structure of industry in northern Finland, in electronics and telecommunications in particular. Oulu has, in fact, become a national centre in these fields and employs an estimated 10,000 people regionally. The number of students has steadily increased from a few hundred in the early years to 12,000 by the early 1990s.

Despite strong support (bordering on a popular movement) at the beginning, local support for the university has been more in the form of material assistance and cooperation than financial. In Finland, where all universities are state-run, direct financial support at the local level is limited. In contrast, different forms of cooperation between universities and regional officials, as well as between the university and area business, is intensive indeed. The University of Oulu has been a forerunner in this respect and has had a significant impact on reshaping the structure of business in northern Finland. One indication of this is the amount of outside (non-state) funding the university was able to secure as project funding based on these cooperative relations. In 1996 the university had 164.5 million Finnmarks (US$29.9 million) in such funding, or 21.5 per cent of its total budget. Since the recession, all the universities in Finland have increased cooperation and networking. In addition to its ties with the University of Lapland, the University of Oulu has cooperative educational programmes with the Universities of Kuopio, Vaasa and Jyvaskyla.

With good reason one can say that the University of Oulu has exceeded even the most ambitious goals set for it when it was founded. When the positive regional impacts of Finnish universities are being discussed, the University of Oulu is often mentioned as a leading example. The university has had a substantial impact on social services (health care and education), and its Faculties of Technology and science have made a singular contribution to the creation of a new industrial infrastructure in the region. Crucial to the transfer of technology is the Science Park, established at the university in the 1980s. The Science Park has specialised in the transfer of technology both from the university to the region and between regions. At present, some 107 businesses operate in the Science Park, providing a total of 2,200 jobs.

The founding of the University of Lapland

Although the network of regional universities was comprehensive by the 1970s, pressure still existed to establish new institutions in Lapland, eastern Finland and Ostrobothnia. For example, Lapland had had a local university society as far back as the early 1960s whose aim was to establish first temporary, and later permanent, university-level education in the region.

Expanding welfare services meant increased educational provision throughout the country in law, social work, library sciences and other fields. In an effort to coordinate new projects nationally and address local pressures, the Ministry of Education set up a number of committees in 1974 to determine the need for new universities.

Drawing on the recommendations made in the committee reports, the Ministry set up a committee in 1997 to plan the first phase of the University of Lapland in Rovaniemi. No decision had been made on establishing a new university at that point, but the wording of the committee's responsibilities left no room for doubt: it was the Ministry's intention to establish a university in northern Finland and this was to be located in Rovaniemi. No other similar projects for other regions were being supported by the Ministry.

On the basis of the committee's work, the government presented a bill in the autumn of 1978, which was approved by Parliament in January 1979. The University of Lapland started up in March of that same year, with the first students being admitted the following autumn.

If anything, the struggle to establish a new university was even tougher than that which had taken place two decades earlier in Oulu. The ranks of the opponents included – and this was no surprise! – the leadership of the University of Oulu. In Lapland, as in Oulu, what made the difference was the initiative of local people and the direct links between the region and the decision-makers in high state positions, the government and the president. Just as the University of Oulu had its Minister of Education (Saalasti) from the Oulu constituency, Lapland had a minister (the Minister of Justice, Tuure Salo) who was, at the same time, mayor of the city of Rovaniemi. Clearly, Salo was in a position to expedite matters by appealing to the increasing need for trained lawyers.

The university began in rented premises in the autumn of its first year (1979) of operation, and over the next decade acquired a campus of its own. However, the university has grown faster than it can build and is still located on several sites in Rovaniemi. In addition, it has branches in Kemi and Kemijarvi.

With Oulu's focus on basic and applied research in the natural sciences and teaching in medicine and technology, it was natural that the University of Lapland should emphasise fields related to systems of social services which were not represented at the other institution. Since the Master's degree had become the basic qualification for school teachers, education – in particular teacher training – became one of the fields of study at the new university. With the increased need for legal training in the country, the university also became the site of the country's third Law Faculty. Later, in the 1980s, the Faculty of Social Sciences was established. From the outset to the present day its strength has been research and teaching in the field of social work. The same Faculty now includes degree programmes in business administration, public administration, sociology, international relations and tourism.

At the end of the 1980s, the academic base of the university was extended to the fine arts and industrial design with the establishment of what was, at that time, the second training unit in these fields in Finland. Another important addition to the university in the late 1980s was the Arctic Centre, a facility for research on nature, environment and societies in arctic and other northern areas and the site of information services and exhibitions related to that research. With the addition of the Arctic Centre, the scope of the university's work expanded beyond the social sciences to include the natural sciences and technology.

Regional development at the university has been channelled principally through its Continuing Education Centre, though nowadays the Faculties proper have made such work part of their core activities as well. At present the most significant form of cooperation in regional development is the university's participation in projects funded by European Union structural funds in collaboration with regional officials and businesses.

Just as the University of Oulu increased the number of doctors in northern Finland, so too the teacher training programme at the University of Lapland has increased the supply of teachers in Lapland. The university programmes have also had a direct impact on the availability of legal and social services in the region. Before the University of Lapland was founded, there was a shortage of school teachers in the province of Lapland, but this was quickly rectified as the university's graduates began to enter the local job market. In fact, by the beginning of the 1990s, the situation in Lapland – and in all of northern Finland – was better than elsewhere in the country (Toivonen, 1995). Developments where legal and social services are concerned followed essentially the same pattern. Previous shortages and deficiencies in these services have been overcome and the level of services now often surpasses that found in southern Finland.

The University of Lapland has not been able to address the needs of industry in the region to the same extent as the University of Oulu with its Faculty of Technology. However, it has made a significant contribution to regional development through its Continuing Education Centre (entrepreneurial training in particular) and its programmes of research and training in the industrial arts. Design and development projects at the university involving the new media, industrial design and industrial arts are one example of the direct channels through which the university works with and for the local business ccommunity. The concrete link in such activities is the Design Park, which spawned more than ten businesses in its first year of operation. Similar connections have been set up between research and education in tourism and regional enterprises. The Department of Tourism is part of the national network of know-how in the field, the goal of which is to produce innovations to benefit businesses at the practical level.

The number of students and teaching staff at the University of Lapland has increased steadily. Between 1979 and 1996 the number of students increased from 300 to over 3,000 and the number of teaching staff from a handful to 205. It differs in structure from the University of Oulu, where Faculties have large numbers of students and staff. Annual admissions at the University of Lapland to the various degree programmes are small, which means intense competition for the places available. Throughout its history, the university has in fact been one of the four most selective institutions in the country (and one of the top four in number of applicants per place available). This has also guaranteed a student body of high calibre.

Like other universities, the University of Lapland gets most of its funding through the state budget. Regional and local support and the need for external funding have become increasingly important, however. Municipalities and businesses in the region have to date donated three professorial chairs, this contribution being complemented by cooperation between the University of Lapland and the regional development authority – the regional government – which has been instrumental in implementing EU-funded projects. This external funding accounted for a full 35.9 per cent of the university budget in 1996.

The involvement of the university in regional development has contributed a great deal to the regional development programmes in Lapland which form the basis for projects funded through the EU. In this way the university has not only focused its efforts on key regional development programmes, but also has been the largest single recipient of the funding provided through the structural funds.

As a small university and the northernmost institution in the country, the University of Lapland has had to pay particular attention to its image and work especially hard to ensure its own development. The motto it has adopted is 'Northern Expert – International Educator'. Living up to this has meant active participation in developing the livelihoods and cultures of northern Finland as well as cooperation with the universities and research institutes of the circumpolar north. The university has also actively pursued the goal of making the northern dimension, as a Finnish national initiative, part of both the internal and foreign policy of the European Union.

Despite difficult economic times, it has been possible to develop the university steadily. The budget has been increased 10–20 per cent annually and has already surpassed that of many of the older institutions. The

University of Lapland and the University of Oulu maintain a permanent cooperative body, the Meri-Lappi Institute, a joint research and training facility located in Kemi. Networking with other universities nationally has taken place primarily in the fields of research and teaching in tourism and educational programmes in Russian competence.

On balance, the University of Lapland has also clearly exceeded the quantitative and qualitative goals set for it when it was founded. The original intention was to establish a small university in northern Finland for the social sciences, one which would round out what the University of Oulu had to offer. However, the University of Lapland has grown well beyond this original mission to become a versatile engine for research and development in the region.

The role of the northern universities in regional development in Finland

The social development of Northern Finland from the 1960s to the 1990s

As we have seen, through the 1950s northern Finland was poorly integrated in economic as well as cultural terms from both the national and the international point of view. There was a marked difference in the availability and quantity of business and social services between the northern and the southern parts of the country.

It is interesting to ponder how much social development contributed to the founding of the universities in northern Finland or, conversely, how much the founding of these institutions contributed to the social development of these regions. Clearly, one crucial force leading to the founding of the University of Oulu was an increased awareness that the northern regions were falling behind and that a university could contribute to eliminating this and other problems. By contrast, the central impetus behind the decision to establish the University of Lapland was a vision of the positive impact a university could have – in other words, a conscious effort to influence social development through the university.

The University of Oulu did not have time to affect the structural change which occurred in the 1960s and 1970s and which sparked the wave of emigration to Sweden. For the most part, those emigrating to Sweden were poorly educated and often unskilled. However, the university had a positive impact on the structural change of the 1990s, producing new, high-tech businesses and jobs in the region which have persuaded people to relocate in the Oulu region.

The situation of the University of Lapland today is much like that of the University of Oulu during the structural changes of the 1960s and 1970s. The University of Lapland has not had the time to influence the ongoing structural change in the region or the resultant emigration. However, the expansion of fields of study and endeavour at the university has helped keep population trends in Rovaniemi positive, although it has not achieved anything like the attraction of Oulu. Yet, if developments in Oulu are any guide, within a decade Rovaniemi will attract people with its strong service sector and advancements in computer applications.

The impact of social development on universities or of universities on social development is not a one-way affair, but reciprocal. A certain lag is involved: it takes time before the social need is felt for a particular activity and a research and education unit is set up at the university to address this need; it also takes time before this unit begins to have an appreciable impact on social development. The relationship between social development and higher education and research is thus dialectical; each draws strength from the other.

What do we mean by the impact of universities?

The impact of universities can be assessed from a number of perspectives depending on the purposes of the observer. One can speak of a direct and indirect, or an active and passive impact. Several direct impacts are apparent. There is the impact on education, which includes not only the impact of instruction but its implications for student recruitment and the number, quality, placement and employment of graduates. There is the impact on research, which can be assessed by looking at the significance of the research done at the university for its stakeholder groups and how this research can be utilised by them. There is the impact on adult education in terms of enhancing the productivity of this education. There is the impact on the transfer of knowledge and technology in terms of the reshaping of economic life in the region. Several indirect impacts are also evident. There is the economic impact in terms of the added value which the university, with its students and staff, contributes to the community in which it is located, as well as the scope for development made available to the university's stakeholders through this contribution. There is also an indirect cultural impact which consists of both the direct political participation of the members of the university community and the strengthening of regional identity engendered by the university. These then increase the political weight of the region in the national context. Another indirect impact is the increase in the internationalisation created by both faculty and student linkages beyond national boundaries.

The point of departure in assessing a university's impact is the institution's overall interaction with others. Such an assessment should consider the goals which the university has set for itself as well as any unanticipated views and expectations concerning the institution that arise from outside it.

Generally speaking, universities have reached a point where the traditional (classical) model of the university is evolving to one in which a university can be seen as an organisation of experts responding to changes in the environment. In practice, universities today attempt to strike a balance between their pursuing pure research and the desire to respond rapidly to changes in the world around them. The emphasis on application alongside – or even in preference to – basic research, the training of a new breed of experts (focused training) and the establishment of systems of funding to serve these ends all affect what a university produces and the impact it will have. Reproducing the scientific system under present circumstances is more demanding than ever, as universities must concern themselves with efficiency, productivity and economy while pursuing their basic mission.

The impact a university's activities have can be assessed from individual, institutional and societal points of view. All activities have either desirable or undesirable effects on an institution's environment; and these impacts may manifest themselves in very different ways over time, ranging from studies or degrees representing specific applications of knowledge to changes affecting the scientific paradigm.

In assessing the impact of the education provided by a university at the societal level, one must look not only at quantitative criteria but also at the applications which the graduates' knowledge and skills make possible and the graduates' ability to apply what they have learned; that is, their expertise.

The impact of research is even harder to capture using quantitative indicators. It is only the applicability of knowledge gained through research and the added value of applications which will result in research having an impact. The period of time over which this takes place may be long indeed. Rapid innovations in applied research can produce noticeable impacts very quickly; innovations in basic research, however, may not yield applications for a very long time, with demonstrable impacts not being seen until decades or perhaps even centuries later.

The economic and cultural impact of a university can be seen in the quantitative terms described above, or in terms of indirect or cumulative impacts; the institutional impact of a university manifests as various types of economic activity (e.g. restaurants and the activities in them) or as cultural processes, such as a heightened interest in the arts.

The social and cultural impacts of the universities in northern Finland

In the light of the above breakdown of impacts, the first thing to be said concerning the educational impact of the two universities is that both recruit their students primarily from northern Finland. In both institutions, half the students come from the province in which the university is located, a quarter are from the neighbouring province and the remainder from elsewhere in Finland or abroad. The recruitment profile of the two institutions is very similar, despite the differences in the fields of study they offer.

Clearly, without universities in their region, the opportunities for higher education available to people in northern Finland would be inferior to those enjoyed elsewhere in the country. This would also have a direct impact on the level of education in the region and, accordingly, on the structure of the economy and people's opportunities to earn a living. It is only with its universities that northern Finland can maintain its present position both nationally and internationally.

The picture is essentially the same if one looks at the placement of graduates in the region. Approximately half the graduates settle in the same province – 54.4 per cent for the University of Oulu and Oulu province and 49 per cent for the University of Lapland and Lapland province. Only the universities in the Helsinki region can boast a higher rate. Moreover, 17.8 per cent of the graduates of the University of Oulu settle in the neighbouring province of Lapland and 15 per cent of the graduates of the University of Lapland settle in the neighbouring province of Oulu. Employment for graduates has also been good, which is one indication of the educational impact of the universities.

As far as the impact of research is concerned, the conclusions are not as straightforward, except in the case of applied technological research and product development. Telecommunications technology and industrial design have been the principal fields where university-level research and development have yielded direct benefits for businesses in the region.

Both academic and non-academic adult education has been organised at both institutions through continuing education centres. In relation to the university operations overall, this activity has been more extensive at the University of Lapland, where the number of students taking part in adult education through the Open University and the Continuing Education Centre (7,000) is more than double the number of degree students proper (3,000).

The transfer of knowledge and technology and the consequent reshaping of livelihoods in the region have taken place at both universities through their science parks (The Technology Village in Oulu and the Design Park in Lapland).

As far as indirect impacts are concerned, it is the local impact of the universities which has been the most significant. It has been estimated that every full-time position at either university ultimately creates 2.5 jobs in the local community. Accordingly, the University of Oulu has generated 10,000 jobs locally and the University of Lapland 1,250.

Cultural and political impacts are naturally harder to assess in precise terms. Both universities have played a crucial role in strengthening regional identity. Their work has created a foundation for, and done much to promote, the building of a more equitable society regionally. In Oulu especially, the success of the university has clearly enhanced the weight of the region in national decision-making.

Traditionally, universities have been the first forces of internationalisation in their regions, and this has certainly been the case in northern Finland as well, although Lapland has always been far more international than Oulu owing to its traditions of tourism and cooperation with the other Nordic countries. The work of both universities has done much to boost internationalisation in their respective regions, attracting more international students and staff to these areas and, with them, new cultural features.

In 1989, at the First Circumpolar Universities Cooperation Conference, at Lakehead University in Thunder Bay, Ontario, I had the occasion to provide the following assessment of the impact of the two universities:

> Thanks to its universities, northern Finland, which once had the poorest public services in the country, can boast of the best teacher situation, while other public services (health care, social services, legal services) are at least on a par with those in southern Finland. The development of an academic work force in northern Finland has been considerably faster than in the rest of the country.
>
> (Riepula, 1991: 15)

Since that time the impact of the universities on society has been channelled more distinctly through the private sector. Their mission remains that of ensuring a high-level system of public services in their regions by training teachers, doctors, social workers, lawyers and administrative professionals; however, they increasingly endeavour through research and education to produce knowledge, which, refined into innovations, can provide the foundation for new business activities.

Conclusion

Knowledge has become an increasingly important factor of production in all developed societies. The economy of such societies is based above all on knowledge. Only regions which can themselves produce and process relevant information and knowledge have any hope of succeeding in global competition. That is precisely why northern Finland needs its universities.

References

Central Statistical Office (1970–80) *Statistical Yearbook of Finland* (Helsinki).

Julka, Liisa ja Kyosti (1983) *Oulun yliopiston perustamisen historia [The Founding of the University of Oulu]* (Rovaniemi: Historical Association of Northern Finland).

Kero, Reino (1974) *Migration from Finland to North America in the Years between the United States Civil War and the First World War* (Turku: The Institute of Migration, University of Turku).

Northern Finland Working Group (1998) *The Strategy for Northern Finland* (Oulu).

Rantakaillo, Paula (1996) *Mita on syntya Pohjois-Suomeen [What it is to be Born in Northern Finland]* (Acta Universitatis Ouliensis F6).

Riepula, Esko (1991) 'The Impact of Universities on the Economic and Social Development of Northern Finland', pp. 13–17 in Lakehead Centre for Northern Studies, *The Role of Circumpolar Universities in Northern Development* (Thunder Bay: Lakehead University Centre for Northern Studies).

Toivonen, Klaus (1995) *Lapin yliopisten yhteiskunnallinen vaikuttavuus [Social Impact of the University of Lapland]* (University of Lapland Newsletter, KIDE 5).

Ursin, Martti (1980) *Pohjois-Suomen tuhot ja jalleenrakennus saksalaissodan 1944–1945 jalkeen [The Reconstruction of Northern Finland after the German War 1944–1945]* (Rovaniemi: The Historical Association of Northern Finland).

3
The University of Umeå – The University of Northern Sweden
Kjell Lundmark

Introduction

In government reports as well as in weather forecasts the northern part of Sweden is commonly referred to as Norrland. Norrland has always been seen as something a bit different from the rest of Sweden. It differs from the southern regions of the country with respect to its ecology, economy, politics and culture. Even though many of these differences can be ascribed to popular stereotypes, facts and figures still paint a distinctive portrait. To start with there is the size of the area. Norrland covers almost 60 per cent of the total land area of Sweden, but within this vast domain, there are few people – just 13 per cent of the total Swedish population. The climate is also somewhat distinctive and challenging. It has short, cool summers and long, dark winters. It represents in the minds of most Swedes a remote and harsh land. It also has the reputation of being a frontier area in terms of its economic and social development. Historically, it was settled later than other parts of the country. It has traditionally had a natural resource-based economy. It has confronted a number of social and economic problems associated with its peripheral status. It is within this distinctive context that post-secondary education has emerged in northern Sweden.

The tale of post-secondary education in Norrland is closely linked to the story of the development of the University of Umeå. This institution of higher education was founded in September 1965. Its establishment represented the end of a twenty-year struggle to create a university in northern Sweden. The Swedish government's decision to establish a new research university in Umeå finally gave this under-served region of the country a share in the nation's higher educational system.

The provision of higher education could be seen by Swedes of the day as a goal in itself. There has always been a strong faith in the inherent value of advanced education and the desirability of having it distributed throughout the country. Yet there were other, more regionally-specific aspirations that were highlighted in the founding of the University of Umeå. It was fervently believed that the youth of the north could now have access to higher education in their own region. Hopefully this would stem the steady migration of young northerners from the area. The north could educate and provide professionals and specialists for Norrland, a region long-plagued by insufficient numbers of highly educated people. It was also hoped that the new university would contribute to economic growth and social development in a peripheral region.

Thirty-five years after the official inauguration of the University of Umeå, most observers seem to agree that the establishment of the university in the northern portion of Sweden has been an overall success. However, success can takes many forms – with several twists and turns. In this chapter the development of the University of Umeå is described, starting with the regional setting of this university of northern Sweden. This is followed by a thumbnail sketch of the overall higher education system in Sweden. The establishment and development of a university in the north can be seen as an integral part of the restructuring of the higher education system in Sweden that began in the 1960s. The focus of the chapter then shifts to the specific story of the creation of the University of Umeå. What were the goals, and what were the national and local aspirations? How did this project evolve? What were its short-term consequences? This discussion is followed by an examination of the University of Umeå's longer-term impact at both a national and a regional level. Special consideration is given to the interaction between Swedish regional policy and the evolution of higher education policy in the country. The chapter concludes with a more general discussion of how the development of the University of Umeå has had a distinct impact on its surrounding community and region.

The context: northern Sweden

From the era of its industrialisation in the late nineteenth century, Norrland has traditionally been a raw material-producing region. It has had an economy based on agriculture, forestry and mining. The continued rapid exploitation of its natural resource base in the twentieth century meant an initial economic burst of activity followed by a worrying rural decline. In the period between 1940 and 1970, Norrland had a net out-migration of some 200,000. At the same time, within Norrland, there was a movement of people from the inland areas to the coastal cities, with a steady decline of the smaller inland settlements (Näslund and Persson, 1972; Johansson, 1989; Oscarsson, 1989).

During the first half of the twentieth century, the economic and social challenges facing the region were quite severe. By almost any measure, Norrland was an underdeveloped and underprivileged region in comparison to the rest of Sweden. Its communication and transportation networks were backward. Much of its housing stock was substandard. Employment opportunities were limited. Access to health, education and other social services were limited. The general social welfare of the society compared unfavourably with that which existed in the southern regions of the country. This condition continued well into the post-war era.

While the rest of Sweden experienced a period of prolonged economic growth in the 1950s and 1960s, this national prosperity had only a marginal impact on Norrland. During the first half of the 1960s, 20,000 jobs – out of a total of some 81,000 – were lost in its agricultural and forestry sectors (Näslund and Persson, 1972). During 1965–70, employment decreased by more than 15 per cent in a third of the municipalities of the region (ibid.). At the same time, there was further out-migration from the inland resource and agricultural communities to the coastal cities draining the inland areas of even more people.

In the first half of the 1970s, this pattern of regional decline subsided and out-migration from Norrland to the south of Sweden ceased. There was a small growth in the region's population, however this was heavily concentrated in the coastal cities. The rural, inland communities continued to suffer from loss of jobs and people. Unemployment rates in Norrland were still substantially higher than those in the rest of the country.

In the period between 1975 and 1980 there were dramatic dislocations in Sweden's forestry and steel industries caused by an energy crisis. Employment in these industries was down as much as 8 per cent for the country as a whole (SOU, 1984: 74). The counties of Norrland too experienced the negative consequences of this economic downturn. Their large, natural resource-based economies were again imperilled.

The 1980s witnessed a return to economic prosperity in the major growth areas of the country. These regions are well to the south of Norrland. They include the Stockholm metropolitan region in central Sweden and the southern corridor between Gothenburg and Malmö. In Norrland, the main coastal cities grew somewhat during the 1980s. However, the inland communities continued to suffer from economic decline and out-migration. One third of the municipalities in Norrland experienced population declines of more than 30 per cent between 1960 and 1990.

In the early 1990s, the whole country experienced a period of severe economic recession. The nation faced unemployment rates that had only previously been seen in the north. The region of Norrland was also buffeted by the hard economic times. The north once again faced population losses. The drainage of people from the inland communities to the coastal cities accelerated. The only real growth-pole in the region throughout the decade was the city of Umeå. The university town of Norrland was beginning to follow a general pattern seen elsewhere in Sweden where steady population growth was taking place in the university towns of Uppsala, Lund and Linköping.

Population Figures in Cities in the North of Sweden

	1965	1970	1975	1980	1985	1990	1995	1999
Umeå	61,296	67,799	73,977	79,930	84,192	90,004	99,249	103,912
Sundsvall	85,883	89,853	93,368	94,358	93,569	93,404	94,815	93,509
Skellefteå	71,818	71,827	72,120	73,647	74,329	74,720	75,822	73,020
Luleå	52,306	57,838	64,322	67,190	66,811	67,903	70,694	71,305
ÖrnskÖldsvik	60,700	60,495	60,152	60,665	59,918	59,225	58,663	56,211
Östersund	42,931	48,918	53,252	55,440	56,407	57,733	59,730	58,431
Students at Umeå University	1,801	7,049	5,894	7,137	10,066	11,995	22,085	24,131

Part of the continuing development problem faced by Norrland has been the predominance of its natural resource-based economy. Much of the initial economic growth – and subsequent decline of the region – can be associated with the changing fortunes of the timber, hydroelectric and mining industries. Frequently referred to as the 'forest counties', Norrland continues even today to be the home of major wood products and pulp and paper industries. Other types of industrial enterprises – including metal, machinery and automobile production – have tended to come late to the region and have been concentrated in its coastal cities. Of the top twenty-five industrial municipalities found in Sweden today, only four can be found in Norrland.

In recent years, there has been a steady growth in the service and public sectors of the region's economy. None the less, unemployment levels remain high in the area and there is a concern that jobs in the new industries of the technological age may pass by the region if insufficient resources are devoted to job training and advanced education. In such a context, the establishment of a major university is seen as a significant contribution to the future economic diversification of the region.

The higher education system in Sweden

The higher education system in Sweden was, until the beginning of the 1960s, a highly elitist system. In 1955, only 3.7 students per 1,000 inhabitants enrolled in the Swedish higher education system. This was in marked contrast to the more inclusive systems of the United States and Canada which reported figures of 16.2 and 6.4 respectively (Lane, 1983). At that time, there were only four universities in the country: Uppsala, Lund, Stockholm and Gothenburg. They were organised in a tight, centralised system reporting to the government and educational bureaucracy in Stockholm. Below the government itself there was an Office of the Chancellor of the Universities, which had been established in 1852. The Office oversaw the various activities of the four universities and helped to coordinate funding and planning for the national system. This organisational structure remained unchanged for many years. During the 1950s and 1960s some minor reforms were made focusing on new directions in higher education. However, it was not until the 1970s, following a major restructuring of the primary, secondary and high school systems of the country, that it was decided that the Swedish university system required a radical transformation.

The period of the 1960s and 1970s witnessed a sharp increase in the number of students desiring admittance to Swedish post-secondary schools. Responding to this demand, the Swedish government created a number of new universities and university colleges. It also brought forward a series of higher education reforms which restructured the old system in many ways. These reforms introduced a broader concept of higher education, a change in the rules governing student access to the system and, not the least significant, a distinctive regional dimension to the planning of the higher education system.

The guiding idea behind these reforms was the belief that there should be an inclusive national education policy. It would direct the flow of educational services from the primary schools to higher education institutions. It was believed that the education system should be planned in its totality and aimed at broadening the overall development goals of the society. These general goals were expressed in grand terms such as democracy, equality, growth, efficiency and freedom of choice. The importance of linking education to the overall needs of the labour market was also noted.

Given the broad agenda of this reform message, a distinct regional feature of these proposals soon emerged. It was clear from the outset that if the Swedish higher education system desired coherent results across the entire nation, a level of regional planning would be required. This meant the establishment of a decentralised system where the activities of the various higher education institutions could be adjusted to reflect each region's industrial structure and labour market needs. The existing imbalances in regional access to higher education and in labour market demand could be cured by a planned higher education system. Higher education would in the future be planned and distributed in a more equitable way so that different social groups, different regions and different forms of delivery systems would be represented.

Under the new system which emerged in Sweden in the late 1970s, the country was to be divided into six higher education regions. Each of these was to be governed by a regional educational board. This board was to be composed of representatives from the universities and professional schools within the region as well as public members appointed by the government.

The board had three goals. Its first was to broaden and differentiate the range of higher education options in the region. The second goal was to increase access to higher education – especially for non-traditional student groups. Finally, the board sought to develop higher education opportunities as a means to meet the needs of the labour market and to provide support for the renewal of business in the region.

One of the six higher education regions that was created in the late 1970s was for the northern region of the country. It was named the Umeå Higher Education Region. This region covered the four northernmost counties of the country. Through this action, northern Sweden was recognised as being on equal terms with the rest of Sweden. With the establishment of the University of Umeå in 1965, Norrland could claim to be the home of the newest university in the country.

Within the Norrland region, three other state higher education units were also established. Since 1971, there was the Institute of Technology in the City of Luleå, some 300 kilometres north of Umeå. Since 1970 and 1971, respectively, there were also more limited schools of higher education in Sundsvall/Härnösand and in Östersund. The unit in Sundsvall/Härnösand started as a decentralised university training site mainly rooted in the old teacher training school. Begining with some 600 students in 1970, its student population grew to number over 1,000 students some six years later. The unit in Östersund started in 1971 as a school for social work which enrolled some

60 students. Over the course of the next six years, it student numbers rose to 1,000.

Northern Sweden, so long lacking institutions of higher education, had secured by the mid-1970s not only the University of Umeå, but also post-secondary schools in the cities of Luleå, Sundsvall, Härnösand and Öster-sund. Other cities in Norrland also expressed their interest in participating in this higher education expansion. Government efforts to address problems of access and appropriate labour market development were paying substantial regional development dividends. Local community leaders began to view post-secondary education as providing a fast track for community economic diversification. Many wanted their piece of the post-secondary education bonanza.

Such sentiments could have easily come together as a threat to the development path of the major institution of the region – the University of Umeå. In this huge but sparsely populated Norrland one could now suddenly see as many places with permanent resources for higher education as one could see in other parts of Sweden. Why should the government invest further resources? From the Umeå perspective, maintaining influence over the northern regional higher education board in the north was one way to control how this new landscape of many higher education institutions in Norrland should develop.

A clear threat to the development of the University of Umeå was if the other northern institutions and cities should go to Stockholm and lobby for their individual needs. Having a regional, coordinating board might inhibit this somewhat. This idea of a regional board actually emanated from Umeå. Scholars from that university had been the architects who designed the system of a regional level of planning between the Office of the Chancellor of the Universities and the several Swedish universities and institutions of higher education. Responding to the Commission of Inquiry on Higher Education of 1968, the administration of the University of Umeå had argued for more coordination in the planning of higher education in the country – especially in Norrland. Although they clad their general arguments for coordination in the rhetoric of efficiency and accountability, pure institutional self-interest was operative as well.

After ten years of operation this system of six higher education regions gradually dissolved. In 1988 the regional educational boards were abandoned. Four years later, the National Agency for Universities and Colleges was reorganised into three smaller units. The new non-socialist government, which came into office in 1992, launched a new reform of the higher education system. Universities and other post-secondary education institutions would now have their independence restored. The rather rigorous and planned system of higher education that had emerged in the late 1970s was largely abandoned. Some institutions were actually removed from direct government control. Defunct wage-earners funds were used to finance these 'privatised' institutions. This decentralising wave also carried with it various elements of marketplace-inspired promotion and development activities. Every Swedish university or university college was to chart its own course. The University of Umeå and the other institutions in Norrland now had to prove their merits in direct competition with the old established universities in the south. They also had to face challenges from a class of 'new' universities established in the final years of the twentieth century.

A university of the north

The creation of the University of Umeå in 1965 was emblematic of the dramatic changes sweeping through higher education in Sweden during that era. The 1960s and 1970s saw the traditional higher education goals of achievement and efficiency being downgraded somewhat. In their place, broader social goals now guided politicians and policy-makers. Increasing numbers of students were demanding entrance into the Swedish universities. Their demands for equal access to post-secondary education inspired other groups – including regional representatives – to state their case for greater geographic democracy. Their call for a university in the north was based upon a long-perceived sense of regional injustice.

As early as the 1930s, the Swedish government had undertaken an inquiry into the nature of social and economic disparities in the north of the country. This 'Norrland Inquiry' had attributed some of the region's disadvantages to its inability to secure various professional services – especially in the areas of health and education. In addition to having an ailing, natural resource-based economy, Norrland lacked doctors, dentists and teachers. It had become an urgent task to bring such professionals to the region. But from where could such individuals be recruited? Would it not be better to train such professionals in new higher education institutions in Norrland?

Discussion of the creation of a new university in the north of Sweden was well underway at the national level by the mid-1950s. Given the complete lack of higher education institutions in Norrland, the people of the region could make a strong case that the north of Sweden deserved a new university. The government soon became the target of many local lobbyists from the north who argued that their individual communities were the logical sites for such a university.

In 1955, the Swedish government appointed a university commission to investigate the future of the entire higher education system. Cognisant of a predicted explosive increase in the number of students applying for entry to national universities, the commission considered a variety of ways of expanding access. Among other means, the commission was to inquire into the conditions for creating a new university in Norrland. Unfortunately for the people of the north, the commission's final report was a disappointment. Expansion should, according to the commission, take place within the traditional structures. In reality, that meant existing universities in the south should grow.

However, other initiatives in Norrland had already been successful. These earlier initiatives had laid the foundation for the creation of the University of Umeå. As early as 1951, the Swedish government had decided to establish a large depository library in the capital of Västerbotten. It was to receive all books and documents published in the country. This action was followed by the creation of a dental school in Umeå in 1956. Three years later, a new medical school was established. These three important decisions paved way for the creation of a university in Umeå a decade later.

As noted above, the 'Norrland Inquiry' had called for an improvement in the health and educational services that were available in the north of the country. The establishment of the new university and the associated medical and teacher training schools represented clear progress towards such goals. Very quickly, the doctors, dentists and teachers who were educated in Umeå began to serve the Norrland community. By the mid-1980s more than 70 per cent of the dentists working in the northern provinces of Sweden had received their education at the University in Umeå.

Many of the major arguments supporting the creation of a university in Norrland were based on the broad principles of justice and equity. The north ought to have the same right of access to higher education that was already enjoyed in southern Sweden. Equally persuasive were the promised improvements in health care, education and community welfare that would accompany investment in higher education in the region. There were also arguments in favour of the creation of a university which emphasised its creative role in stimulating a local and regional profile and identity. The argument was made that a university in the north could serve as a source of 'energy' for the intellectual life in northern Sweden. In still broader terms it was argued that the university could play a role in preserving and stimulating local cultures of the region. In other words, the university could have a special regional or local profile that would be reflected in its teaching, research and service roles. These arguments combined to suggest that the University of Umeå should be a 'different university'. It should always reflect its regional setting.

During the 1950s, the other cities in Norrland competed fiercely to become the location of the new university in the north. Although the central authorities in Stockholm tried to argue that the units of higher education already established in Umeå would in no way unfairly influence the final siting of the new university, their mere existence implied more higher education would come to the Västerbotten capital. As the need to expand access to the higher education system accelerated in the 1960s, economy of scale factors increasingly dictated that Umeå be the site for most of these endeavours.

As this short history suggests, however, the creation of the University of Umeå in 1965 was not simply the successful implementation of a single coherent plan for higher education in the north of Sweden. The University of Umeå was developed gradually, in a series of stops and starts. One observer has suggested that its growth took place in accordance with 'a snowball or avalanche-like principle' (Lane, 1983). Once one decision was taken to commit resources to its growth, others soon followed. Investments in buildings and staff followed close upon each other.

Once the new university had been inaugurated in 1965 it, as well as the city of Umeå, had to address and react to new challenges. The first of these was to deal with the rapid expansion of student numbers in the late 1960s – followed by their rapid decline in the 1970s. In 1965, the student enrolment at the new University of Umeå was around 2,000. Over the next five years the institution more than tripled this figure, growing at a much faster rate than the older, more established universities in the south of Sweden. Such rapid growth put tremendous pressure on both the university and the surrounding community, which was not used to having such a significant student population in its midst. Demands for housing, transportation and social services were voiced in Umeå, causing some alarm on the part of long-term residents. On a more positive note, such agitation also resulted in greater investment in the community by both the public and private sectors. The university, and its students and staff, were becoming important contributors to the social and economic growth of the community. This reality became all the more apparent in the mid-1970s when student enrolments dropped in response to declining economic and demographic factors.

The 1970s became a period of consolidation and continuing challenges for the new university. During much of this period enrolment figures did not increase significantly. Nor did faculty and staff numbers grow appreciably. After the flurry of excitement associated with the opening of the new institution, more careful consideration was given to how the institution might live up to all the expectations placed upon it.

Swedish regional policy also went into a new phase, beginning in the 1970s. The 1960s had witnessed a regional policy focused on the concept of modernisation. The regional policy of the 1970s became more interested in the ideas of structure and planning. From this latter perspective, the public sector itself was introduced as an important actor in development strategies. Public investments could promote growth and create jobs throughout the country – especially in economically depressed regions such as Norrland.

The new regional policy was also grounded in the growth-pole theory. It stressed the spontaneous development of industry, the concentration of expanding branch plants and the focusing of administration in metropolitan regions. This policy had a number of implications for the Swedish higher education system as well. Higher education resources could be used to stimulate innovation and development. Within a planned growth-pole structure, higher education institutions could serve as an important factor determining the development of industrial life. The creation of the Institute of Technology in Luleå, in 1971, can be seen in this perspective. This was followed by other reforms to the Swedish system of higher education that resulted in other major cities in Norrland receiving higher education institutions as well. As noted earlier, in 1970 a School of Higher Education was set up in Härnösand/Sundsvall and in 1971 a School of Social Work was established in Östersund. It was firmly believed that by delivering such higher education resources to the region, economic and social development would be stimulated in specific fields.

Part of the initial growth-phase for the University of Umeå during the late 1960s can be ascribed to the general expansion of the higher education system in Sweden. However, its potential contribution to the regional development of the area was always in the forefront of the minds of government planners. In 1968, almost nine out of ten students enrolling at the University of had Umeå their origins in Norrland. This figure gradually changed so that by the mid-1970s almost one in five students enrolling came from outside Norrland. Yet the 'local' presence became even more apparent. In the late 1960s as many as one in six students enrolling in the institution came from the city of Umeå. That figure continued to hold even during the declining enrollment years of the 1970s.

The University of Umeå attempted to meet the declining student numbers of the 1970s with a policy of diversification. This meant broadening the number of courses offered, opening up new research and education centres and engaging in distance education. The university's goal was to keep as much as possible of the day-to-day administrative and research operations in Umeå. However, certain teaching and extramural activities were to take place in other cities in Norrland. The key to the university's regional outreach was its distance learning initiatives. By 1975 the University of Umeå had almost 40 per cent of its students enrolled in the distance learning system throughout Sweden (Holm and Wiberg, 1995).

The 1980s witnessed some recovery in student numbers. The growth was not impressive though, and there were some years when the number of students actually declined. This challenge was met with additional distance education and other outreach programmes. Working with a number of inland communities in Norrland, for example, the university, launched a special project aimed at creating local study centres in smaller towns and villages. This special access project was funded by the Swedish Ministry of Industry from 1987 to 1993.

The 1990s saw student numbers at the University of Umeå grow rapidly once again. From around 10,000 students in 1990, the university now numbers its enrolment at more than 25,000. The university is also acquiring its own share of externally funded research. In this regard it compares favourably with the older, established universities in the south. Its faculty and researchers publish widely and have earned international reputations. The university in the north has grown, matured and at last been able to discard its old soubriquet of 'The Academy in the Big Forest'.

Town and gown

As noted above, national policy-makers frequently set 'regional' development goals for the new university in Norrland. None the less, much of the actual impact of the University of Umeå experienced in its first few decades of operation was at the 'local' level. The primary beneficiary has been the city of Umeå. In Norrland as a whole, the coastal cities have grown somewhat over the last decade, but the inland communities are still suffering from out-migration. The city of Umeå has led in population growth in all of Norrland during the 1990s. No one disputes the important role the university has played in facilitating this population growth.

Population figures for the past few decades clearly reflect the rapid growth that the city of Umeå has experienced since the establishment of the university. From the beginning of the 1960s, the city has grown from a fairly small town of some 50,000 inhabitants to become the 'Capital of the North' with a population of more than 100,000 at the start of the new millennium. The city has not simply grown; it has become a 'young' city as well. The average age in Umeå is now well below the figures for Sweden as a whole. Likewise, the average labour participation rate and the average disposable income of Umeå residents is higher than those of southern Sweden.

Forestry, paper and pulp dominated industrial structure of Umeå immediately after the Second World War, as did those sectors in many coastal cities throughout Norrland. Even if the natural resource economy expanded somewhat from the 1940s to the 1960s, the real expansion in regional employment during the period took place in the public sector. This was particularly true for the Umeå region. The city became increasingly a centre for public administration and the delivery of health care. Already the seat of the county government, Umeå quickly became the administrative centre for other state agencies in the north of Sweden. The Court of Appeal for Upper Norrland was located there. Likewise two of the Swedish military regiments were based in the community. This meant that the central government had a significant presence in the city's economy.

The establishment of the new University of Umeå meant that the dominance of the public sector in the local economy was to be strengthened even further. The university's contribution to the local labour market has been estimated at close to 10 per cent. From 1965 to 1995 the university accounted for 25 per cent of the city's economic growth (Holm and Wiberg, 1995). The university's role as a 'magnet' attracting other public and private investment would add to that figure. In its early years, in the late 1960s, the university directly employed almost 1,000 individuals. Today, the university employs almost 4,000 people. It has become third largest employer in the city.

While very few dispute the fact that the university has had a positive effect on the local economy, there is some debate over the size of its impact. Growing gradually over a number of years, the extent of the university's economic contribution to the community is not always immediately apparent. Today the university's total expenditure is more than $250 million per year. Salaries paid to faculty and support staff account for more than half that sum. Even when state and local taxes deducted from this sum are taken into consideration, the economic impact on local consumption is dramatic. In one study from the mid-1990s, the direct economic contribution of the university and its students to the local economy was estimated to be at least $188 million a year (Holm and Wiberg, 1995). To that was added the multiplier and indirect effects of such spending, which increased the figure by an additional third. This figure should be seen in relation to the overall budget of the city of Umeå, which is about $412 million per year.

A frequently asked question relates to the extent to which the university has contributed to the development of trade and industry in the region. Has the university fostered entrepreneurship and played a role in the creation of new firms or the development and expansion old ones? There are at least three ways in which a university can contribute to the industrial development in a region. First, its contribution can come from the supply side. A university delivers educated labour to the market-place. All firms, even local firms, can more easily recruit high skilled personnel if they are educated in the local region. In this respect the university plays a vital role in industrial development. Another way that a university can make a contribution is by functioning as a 'magnet' encouraging trade and business enterprises to locate their development and production units close to them. They can facilitate the construction of science parks or other business 'incubators'. A third way is by means of entrepreneurial spin-offs associated with research conducted on the campus or in cooperation with university personnel. The economic impact on local economies through the production of new goods and services can be immense. In one study covering the years from 1989–95 the city of Umeå and its university compared favourably with other Swedish university towns in the number and quality of new business enterprises established in their region (Holm and Wiberg, 1995).

The institutions of higher education in Norrland have also been adept in the education and training of specialists in a number of fields. Both the University of Umeå and the newer Luleå Technological University have sought to use their campuses as launch pads for regionally relevant research in science and technology. There are and have been several direct entrepreneurial spin-offs associated with such initiatives. While these universities have served as useful development 'magnets', their impact has been somewhat uneven. There are some examples where the University of Umeå has attracted firms from the private sector to locate in its immediate environs. These include large businesses like Ericsson in telecommunication and Pharmacia & Upjohn and Astra in pharmaceuticals and medical products. However, most examples of 'magnet' investment are to be found in the public sector. Especially during the 1970s, a large number of public research institutions were established or even relocated to Umeå on the strength of the environmental research taking place at the university.

There is still another development role that is sometimes allotted to new universities. It is frequently suggested that they contribute to the social capital in a community. As such, they should have a general social and cultural development role. Arguments of this kind had been mooted since the University of Umeå was first established. Northerners argued that the new university should make a distinct cultural contribution to the region. The southern communities of Sweden with their long-established universities had major libraries, museums, publishing companies and performance centres. Norrland should not be left wanting.

In the initial planning stage for the University of Umeå it had been suggested that a Faculty of Arts and a training and research centre in the humanities be established. These proposals were rejected by national planners, who suggested that the university had to answer to more practical and immediate questions of access, professional training and economic development. However, once the new university was established with Science and Social Science Faculties, the debate again turned to the importance of creating an Arts Faculty as well. Although the government had actually made a decision as early as 1965 that there should be an Arts Faculty at the university, the implementation of this decision was left to the traditional budgetary process. In doing so, it was inevitably delayed. Umeå could not rely on any special treatment in the allocation of funding following its inauguration. It had to compete with the older universities in the traditionally uncertain budgetary process.

The University of Umeå was able to open a Humanities Faculty in 1968. Besides conducting its own teaching and research, this academic unit within the university has taken on special responsibility to encourage the cultural life of the campus and the surrounding community. Some part of its training and research facilities also serve the general public. There is now a university art gallery linked to the Humanities Faculty with permanent exhibits from The National Museum of Art in Stockholm. The gallery also functions as a general art gallery for the city and the region. The Design School has its own gallery for exhibitions open to the public. Within the community of Umeå a number of art galleries have developed as spin-offs from the Art School and the Design School.

University faculty, staff and students are very active in the cultural life of Umeå. The organisation of chamber music festivals, jazz and blues festivals, photography exhibitions and film festivals is often undertaken by university personnel. They are seen as important initiators and driving forces in the staging of such cultural activities. Local theatre groups and choirs often count on the active participation of members from the university world. Students and university staff also constitute an important audience for publicly financed as well as private cultural exhibitions and shows. The presence of the university is also given special attention in proposals from the city and regional governments to expand cultural performance sites. For instance, in 1974 a new opera house and a Symphony Orchestra of Norrland were established with the support of state and regional resources. Other cities in Norrland with equally good musical reputations could have provided interesting locations for this cultural initiative. However, the university town had a strong advantage.

Another potential impact that a university might have on the social and cultural development of the region relates to its research and inquiry into the local environment. Does it seek to investigate and develop knowledge on the history, culture and traditions of the area? There was much discussion during the planning stages of the university concerning how the new institution might shed new light on these aspects of Norrland. However, much of this local orientation was relegated to the sidelines when it came to the practical implementation of the university proposal. The academic chairs and subject fields that were created at the outset of the university's operations were mainly in the traditional areas found at the older Swedish universities. Once the university was established, regional priorities gave way to a more universal orientation. The new university could not afford to be accused of being narrow and parochial in its perspective.

It should be noted, however, that in the following years, there has been a considerable amount of research and teaching undertaken in the fields of archeology, economic history, ethnology, history, arts, literature and language (Lappish) which has contributed to new perspectives on the region. One interesting result of this northern perspective has been the production of the four-volume *Encyclopedia of Norrland*. It styles itself as 'An Encyclopedia of the Scientific Foundation of the Norrland Region'. The project was undertaken predominantly by researchers from the University of Umeå, the Institute of Technology in Luleå and other higher education institutions in the region.

Conclusions

The major arguments for the establishment a university in Norrland were built upon a mix of theoretical as well as practical goals. There were the general goals of justice and equality: the north of Sweden ought to have its fair share of the higher education system. The creation of a university in Norrland was also seen as a means to attain other regional policy goals. The building of the university was part of a broad strategy to strengthen and develop the northern provinces. The institution would train professionals. It would serve as a catalyst for economic growth and diversification. It would encourage cultural development. Each of these objectives would be addressed in turn.

When the Dental Institute and the Medical School were founded in Umeå in the early 1950s post-secondary education in Norrland had only one goal. These institutions were created to provide the northern region with professionals. This, however, could also be seen as a means to other, broader goals, including regional justice and equality. The northern part of Sweden should have its fair share of higher education resources. Higher education is a goal in itself and should accordingly be evenly distributed over the country. When higher education is looked upon as a means to other ends several additional objectives can be identified. A university in Umeå could provide training for a variety of specialists beyond education and health care that might equally contribute to the region. A university could, thanks to its location, contribute to the development of other public institutions and business enterprises.

The creation of a new university in the north, the University of Umeå, is often referred to as a very successful – if not the most successful – example of Swedish regional policy. This apparent success, however, requires answers to important questions. To what extent has the University of Umeå and other higher education institutions in the north of Sweden contributed to regional justice and equality? To what extent has a university located in Norrland contributed to regional development? Has it provided greater regional access to university education? Has it increased the availability of educated professionals in the area? Has a university of the north of Sweden had an important impact on the social and cultural development of the region?

One can open this discussion with a consideration of the impact which the University of Umeå has had on population growth within the region. The figures are indisputable. The city of Umeå has been one of the fastest-growing towns in Sweden since the early 1960s. This trend continues today and clearly demonstrates the ability of the university not only to keep young people from the region from moving to the south, but also to attract new residents. Many of the latter are young, well-educated and trained.

One can turn next to the socio-economic development impact of the new northern university. Here there is no single indicator to measure the overall contribution of the institution to the regional economy. All the individual figures, however, point in the same direction. The establishment of a university in Umeå has been conducive to sustained socio-economic development in the city and region. Umeå and Norrland have gained from the university's training of specialists. The majority of the students educated in Umeå as doctors, dentists and teachers now live and pursue their professions in Norrland. The university has also made a positive contribution to the region's overall employment figures and has raised the standard of living in these northern communities.

Finally, looking at the questions of access to higher education and the possibilities for social mobility the positive trends are the same. The proportion of students from Norrland enrolling in higher education has risen dramatically since the university opened. This northern institution has become an attractive alternative to moving south for education. Equally significant, the number of working-class students has been higher in Umeå than in other Swedish universities. All in all, if one looks at the university's impact on service to the local and regional community, the message is the same – the university has made a difference.

References

Beckman, B. and Carling, A. (1989) *Förhandlingsekonomin i regionalpolitiken* (Stockholm: Allmänna Förlaget, Ds A 1989: 28).

Bergendal, G. (1977) *Higher Education and Manpower Planning in Sweden* (Stockholm: The National Swedish Board of Universities and Colleges 1977, Liber Läromedel/ Utbildningsförlaget).

Carlbom, T. (1950 B 1965) *Högskolelokaliseringen i Sverige* (Stockholm: Almqvist & Wiksell).

Dahllöf, U. (1990) *Högre utbildning i komparativt perspektiv* (Pedagogiska institutionen Uppsala, Pedagogisk forskning i Uppsala 95).

Dahllöf, U. *Reforming Higher Education and External Studies in Sweden and Australia* (Uppsala: Studies in Education 3).

Dahllöf, U. and Selander S. (eds) (1996) *Expanding Colleges and New Universities* (Uppsala Studies in Education 66).

Holm, E. and Wiberg, U. (eds) (1995) *Samhällseffekter av Umeå universitet* (Umeå University: CERUM Regional Dimensions Working Paper No. 1).

Johansson, M. (1989) *A Brief Overview of Regional Development in the Nordic Countries* (NordREFO).

Lane, L.-E. (1983) *Creating the University of Norrland* (Stockholm: Liber, Umeå Studies in Politics and Administration).

Larsson, L.-G. and Elgqvist-Saltzman I. (1995) *Ett universitet växer fram* (Umeå: Norrlands universitetsförlag).

Lorendahl, B. and Persson, L.-O. (eds) (1992) *Utbildning för utkanter Rapport 1992: 5* (Högskolan i Östersund).

Lundgren, N.-G. (1991) *Högskolan i Luleå och Norbottens utveckling* (Luleå: Länsstyrelsen i Norrbottens län).

Länstyrelserna i Västernorrlands, Jämtlands, Västerbottens och Norrbottens län (1986) *Kunskap och utveckling i Umeå högskoleregion* (Umeå: Länsstyrelsernas regionalpolitiska riktlinjer för statlig högskoleutbildning och forskning i Umeå högskoleregion).

Näslund, M. and Persson, S. (1972) *Regionalpolitik. Igar, i dag, i morgon* (Stockholm, Norstedts).

NordREFO (1993: 4) 'Högskolene i nord-skandinavia: drivkrefter for regional näringsutveckling'. *Norländsk uppslagsbok 1993: 96* (Höganäs, Bra Böcker).

NordREFO (1987) *Regionstyrelsen i Umeå högskoleregion: 10 år i Norr* (Umea: Centraltryckeriet).

OECD (1979) *Education and Regional Development* (Paris: Technical Reports. Volume II).

Oscarsson, G. (1989) 'Regional Policies in the Nordic Countries: Origins, Development and Future'. In NordREFO, *The Long-Term Future of Regional Policy: a Nordic View.*

SOU (1969: 49) Inrikesdepartementet. *Lokaliserings-och regionalpolitik.*

SOU (1984: 74) Industridepartementet. *Regional Utveckling och mellanregional utjärnning.*

SOU (1989: 55) Arbetsmarknadsdepartementet. *Fungerande regioner i samspel.*

TemaNord (1995: 518) *Universitet och region: samarbeid mellom universiteter og regionalt naringsliv i Norden.*

Umeå universitet 25 år. Umeå universitet 1990.

Wiberg, U. (ed.) (1993) *Botnianatverket. En strategisk allians mellan nordliga kunskapsstäder* (Umeå: CERUM).

4
The University of Tromsø

Peter Arbo and Narve Fulsås

Introduction

When Norway got its first university in 1811, the country was still in union with Denmark. The main arguments for establishing the university were that Norwegians should be given the same educational opportunities as Danes, Norwegian society should have a better supply of university-trained professionals and that a university would benefit the development of the country's industries. In addition, some academics saw a new university as an opportunity to reform the university curriculum. The University of Copenhagen was considered to be old-fashioned and out of touch with the development of newer and more utilitarian branches of knowledge.

Similar considerations were prominent when the Norwegian Parliament (Stortinget) in 1968 decided to locate the country's fourth university in Tromsø. Thus, the regionalisation of higher education in the last part of the twentieth century can be seen as a process akin to the nationalisation of higher education some 150–200 years earlier. From a regional policy point of view, the decision to create a university in northern Norway may also be regarded as one of the most successful government initiatives for the region.

In this chapter we will examine the role of the University of Tromsø in the development of northern Norway. The chapter starts with a brief account of the regional context. It proceeds with an outline of the Norwegian higher education system, followed by a description of the founding process and the expansion of the university. In the subsequent sections we assess the regional impact of the university and discuss the effects in the light of shifting expectations the university has met with. Finally, future challenges are identified and reflected upon.

The regional context

Northern Norway comprises the counties of Nordland, Troms and Finnmark. The total area is 113,000 square kilometres, which means that the region covers an area roughly equivalent to Denmark, the Netherlands and Belgium combined. Northern Norway borders on Sweden, Finland and Russia. The inhabitants of this part of the country are mainly of Norwegian, Saami and Finnish descent and total 463,000 people, which is 10.4 per cent of Norway's population. The three counties which make up the region embrace 89 municipalities, each with its own local government. Tromsø is the biggest town in the north, with a total of 58,000 inhabitants. Among Norway's municipalities, it is the seventh largest. Most of the municipalities in the region are very small, 75 per cent have fewer than 5,000 inhabitants.

Northern Norway has traditionally been regarded as the least developed part of the country. Well into the twentieth century the area was less industrialised and less urbanised than the south, and the economy had a strong element of household production. In 1946, 46 per cent of the population were still occupied in the primary industries, usually combining in different forms small-scale fishing, farming, forestry and reindeer herding. During the war, Finnmark and the northern part of Troms were almost completely destroyed as the German troops withdrew from the advancing Soviet army. Consequently, the Norwegian state put extensive effort into rebuilding and developing the area after the war. These undertakings echoed the general programme of the Labour government to modernise the country and raise the standard of living. In 1951 a ten-year regional development programme was launched. The main objective was to enhance industrialisation. When regional policy was institutionalised in Norway at the beginning of the 1960s, it was, in fact, modelled on these efforts to modernise northern Norway.

This reconstruction and politically supported industrialisation contributed to a long period of rapid economic growth. Employment in primary industries was greatly reduced, and the most marginal rural settlements were depopulated. The surplus of labour was absorbed by the growing manufacturing industry, which benefited from expanding international markets. In spite of net migration from the region, the population increased due to relatively high fertility rates, notably in the rural areas. Total employment in manufacturing reached its peak in northern Norway in 1981. In the meantime, the expansion of public services gradually opened an alternative field of occupation. This process was spurred during the 1970s, when the oil revenues from the North Sea began to have an effect and the government tried to recapture popular support after the defeat in the 1972 general referendum on Norwegian EEC membership. In the same decade women began to enter the labour market in large numbers. The expansion and decentralisation of the welfare state created new jobs in health care, social services, education and administration. Improvements in transportation and communications also facilitated the development of more integrated regional labour markets, making commuting an alternative to resettlement. Although geographically rather evenly distributed, the new workplaces were mainly created in municipal centres and towns attributed regional public functions, which consequently have been the growth poles of the region since the 1960s.

In the course of a few decades, northern Norway was transformed from an almost pre-industrial economy to a predominantly service economy. The process entailed a levelling-out of most of the earlier regional disparities in Norway. Today, the region is comparable to the rest of the country in terms of settlement structure, employment pattern, income level, housing conditions, leisure activites, etc. Approximately 7 per cent of the working population in northern Norway is now employed in primary industries, 18 per cent in secondary industries and 75 per cent in the service sector. This pattern is broadly similar to the national average. However, the range of industries is narrower the further north we move. The proportion of workers employed in most industrial sectors and market-oriented services is much lower in northern Norway than in the rest of the country, while the opposite is the case in a few industries such as fisheries, metals, construction and tourism. Northern Norway also has a high proportion of civil servants. The public sector employs about 40 per cent of the labour force. If we include semi-public industries such as electricity and water supply, transportation, post and telecommunications, and cultural services, approximately 50 per cent of employment in northern Norway is connected to the public sector. Hence, the economy of the region is, to a great extent, dependent upon income from raw materials-based industries and public funds.

Registered unemployment in northern Norway is low. In 1998, the annual average was 3.1 per cent of the working poulation in Nordland, 2.7 per cent in Troms and 4.5 per cent in Finnmark, as compared to a national average of 2.4 percent. These figures reflect the present healthy state of the Norwegian economy. But in prosperous periods with high demand for labour, the net migration from northern Norway also tends to increase. In the last few years the net migration to the south has been substantial. In the wake of the urbanisation and growing female participation in education and work, there has also been a drop in the fertility rates, which means that the net natural increase in the total population no longer exceeds the number of people moving out of the region. Many small communities have experienced a change in the composition of their sex and age distribution, thus fewer women and older men are left behind in there communities. Today, even the larger towns in northern Norway are faced with zero population growth.

The system of higher education

The school system in Norway is primarily public. The municipalities are responsible for the compulsory ten year primary schools, the counties for upper secondary education, and the national government is in charge of higher education. The normal admission requirement for higher education in Norway is a General Certificate of Education. Students have a total of at least twelve years' education below university or college level.[1] Almost all pupils continue from compulsory school to advanced level studies.

Like other OECD countries, post-war Norway has experienced a growing demand for upper secondary and higher education. Education has also been given higher priority by the government and has been promoted as an instrument to enhance democracy, bring about social equality and foster economic development. By the end of the 1950s, the government began to realise that a shortage of academic labour could arise if educational capacity did not expand. When student enrolment increased rapidly during the 1960s, several initiatives were taken to reform the higher education system. First, in 1968, the decision was made to erect new universities in Trondheim and Tromsø to supplement the older universities of Oslo (1811) and Bergen (1946). Second, a new system of regional colleges (*distriktshogskoler*) was introduced, basically intended to provide more short-term vocational education. These initiatives were, on the one hand, an attempt to lend the established universities some relief from the huge influx of new students and to make the system of higher education more flexible. On the other hand, they must be seen as a response to the strong welfare claims of the regions, eager to take part in 'the education society' and to stimulate economic and social development. In accordance with the general trend of welfare services, education was decentralised as well.

During the 1970s and early 1980s, a number of regional colleges were established. Concurrently, several former upper secondary educational institutions acquired the status of higher educational institutions (i.e.

colleges of education, colleges of engineering, colleges of social work, conservatories of music). This triggered a kind of 'academic drift'. Gradually most of the institutions in the regional system developed research activities. In education the colleges moved into academic territory and extended their curricula to embrace courses that were formerly considered to be classic university subjects. With the support of the Ministry of Local Government and Labour (KAD), regional research foundations were established, with close links to the regional colleges. A new wave of structural reforms was launched in the late 1980s and early 1990s. First, the idea of 'Network Norway' was introduced, demanding stronger specialisation, cooperation and communication between the institutions of highr education and research. Second, several colleges were merged to administratively. In 1996 the University of Trondheim merged with the much older Norwegian Institute of Technology (founded in 1910) to form the Norwegian University of Science and Technology (NTNU).

Today, the system of higher education in Norway consists of four universities, six specialised colleges at university level[2] and 26 state colleges (former regional colleges). These institutions are owned by the state and are largely financed by the national budget via the Ministry of Church Affairs, Education and Research (KUF). In addition, there are some private educational institutions receiving government financial support, of which The Norwegian School of Management is the largest.

Since the end of the 1980s, Norway has seen a tremendous growth in the student population. Between 1988 and 1998 it increased by 71 per cent, from 101,000 to 173,000. The number of students coming from northern Norway has increased at the same rate, from less than 12,000 to more than 20,000. About 43 per cent of Norwegian students are university students. About, half of all schoolchildren go on to higher education. An important aspect of this growth is the eradication of sex discrimination, so that women now constitute the majority of students.

Today, there are seven state colleges in northern Norway. They are located in Nesna, Bodo, Narvik, Harstad, Tromso, Alta and Guovdageaidnu. Guovdageaidnu is a Saami college. The colleges offer a broad range of studies from professional degrees in engineering, education and nursing, to university-level studies in various fields. In 1998, the colleges of northern Norway had a total of 10,300 students and about 1,200 employees. The University of Tromsø is the largest of the higher educational institutions in the region. The university consists of six Faculty units: the Faculty of Humanities, the Faculty of Law, the Faculty of Medicine, the Faculty of Social Sciences, the Faculty of Science and the Norwegian College of Fisheries. These are subdivided into 39 depart-ments. In addition, the university includes the Centre for Teacher Education and Further Education (UNIKOM), Tromsø University Museum, the University Library and four research coordinating centres: the Roald Amundsen Centre for Arctic Research, the Centre for Environment and Development Studies the Centre for Saami Studies and the Centre for Women's Research and Women in Research. Graduate degrees are offered in natural sciences, humanities and social sciences, while professional degrees are offered in engineering, law, medicine, pharmacy, psychology and fishery sciences. In 1998, the university had 6,300 students, of which 53 per cent were women. The total staff was about 1,400 employees. More than half of the employees are academic staff, while the remainder fill tech-nical or administrative positions.

The foundation and evolution of the university

The idea of a university in Tromsø was first voiced in 1918. Addressing the problems of recruitment and high turnover among clergymen and medical practitioners in the region, a local merchant argued that creating a university in northern Norway was the only effective solution. The same arguments, in fact, were employed when Parliament took its deci-sion fifty years later. The prelude to this decision started with a govern-ment committee (the Kleppe Committee) which came together in 1960 to prepare a ten-year plan for the development of higher education. Although the committee urged a doubling of the capacity, it assumed that this could take place within the established educational institutions. However, in the White Paper presented to Parliament, the Ministry of Education added that northern Norway ought to have its own institution of higher education. This was approved by Parliament, and a new com-mittee, the Ruud Committee, was formed in 1963 to investigate the necessity of opening a university in Tromsø.

While the Kleppe Committee was preoccupied with cost-effective solu-tions to the national capacity problems, the Ruud Committee empha-sised the uneven regional distribution of educational opportunities and supply of academic labour. The work of the committee coincided with a heated public debate on the lack of medical officers of health, especially in northern Norway. The committee stated that the problem could be solved only by educating more doctors in the region. Based on research by one of the committee members, it argued that if young people from northern Norway could go to a university in their home region, they would be more likely to stay there after graduation.

The choice of Tromsø as the site of the new university was not disputed. Over the years, several scientific institutons had emerged in Tromsø. In 1872 a museum of natural and cultural history was established, and in 1918 a geophysical institute was added. This, after a few years, split into a meteorological institute and the Northern Lights Observatory. In addition, a teachers' college had been in operation since the early nineteenth century. This meant that a small scientific community already existed in Tromsø. Furthermore, Tromsø is located in the middle of northern Norway and has long enjoyed a reputation as the gateway to the Arctic. What created controversy, though, was the proposal to include medical training at the new university. The established institutions in the health sector, and the associated organisations and politicians, were overwhelmingly in favour of locating Norway's third medical school in Trondheim. It was the competition between Tromsø and Trondheim that gave momentum to the local campaign for the university. Althought the demand for a univerity in the north had existed for several decades, local action in support of the project had been sporadic until the mid-1960s. Before the government expressed the need for an institution of higher education in northern Norway in 1962, people in Tromsø thought it would take generations to see the dream of a university fulfilled.

The Minister of Education finally decided to opt for Tromsø with respect to the medical school. Tromsø was chosen for welfare and regional policy reasons. The planning began immediately after the parliamentary decision in 1968. Headed by a professor of medicine from Oslo, the provisional university board launched an offensive strategy for the establishment of the university. The board wanted to avoid a protracted planning period. Concrete results were deemed necessary to maintain political backing. Hence, research and education should commence from the outset while the planning of the permanent university facilities took place. The strategy was a success. Between 1971 and 1974 the government alloted 378 positions, of which 185 were scientific, to the University of Tromsø. The first 420 students were admitted in 1972. This rapid expansion of activities marked something new. Traditionally, new universities had been very small and very slow-growing institutions. But during the 1960s both the Norwegian and many other governments changed their stance, and tried to more on from the old pattern. The timing was important. The University of Tromsø came early enough to enjoy the expansion period of Norwegian higher education, which ended in 1973.

The recruitment of staff to the new university was easier than expected. First, many academics from northern Norway who lived elsewhere were eager to return and take part in the project. Second, the University of Tromsø was associated with progress and a reform ideology, which had a considerable appeal to people who wanted to experiment with new ideas. Third, the vacant positions provided an opportunity to climb the academic career ladder for those who were willing to move in order to realise their ambitions.

When Parliament decided to create a new university in Tromsø, the specific location of the new university was not specified. Intense conflict soon arose between the university board and the local authorities. The university strongly preferred an attractive site on the southern part of Tromsø island, while the municipality wanted to use the establishment of the university as a means to develop the northern part of the island and to channel the growth of the town away from the urban centre. The conflict was resolved by Parliament, which supported the local authorities. The provisional board had greater success when it came to the organisation of the planning and construction process. The Directorate of Public Construction and Property joined with the University of Tromsø, and set up a local planning department in Tromsø. This was a novel model, with a more decentralised control of activities. An open and flexible plan for a modern campus, three kilometres north of the city centre, was outlined. The first stage of construction was finalised between 1978 and 1983, including the, the university library, science social sciences and humanities blocks.

The period from 1974 to 1988 was a more difficult one for the university. At the national level, the main structural reforms of higher education had been accomplished and a general mood of reform exhaustion prevailed. The higher educational budgets also became tighter even though they had to accommodate the expansion of the regional colleges. Although the University of Tromsø was favoured by the government as compared to the other universities, a huge gap opened between expectations created by the initial plans and the new budget realities. Moreover, the number of students increased much more slowly than expected. The goal had been for the university to reach 2,000–2,200 students by 1980, but the number stabilised below 1,700. As the only quantified measure for development, these figures acquired very strong symbolic significance. The stagnation was amplified when the planning of the new hospital and medical institutions ran into deep crisis in the beginning of the 1980s, and the whole project had to be scaled down.

The slow student growth rate was not unique to the University of Tromsø. All the universities had to compete for students with the new regional colleges. In this respect, the University of Tromsø was hit by the effects of the same decentralisation policy that had brought about the university in the first place. The university, however, paid special attention to the fact that the region still had a substantial 'leakage' of students to the south. In the county of Nordland, three-quarters of students still preferred to study in Oslo, Bergen or Trondheim. The University of Tromsø realised that to turn the tide, it had to broaden its courses. After failing to obtain a new Bachelor of Commerce degree for Tromsø, the university was allowed to start Law Studies, which gained it many new students. Favourable demographic trends also contributed to an increase in the number of students from the mid-1980s on. But since relevant age cohorts would shrink in the 1990s, the recruitment of students continued to be a matter of great concern. Early in the 1980s the university had hoped to reach a target of 3,000 students by 1990, but after a few years that target was deferred to 1995.

The student explosion after 1988 came as a surprise. In 1989 the number of students passed 3,000, and the increase continued until 1996, when the University of Tromsø reached a total of more than 6,000 students. Thus, from 1986 to 1996 the number of students tripled. This influx was the combined effect of more young people, growing unemployment; the abolition of sex discrimination; and a general increase in the demand for higher education. The University of Tromsø also adopted a policy of accommodating the situation. While the other universities imposed restrictions on access to previously open education, the University of Tromsø decided to keep its courses open to all qualified applicants. The university board had learned from experience that the number of students was the single most imprtant factor in attempts to solicit more resources from the government. They wanted to utilise the growth in student numbers as a means to consolidate small programmes and expand services. The strategy was a success. The first half of the 1990s was the strongest period of growth in the history of the University of Tromsø since the founding years in the early 1970s.

The regional effects of the university

To assess the regional role of the University of Tromsø, it is convenient to distinguish five ways in which a university can affect regional development: by a demand effect; a supply effect; a magnet effect; a research-based innovation effect; and a socio-cultural effect.

First, a university brings with it a demand for goods and services. The construction and running of a university create a market for construction companies as well as a multiplicity of suppliers and subcontractors. The staff and students also represent an inflow of money. By spending their incomes they directly and indirectly contribute to the level of economic activity in the region. These demand effects are amplified if the establishment of the university leads to an upgrading and modernisation of a local hospital or other institution with auxiliary functions for the university. To take just one example: in Tromsø the building of a new regional hospital was an integral part of the decision to erect the university.

As an indication of the demand effects of the University of Tromsø, one should note that the university budgets have included total investments of US$250 million. The new regional hospital has been allotted approximately the same amount of investments. The university and the Student Welfare Organisation have also built residences and kindergartens for staff and students, and in 1995 the Tromsø Research Park opened. In all these projects the construction activities have relied heavily on regional construction companies, architects and consultants. Before Norway signed the European Economic Space Agreement and had to submit to the new rules on non-discriminatory use of general tender in public procurements in 1994, the local policy was to utilise and enhance the competencies of northern Norwegian firms. Likewise, the new institutions have created an enlarged market for the suppliers of computers and software, office equipment, scientific instruments and various professional services. Consequently, many companies have set up subsidiaries in Tromsø to serve their customers. The annual budget of the university is about US$68 million, exclusive of money for new buildings and large equipment. Half of this is staff salaries, of which a large share is spent locally. Moreover, the students probably spend some US$56.25 million during the academic year. In sum, this means a lot to local retail services, restaurants and transportation companies in the region. The population growth of Tromsø, from 38,000 inhabitants in 1970 to 58,000 inhabitants in 1999, must be seen in light of the massive inflow of money which has followed the establishment of the university.

Second, a university is unlike other organisations. It produces graduates and thereby alters the supply and composition of the regional labour force. In fact, the establishment of a new university always has a mobilising effect, inducing more people to engage in higher education. Statistics show that on average between 70 and 75 per cent of the students at the University of Tromsø have come from the region, 25–30 percent from the Tromsø area alone. Foreign students comprise 4–7 per cent. The proportion of students from outside northern Norway increased at the beginning of the 1990s. The investigations undertaken also tell us that most graduates settle in the region. From 1973 to 1996, about 3,000 people received a Master's or a PhD degree from the university. Two-thirds of these were living in northern Norway by the end of 1966. Except from the southern part of Nordland, almost every municipality in the region have both sent young people to the university and received higher-level graduates from the university. By the end of 1966, nearly 40 per cent had settled in the educational centre. Of graduates originally from northern Norway, some three-quarters remain in the region; whereas three-quarters of graduates from other parts of the country leave the region after graduation. A survey conducted some years ago on medical graduates showed that 83 per cent of northern Norwegian students were living in the region five years after graduation. The comparative number for students coming from the southern part of Norway was 40 per cent. Nevertheless, a third of university students from northern Norway go to universities outside the region.

The formal educational level of the labour force used to be much lower in northern Norway than in southern Norway. This difference has almost disappeared over the last two decades. According to the latest figures (from 1988), 25 per cent of all workers in northern Norway have a higher education, while the national average is 27.5 per cent. The propensity to study among the young people of northern Norway is now approaching the national average. Only the county of Finnmark is lagging behind somewhat. To reach students throughout the region, the University of Tromsø has also been engaged in extension and distance learning courses. The full extent of the contributions made by the graduates is difficult to assess. However, what we do know is that the largest percentage of graduates have found occupations in the public sector. Among the working population of northern Norway with more than two years of higher education, nearly 80 per cent are employed by government. The region has become much better equipped with doctors, nurses, teachers and planners, in line with one of the main arguments for establishing the University of Tromsø. Yet graduates have also gone to private businesses and taken part in the restructuring and revitalisation of companies, notably within aquaculture and the fishing industry. Likewise, many of the newer and more advanced companies set up in recent years in the fields of computing, electronics and professional services have recruited graduates from the University of Tromsø.

Third, establishing a university has a magnet effect on well-qualified people and companies searching for such personnel. Research institutions with a good reputation may also attract companies eager to benefit from the research activites. In the past, the sense of remoteness and professional isolation was probably one of the most important hindrances to recruiting and retaining academics in northern Norway. Today, the university acts as a regional point of reference and a centre for further education and training. Thus, the professional isolation has been broken. Several companies report that they regard Tromsø as a favoured location due to the supply of graduate job candidates. However, until recently very few private business companies have set up subsidiaries in Tromsø with the prime intention of cooperating and keeping in touch with university research. The university has mainly had a magnet effect on public or quasi-public research activities. Not unsurprisingly, research has bred more research. Among these new institutions are: the Tromsø Satellite Station; the Norwegian Institute for Fishery and Aquaculture reearch; the NORUT Research Group; the Telenor Research and Development; the Norwegian Institute for Air Research; the Norwegian Institute for Water Research; the Norwegian Institute for Arctic Veterinary Medicine; and the Norwegian Polar Institute. Several of the institutes are now located in a recently completed Polar Environmental Centre. In total, these new research organisations have a scientific and technical staff of nearly 500 people.

Fourth, scientific results can be exploited by industry. The commercialisation of research follows various routes. Research can provide ideas for, or help test out, new products, processes, management systems, modes of marketing and distribution, and other kinds of innovations. Moreover, research can improve company decisions by providing knowledge about the environments companies function in, thereby reducing uncertainty, i.e. mapping natural resources, monitoring market developments, doing benchmarking, analysing trade barriers, communicating cultural understanding and the like. Communities of researchers are also nodes in international academic networks and can act as bridges to international partners for companies. Finally, research may affect political decision having an influence on the business sector, which means it has indirect economic effects. Surveying all these kinds of research-based effects is a complicated matter.

The research activities at the University of Tromsø cover a wide range of topics, although in many fields the empirical attention and scientific commitments are concentrated on Arctic conditions and issues related to northern Norway. Four centres of gravity can be distinguished. The first of these is medicine, which involves about a third of the academic personnel at the university. Important research areas are biochemistry, molecular biology and genetics, biotechnology, pharmacy, microbiology, community medicine, telemedicine and clinical research. The medical departments cooperate closely with the Regional Hospital of Tromsø, which serves as a university hospital. A second is research on natural resources and resource management, with an emphasis on fisheries and aquaculture. Together with the Tromsø-based Norwegian Institute for Fishery and Aquaculture Research, the university runs an aquaculture research station and three research vessels. The third field is computing, telecommunications and satellite remote sensing, including outer space research. The university has the Northern Light Observatory and collaborates with the Tromsø Satellite Station and Andoya Rocket Range. It is also responsible for important research installations such as the EISCAT (European Incoherent Scatter Radar) facilities outside Tromsø and the EISCAT radar and other facilities at Spitzbergen. The fourth main area is the history, social development, culture and multi-linguistic situation of northern Norway and the Barents Region.

Finally, a university has socio-cultural modernising effects. As a bridgehead to an international academic culture and a privileged site for critical reflections, it influences ways of thinking and acting. A university also alters the social structure and pattern of social stratification. The University of Tromsø has increased the regions exposure to outside ideas. The new rationality has been disseminated and can be observed in local media, in public discussion, political life, business associations and cultural activities. In a town like Tromsø, where students and university staff comprise close to 15 per cent of the population, the university inevitably has a great impact on the rest of society. Both the supply of services and the variety in arts, music, film, theatre, sports and outdoor life are strongly influenced by the fact that Tromsø is a university town. However, a university is not only a port for the importation of foreign ideas, but a melting pot and a catalyst for new regional identities. The establishment of the University of Tromsø coincided with a growing wave of regionalism and became part of the same process. The university has raised the profile of the region. It has drawn attention to northern Norway and stimulated interest in and reinterpretation of the language, history and culture of the region. In this sense it has contributed to the formation of regional self-confidence and pride. The same applies to the new ethno-political consciousness among the Saami people. The university has also joined with the municipality to realise specific projects such as a new concert hall, a planetarium on the campus and a local history for Tromsø's 200th anniversary. Another important aspect of is the development of new networks. The university acts as a social arena. As a meeting-place it has given rise to networks which are activated in various fields of social life. To put it another way, the university has enhanced the social and cultural capital of the region.

The meeting of shifting expectations

When Parliament decided to establish the University of Tromsø in the late 1960s, regional policy considerations played a decisive role. The university was expected to give young people from the region equal access to higher education; remedy the lack of academic labour; put northern Norway on the same footing as the rest of the country; and stimulate the general development of the region. The basic arguments expressed a need for greater equality. Hence, the university was part of the project of building the welfare state. The main interest centred on welfare services, public sector occupations and the educational function of the university. However, university policy aims were also put forth. It was emphasised that the university should develop high-quality education and research; recruit students from all over the country; specialise in certain fields of scientific inquiry related to northern Norway; and initiate reforms with the potential of vitalising the other universities as well.

While the university policy objectives have been stable over the years, the regional policy context has changed. Since the beginning of the 1980s, all institutions of higher education have faced new expectations. The universities have become potential seedbeds of innovation and economic restructuring. The legends of Silicon Valley, the Boston Route 128 and the UK Cambridge Phenomenon have reached even the remotest of regions. Now, the universities are regarded as vanguards of the high-tech 'information society'. The main preoccupation is with their contribution to private sector development, and the research function of the university has attained much more attention.

To what degree have these various expectations been met? On a general account, the high-tech visions of a research-based restructuring of regional industry have not been fulfilled. Northern Norway still relies heavily on the exploitation of natural resources and on government budgets. This makes the region vulnerable to marine resource variations, changes in international markets and political decisions. Nevertheless, the university has contributed to a discernible diversification of the economy. It has been the driving force behind the growth of the city of Tromsø, and above all, it has been pivotal to the development of an advanced welfare state in the region. Both the student enrolment and the supply of academic labour have improved substantially. Without the university, the region would have had a much more backward postion in most fields of economic and social life.

The role and prestige of the University of Tromsø in the university system is hard to assess. The accumulation of scientific reputation takes time. New institutions will therefore always face a problem of credibility in their first stage. In addition, institutions in the geographical periphery normally have to cope with prejudices associated with their location. The fact that the university initially tried to profile itself as something different, with more democratic governance, a more interdisciplinary approach and a stronger regional focus and commitment, may be seen as an attempt to withdraw from the traditional standards of evaluation. But most of all it reflected the spirit and ambitions of the first generations of staff and students. During the 1970s the University of Tromsø was labelled 'the red university'. In medicine, social sciences and fishery sciences the university tried to launch alternative studies. However, established academic norms inevitably apply when it comes to appointments, degrees, career patterns and the like. Gradually, the University of Tromsø has become more like the other universities in terms of curriculum, disciplinary structure and faculty organisation.

The pattern of academic mobility indicates an informal hierarchy of prestige: Oslo-based professors are not leaving for Tromsø, while many professors have gone in the other direction. Nevertherless, the turnover among staff has only been slightly higher at the University of Tromsø than at other universities, in spite of the fact that many of those who arrived in the build-up period had no intention of staying permanently. But stability does not necessarily imply quality. Today, low mobility is probably a bigger problem for all the Norwegian universities and colleges than too high a turnover. Since the end of the 1980s, several national evaluations based on peer reviews have been undertaken in various disciplines and academic fields. In these studies the University of Tromsø has a good – in some areas even outstanding – record. So, by and large, the aim of creating an institution of an equivalent standing to the other universities has succeeded. Contrary to what many people thought in the 1960s, it has been possible to persuade academics to settle and develop one of Norway's main centres of learning and research far north of the Arctic Circle.

Future challenges

The Norwegian universities are now facing several challenges. First, the total number of young people in the population is decreasing. Combined with an economic situation with high demand for labour, this is leading to a fall in student enrolment. From 1997 to 1998, most of the universities in Norway witnessed a 10 per cent reduction in student applications. Second, funding of the universities is becoming less generous. In 1990, a new budgetary system was introduced in higher education, which links government spending to the number of students. In the new model the production of grade points and the flow of students through the system are strongly emphasised. Thus, the fall in the enrolment rate has a direct bearing on the resources alloted to the universities. This is amplified by the fact that the government is trying to squeeze expenditures in higher education and research in order to dampen an overheated economy. Third, students have a choice from a widening range of courses and places to study. Private educational institutions have strengthened their role and the digital revolution is making it easier for students to attend courses run by distance education suppliers. Consequently, the universities and colleges are finding themselves in an intensified competition for students. All higher educational institutions are now rapidly moving into the field of further education and training, where there is a potential for new students. To mobilise external resources, they are also seeking new partnerships with industry and government institutions.

In trying to meet these challenges the University of Tromsø has several drawbacks. First, it cannot offer the same range of subjects as the larger and better-established universities. Second, the university has a strong public sector orientation, which reflects the historical connection between the establishment of the university and the building of the welfare state in northern Norway. Today, the public sector is stagnant, while the business sector, notably in the Oslo area, is expanding. These changes are reflected in students' choice of education. Third, the industry of the region has a structure typical of a peripheral region, with branch plants of large industries and small companies engaged in low-tech raw materials production. This means that the university has a narrower labour market for graduates. Furthermore, it makes it more difficult to develop close university–industry partnerships. The large multi-plant companies have their research and development facilities outside the region, while most of the smaller companies lack the human and economic resources to embark on a more comprehensive collaboration with the university.

On the other hand, the University of Tromsø has some advantages over the other Norwegian universities. First, the university has enjoyed strong backing from government. The, national authorities will probably continue to give the university special support for regional policy reasons. Second, being a small and modern university means that the

University of Tromsø can offer better conditions for studying and closer contact between teachers and students than most other universities. Likewise, the university organisation is more manageable and its communications structure facilitates coordinated initiatives in response to new external demands. Third, Tromsø is generally regarded as a pleasant town with an exotic, Arctic flavour. The attractiveness of the university town is important to the recruitment of both students and staff.

However, the future prospects of the university will depend upon its ability to strengthen its academic profile, specialise, develop a regional interface and enlarge its international scope. In these endeavours the university needs to regain some of the entrepreneurial spirit of the early 1970s.

Notes

1. The school admission age was lowered from seven to six years in 1997, so in the future students will have one more year of schooling.
2. The Agricultural College of Norway (1857/93); the Norwegian College of Veterinary Medicine (1935); the Norwegian College of Economics and Business Administration (1936); the Norwegian College of Physical Education and Sport (1968); the State Academy of Music (1973); the Oslo School of Architecture (1964). None of these is located in northern Norway.

5
The Role of the University of Akureyri in Northern Development

Ingi Runar Edvardsson and Thorsteinn Gunnarsson

Introduction

This chapter has a dual purpose. First, it deals with the foundation of the University of Akureyri and its importance for regional development in northern Iceland. Second, it deals with higher education in Iceland, throwing light on some of the country's idiosyncrasies. The chapter begins by introducing the general situation in Iceland, thereby outlining the conditions under which the University of Akureyri operates. This is followed by an analysis of higher education in Iceland and its development. Then, it focuses on the University of Akureyri, describing some of the expectations that its foundation gave rise to and how it has developed subsequently. At this stage, the chapter turns to the university's significance in terms of access to education, economic impact, its effect on vocational education and its effect on various social and cultural aspects of the region. The chapter concludes with an overview of the development of the University of Akureyri and the future opportunities for higher education in the north.

Iceland and the Northern Region

Some of the main characteristics of Iceland are its sparse population, long distances between towns and harsh natural conditions compared with central and southern Europe. However, thanks to the Gulf Stream which provides a relatively mild climate, the country is able to support some agriculture. The total area of Iceland is 103,000 square kilometres and the total population in 1996 was 269,727 (Iceland, 1997). As may be gathered from this, the population is sparse, just 2.6 inhabitants per square kilometre. Due to the fact that the majority of Icelanders live in a relatively restricted area, the proportion of those living in urban population centres is the highest of the Nordic countries at 91.5 per cent. In 1995, only ten population centres had more than 2,000 inhabitants each, which indicates that Icelandic towns are minuscule compared to cities abroad. In addition, there is the special circumstance that 58.4 per cent of the nation live in the area of the capital, which is a considerably higher proportion than in the other Nordic countries. Population growth in Iceland has also been more rapid than in the other Nordic countries or elsewhere in Europe (Gunnarsson, 1993; Olafsdottir and Persson, 1995; Iceland, 1996).

During recent decades Iceland has encountered several problems relating to regional development which remain largely unsolved to this day. The population of rural areas decreased by 27 per cent during the period 1970–91. In 1970 the rural population made up 14 per cent of the nation, but in 1955, this figure had shrunk to 8 per cent. In the countryside and in sparsely populated areas, women are also significantly fewer than men (81 women to every 100 men) and, furthermore, there is a high proportion of old age pensioners (Olafsdottir and Persson, 1995).

Cultural homogeneity is a characteristic of Iceland. From the era of first settlement Icelandic has been the only dominant language among the general population. However, while Iceland was a part of the Danish state in the period from the fourteenth century to 1944 Danish was also important as the language of administration. Religion likewise bears witness to the same phenomenon of homogeneity with 90.5 per cent of the population adhering to the National Lutheran Church. As a consequence religion has not provided a stimulus for the founding of universities, as has been the case in many other countries.

Another distinguishing feature of Iceland is the small number of immigrants. This has resulted historically in the absence of racial miscegenation, although this situation has changed somewhat in recent years. In 1966 only 4.29 per cent of Icelandic citizens were born in another country.

As far as health matters are concerned, the overall situation in Iceland is good, with little regional variation. Iceland boasts one of the world's longest life expectancy rates and the lowest infant mortality rate. The relative number of health personnel per capita in rural districts is generally equal to that of the capital, with the exception of highly specialised disciplines (Edvardsson, 1998: 68–71).

The University of Akureyri serves the whole island of Iceland outside the capital, a population of 108,488. Although some students from the capital enroll each year, about half of the students come from the Eyjafjörður district, which had a population of 20,148 in 1966 (Iceland, 1997). The employment pattern outside the capital is strongly characterised by agriculture, fish processing and industry, whereas trade, communications and the financial sector are highest in the area of the capital. The chief industries in the Eyjafjöður district display a pattern somewhat similar to the capital, although agriculture, fish processing and industry are of greater significance than in Reykjavík, and commerce, communications and services are less prominent. There is considerable variation in economic status from one region to another in Iceland. This tends to be 7–10 per cent below the national average in agricultural districts and 5 per cent above the average in areas where the fishing industry has flourished (Edvardsson, 1998: 23).

The number of high school and university graduates varies significantly regionally. In the case of high school graduates there is little variation according to region, with the exception of West Iceland and the West Fjiords. The low figures in the West Fjiords are noteworthy as they seem to indicate that academic learning has a low priority among young people in the region.

In the period 1995–96, 6,338 students were enrolled in programmes of specialised or university education who have permanent residence in south-west Iceland, 3.6 per cent of the total population of the area. Students residing elsewhere in Iceland make up a total of 1,477, or 1.6 per cent of the population. It is of interest to note that the proportion of specialised and university students is highest outside Reykjavík, in the neighbouring district of Reykjanes, followed by north-east Iceland where the effect of the University of Akureyri is apparent (Iceland, 1997: 32–4, 284–5, 288). This is in accordance with new information regarding the education of different occupational groups according to region, which indicates, for example, that over 40 per cent of employees on the Reykjavík labour market have either completed secondary school or a university degree, while the corresponding figure for West Iceland, the West Fjiords, East Iceland and South Iceland is 17–23 per cent (University of Iceland, 1997: 12).

From the above, it may be gathered that the districts served by the University of Akureyri have two distinguishing traits. First, the employment pattern is less varied than in and around the capital, and there is a marked emphasis on agriculture, fish processing and industry. Second, the proportion of persons with a university education is considerably lower than within the capital.

Higher education in Iceland

The first comprehensive legislation covering the entire higher education system as a whole in Iceland was passed by Parliament (Althingi) as late as 1997. According to this piece of legislation each higher educational institution is directly responsible to the Minister of Education, Research and Culture. Separate legislation passed by the Althingi for each institution defines their main roles in education and research; their responsibilities towards higher authorities; their internal organisation, and their administrative structure.

The higher education system in Iceland has three main levels. First is non-university education which is mainly provided within small, vocational colleges, but universities also offer short courses of study that lead to a non-university diploma. Education that leads to a first degree is the second level and takes place mainly within the universities and university colleges. A first university degree is either, a bachelor's degree or a *candidatus* degree. Graduate education is the third level. This is provided within the universities or university colleges only, and leads to a second university degree below the doctoral level, or to a doctorate. During its first decades university education in Iceland was modelled on the University of Copenhagen. However, since 1960 the structure of tertiary education has been increasingly influenced by the British and American models.

The foundation of the University of Iceland in 1911 marks the beginning of the modern Icelandic system of higher education. This first national university was created by merging three professional schools founded during the previous century (the schools of theology, medicine and law) and adding a Faculty of Arts. Before the founding of the university Icelandic students mainly travelled to Denmark for higher education. The University of Iceland has grown rapidly during this century. The original Faculties have been expanded and new ones have been added to extend the total number from four to nine. The new Faculties are Social Sciences, Natural Sciences, Economics and Business, Engineering and Dentistry.

In recent decades there has been growing pressure from various sectors in Icelandic society to upgrade post-secondary institutions and diversify the current system of higher education to meet the demand for more education and to accommodate an ever increasing number of students. Today, the higher education system in Iceland consists of one conventional university (the University of Iceland), the University of Akureyri and the University College of Education. In addition, there are several technical, vocational and art colleges that offer programmes at the higher education level. The University of Akrureyri is more specialised than the University of Iceland and has far fewer students. A university education is more readily available in the capital where the University of Iceland occupies a dominating position. During the 1995–96 academic year the University of Iceland had 5,199 university students out of a total of 6,601 for the country as a whole. There were 747 additional students at university level that year in seven schools. Of those, 685 (92 per cent) were located in Reykjavík, and 62 (8 per cent) were located at the National Athletics Teacher Training College at Laugarvatn which has now ceased operations (Ministry of Education, 1996: 26). These figures clearly indicate that the mainstream of tertiary education flows through the capital. There are a few specialised paths of higher education in the District of Borgarfjörðour and in Akureyri, but in other parts of Iceland university education is not available.

Like other higher educational institutions in Iceland, the University of Akureyri receives most of its funding through the state budget. However, the need for regional and local support, as well as external funding, has become increasingly important. The Icelandic Freezing Plant Corporations have to date donated one professorial chair in the processing techniques of fish products at the Fisheries Science Department and this kind of cooperation is likely to be extended in the future. Moreover, Akureyri Municipality provided the university with premises in its first years of operation and the Town Council is planning to build a research centre at the university, to be repaid over 25–30 years by the state. External funding amounted to approximately 10 per cent of the university budget in 1997.

The founding of the University of Akureyri

Formal instruction under the auspices of the university began on 5 September, 1987, but the bill creating the university was passed by the National Assembly on 27 April 1988. The opinions expressed by Members of Parliament during the debate on the issue clearly indicate that the main weight behind the decision to establish the university was an emphasis on regional development. The aim was to try to motivate young people to settle in the area and to commence instruction in short programmes of study of a practical nature which would be seen as relevant right from the foundation of the university. During the parliamentary debate, the Minister of Education, Birgir Ísleifur Gunnarsson, said, for example, 'I see a particular reason to rejoice in the fact that the north of Iceland now has a university. It is, in my opinion, an issue of utmost importance in regional development to provide the inhabitants of sparsely populated areas with extensive educational opportunities, maintaining, at the same time, high standards as far as the quality of education is concerned' (Parliamentary Reports, 26 April 1988). There was also a lengthy debate in the Assembly as to whether the University of Akureyri should be a traditional university, combining teaching with research, or an institution which provided instruction in practical subjects only and did not, therefore, deserve the designation of 'university'.

It should be mentioned that the representatives of the University of Iceland and other establishments in Reykjavík were adamantly opposed to the foundation of the new university. They argued that it was an indefensible error of judgement to establish a provincial university while the University of Iceland was starved of funds (Parliamentary Reports, 16 March 1988, 22 March 1988, 26 April 1998).

Originally, the stated purpose of the University of Akureyri was to provide its students with an education that fitted them for various tasks in industry, for positions of responsibility within the community or for further study at university level. Research under the auspices of the university was not included in the original aims. This, however, emerged later in an Act of the National Assembly of 18 May 1992.

Educators and others in Akureyri had talked of founding a university for decades before instruction commenced in the autumn of 1987. Some say that the distinguished poet, Davíd Stefánsson from Fagriskogur, was first officially to air the idea in an address on the occasion of the 100th anniversary of the Municipality of Akureyri in 1962. Ministers of Education appointed three successive committees to consider the foundation of a university in Akureyri, the first in 1982, the second in 1985 and the third in 1986. The first two committees recommended that a progamme of teaching should be instituted in Akureyri, in certain subjects, under the direction of the University of Iceland (University of Akureyri, 1987–92: 1–3). The third committee, appointed by Education Minister Sverrir Hermannsson, proposed that teaching at the university level should commence in the autumn of 1987. In a notice issued by the Ministry of Education on 18 June 1987 the Minister made it known that instruction was to commence in nursing and industrial management in the autumn of the same year. As far as teaching, studies and examinations were concerned, the planners took into account the nursing programme at the University of Iceland and the organisation of management studies at the Technical College in Reykjavík (University of Akureyri, 1987–92: 1–3).

Akureyri Municipality appointed a committee which prepared the basic curricula of the new university. It laid down the schedule of courses, suggesting a teaching programme in five categories; nursing, industrial management, microeconomics, fisheries science and food technology. The main emphasis was placed on short, practical programmes closely allied to industry (University of Akureyri, 1987–92: 1–3).

The current status of the University of Akureyri

The University of Akureyri has grown and prospered since its inauguration. This applies equally to the number of courses offered, the number of students, funding and staff. The university offered a four-year programme of nursing and a two-year programme of industrial management during its first semesters. A four-year programme in fisheries science commenced on 4 January, 1990 and a teacher training department offering a BEd was established in the autumn of 1993. Recent years have also seen an increasing variety of study options offered within these programmes. A teaching programme in total quality management, for example, was added to the Faculty of Management Studies in 1991, and in 1996 the Faculty was granted permission to offer a BSc in management studies. In the autumn of 1998 the Faculty launched studies in computer and information technology and tourism. There have been similar developments within other Faculties. The Faculty of Education initiated courses in pedagogics and curriculum theory in 1994, and a department of early child development in 1995. The department of food technology was introduced in the Faculty of Fisheries Science in 1995 and the Faculty of Health Sciences established a programme in occupational therapy in autumn 1997.

The University of Akureyri initiated a four-year BSc in nursing distance education programme in the West Fjords at Ísafjörður in the autumn semester of 1998. The instruction was conducted with the aid of interactive television and other communications media. A teacher at the University of Akureyri gave simultaneous instruction in Akureyri and Ísafjörður. Students in Ísafjörður interacted with the teacher on a television screen where they listened to a lecture and viewed all the visual materials presented as well as actively engaged in discussion to the same extent as the students in Akureyri. Other distance education media were also utilised, for example, web pages prepared by the instructor, e-mail and fax. A similar distance education programme is now in operation in the eastern part of Iceland and in one town in the southwest.

Student enrolment at the university has been characterised by a pattern of almost constant increase. In the university's first year of operation there were 50 students, whereas in 1997 there were 411. An increase in personnel has gone hand in hand with expanding student numbers and the development of more ambitious academic programmes. It has also managed to attract highly qualified teaching staff. However, there are ominous signs that the brain drain away from teaching posts to more lucrative positions in industry is beginning to impede the progress of the university's aspirations and even to cause some current academic programmes to falter.

The University of Akureyri and the Technical College have decided to investigate the possibility of merging some of their operations, such as those relating to information and registration systems, joint courses and the recruitment of staff. Another significant project is the plan to place the university's teaching and research facilities in one location. In 1995 the university acquired buildings of 2,400 square metres and land totalling 10 hectares in the centre of a new residential area in Akureyri. The new campus is within twenty minutes' walking distance of most residential districts in Akureyri. When the development, the campus is complete, will easily accommodate 1,500–2,000 students. The first phase, that of renovating older buildings and adapting them to their new role, began in 1995 and was completed in 1999. The second phase, the construction of new facilities, is expected to be completed in 2004. The building of a new 2,000 square metre research building is underway along with the preparation for a second phase. Akureyri Municipality has offered to finance the construction of these facilities in return for repayment by the state over 25–30 years. This is now under negotiation. If the outcome is positive, it would be possible to complete the research premises and begin using them by the year 2004.

The development of the new campus is an exciting and challenging project. The facilities will provide an impressive setting for the operations of the university and be one of the hallmarks of the town. The working environment of the students and the staff will be dramatically improved in the new buildings which will be specifically designed for their use.

The University of Akureyri and student access

One of the major roles of the University of Akureyri, and one of the main reasons for establishing it, is to provide much enhanced access to university education in the northern part of Iceland. The local people and government alike argued for the establishment of the university on both access and regional development grounds.

Low participation rates in higher education in rural areas are a reflection of many financial, educational and psychological barriers. The financial barrier is probably the most important, as it is very expensive to send a student to university for one year, more often than not an expense well beyond the means of most families. Another set of barriers to access for rural students is that, typically, they do not do as well in the sciences and languages as students from the larger urban areas. This is partly because fewer physical resources are available, partly because of a shortage of appropriately qualified teachers and partly because rural schools do not concentrate on those subjects required for university entry – the result of family and peer pressure being directed towards the world of practical activities at a relatively early stage. Among the significant psychological barriers for rural students is the widespread belief that a university education is not needed to acquire a well-paid job. Another psychological barrier is the problem of adjustment to going away from home, adapting to a big city and all its attractions, and adjusting to an independent lifestyle (Weller, 1998).

The University of Akureyri has been able to overcome most of these barriers in its short history. The majority of students at the university are relatively mature, with a mean age for males of 28.61 and for females of 28.85. Moreover, 54.7 per cent come from Akureyri and its vicinity, 29.7 per cent from the Reykjavík area and 15.6 per cent from outside both Akureyri and Reykjavík. Thus there is no doubt that the university offers a large number of people the opportunity to study who would otherwise have been deprived.

In a recent survey which included 295 nursing, teaching, industrial management and fisheries science, graduates from the University of Akureyri it was found that 197 (66.8 per cent) live and work in north Iceland, 51 (17.3 per cent) in other districts outside the capital, and 47 (15.9 per cent) in the Reykjavík area (Edvardsson, 1998: 48–9). There is no reason to believe that any tendency was present regarding the choice of domicile by graduates from educational establishments in Reyjavík, such as the University of Iceland or the University College of Education. In 1990, a year before the first nursing candidate graduated from the University of Akureyri, the total membership of the Association of University Graduates in Nursing numbered 530, only 29 (5.5 per cent) of whom were resident outside the capital. Therefore, it is clear that the establishment of the Faculty of Health Sciences at the University of Akureyri has contributed to the increased number of university graduates in nursing residing outside the capital.

Another example of the way in which the University of Akureyri has had a positive influence on regional development is the fact that although half the students in the Fisheries Science Faculty of the University of Akureyri originate from southwest Iceland, 80 per cent of fisheries science graduates find employment with fishing companies located outside the capital. A similar proportion of graduates from other Faculties opt to settle in the provinces.

The University of Akureyri and economic development

The University of Akureyri has had a substantial impact on economic development in northern Iceland by supporting and strengthening industry through its research and development activities, by providing employment opportunities for graduates in the north of Iceland, and by bringing fresh knowledge and ideas to the area. With its powerful computer systems and distance learning programmes, the university has reinforced the foundations of society, adding, at the same time, to the economic multiplication effect, especially in Akureyri.

The regions outside Reykjavík are heavily dependent on agriculture, the fishing industry and manufacturing, as has already been noted. In addition, the proportion of the labour force that is highly educated is relatively low in these areas. Forecasts indicate that jobs in these sectors of the economy will be largely automated and that future demands will enhance the importance of information technology as a condition of economic success. This means that a growing number of scientists, engineers and managers will be needed. Evidently, universities provide a key to future prosperity in rural regions.

The links between the University of Akureyri and industry are strengthened through various cooperative ventures with industrial research institutions. This is evident in the four contracts the university has agreed with industrial research institutions: the Marine Research Institute, the Icelandic Technology Institute, the Icelandic Fisheries Laboratories and the Agricultural Research Institute. The contracts involve cooperation in teaching and research, shared facilities and the co-hiring of specialists who have a contractual obligation to teach at the university. Employees hired under the terms of these cooperative contract have the same rights and obligations within the University of Akureyri as other members of the teaching staff, such as attending Faculty meetings and sitting on committees. They also have the same rights and opportunities to receive research grants and sabbaticals. The university's cooperation with industry's research institutions is most important, for in this way the university gains access to existing research and its results without the expense of establishing the Faculties and hiring the staff. The industrial research facilities also possess vast experience in dealing with industry and commerce. It may benefit any new university to organise its dealings with industry and commerce through such experienced partners as the industry research institutes. It should also be mentioned that the numerous international connections the research institutes enjoy benefit the university.

The University Research Institute has been at the forefront of strengthening the links between the university and industry and commerce. The Institute's experts have worked successfully in service and consulting capacities for various companies and institutions. The future emphasis of the Institute will be strengthening links with the teaching staff and students of the university. Primarily, this will involve placing greater emphasis on linking academic research at the university to consultation and information-sharing with industry and commerce. The university's formative influence on industry and commerce will become ever more visible in this way. Furthermore, the university will seek to align student projects ever closer to the Institute's companies work, so that the problems of industry and commerce will have a stronger voice in the shaping of teaching policy and will be reflected in student projects.

The university has had a tremendous impact on employment in the local economy. Akureyri has about 15,000 inhabitants. In direct terms the university employs about 55 full-time university staff. However, it also boosted print shops, hotels, restaurants, bookshops, computer agencies, travel agencies and airlines through its publications, conferences, investments and transportation of specialists. Moreover, the university has provided schools, hospitals and private firms in the local economy with urgently needed educated personnel. The hiring of university graduates has become far easier in the Eyjafjörður area after the founding of the University of Akureyri. Before 1987, for example, the provincial hospital had to advertise for registered nurses in German, Norwegian, Danish and Swedish journals. Furthermore, university-educated staff have had a tangible impact on the work of teachers and nurses in the northern areas. The nursing director at the hospital in Akureyri and headmasters in the area are in agreement that services have improved thanks to educated staff, as well as to innovation and development. They also point out that the university library is important for the education and training of staff (Johannesdottir, 1997).

Another economic impact related to the University of Akureyri is the spin-off effects. This can be seen in the new companies and institutes that have been founded in Akureyri. One example is the Vilhjalmur Stefansson Arctic Institute, founded in 1998. Another example is the computer company Hugur-Forritunararpjónusta (Programming Service) which established a subsidiary in Akureyri in 1998. One of the key premises for starting up the company there is related to the university, namely, the fact that an information technology cause is being planned which will provide the firm with educated personnel in the near future, as well as facilitating cooperative projects in the years to come.

Another impact of universities and higher education institutions is their investment in computers, distance-learning devices and communications, thereby enhancing the infrastructure of their local economy. This has happened in the case of the University of Akureyri. The economic multiplier effect of the University of Akureyri is worth considering as well. Estimates for 1997 reveal that some ISK 233 million (US$31.6 million) will be allocated to the university budget. Based on the assumption that every krona has a multiplier effect of 1.5 for trade, services and commerce in Akureyri and its vicinity, the economic value of the university amounts to ISK 349.5 (US$47.5 million) million a year.

The University of Akureyri has not succeeded in stemming the decline of traditional industries in the Eyjafjöður region, since general economic developments are very hard to manage. As with the rest of the world's industrialised countries, employment in manufacturing has declined since 1987 in Iceland. However, opportunities in education, health care, research and services have grown steadily in recent decades. It is a recurrent trend where society develops from an industrial into a post-industrial society. The University of Akureyri furthers that development by increasing the number of graduates and educating more professionals to participate in the economy, and by providing research and development for businesses in the local economy.

The University of Akureyri and social and cultural development

The University of Akureyri has had a substantial impact on cultural life in northern Iceland. The first point to be made in this connection is the fact that both the staff and the students of the university are undeniably demanding customers as far as the 'cultural market' is concerned since they are keen patrons of the theatre, concerts and other cultural events. The students frequent cinemas, pubs, cafés and other places of entertainment, thereby strengthening the financial bases of such locales.

However, the extramural summer programme has to be regarded as the university's most important contribution to art and culture in Eyjafjörður. This is a splendid example of the way a university can reach out to the general public with lectures, courses and exhibitions appealing to a wide range of interests. The ivory tower of academe has thrown its doors wide open in the summer, letting in a refreshing breeze from outside, creating contacts with the general population and enhancing popular appreciation of its role within the community.

The University of Akureyri has a positive image in the town and has helped to enhance a confident and independent outlook among the local inhabitants. Both the general public and the administrative sector regard the university as a symbol of progress and innovation. This positive attitude also applies to the national government in Reykjavík, which has demonstrated respect for its value and support for its operations. It is fully understood in the political arena that the university plays a vital part in regional development and in the creation of employment opportunities for young scientists and professionals.

Conclusions

The University of Akureyri was established in the autumn of 1987 with the aim of providing its students with an education well suited to participation in industry or to further academic study. Regional development policies that is, the importance of offering young people a university education in their home town or district, weighed heavily in the decision to embark on this venture. The university has done well in fulfilling the expectations it raised, as can be seen from the fact that 70 per cent of its graduates settled in the north of Iceland after completing their studies. But the university has a more wide-ranging effect. It provides the opportunity to study in the home region; it supports and strengthens industry through its research and development; it provides employment opportunities for graduates in the north of Iceland; it brings fresh knowledge and ideas to the area; and it strengthens the foundations of society with its powerful computer systems and distance learning, as well as adding to the economic multiplier effects, especially in Akureyri.

There is every indication that the University of Akureyri can look to the future with confidence and optimism. It is a rapidly growing institution which has proved its value to society. Apart from traditional instruction which expands every year, distance education programmes aimed at other parts of the country are in the pipeline. Thus the role of the university has evolved, as it has moved from a local university into an institution that serves the whole country. The University of Akureyri and, in fact, all northern educational institutions have become increasingly important for sparsely populated areas, as agriculture and industry decline in importance as providers of employment, whereas the information and knowledge sectors continually increase in importance.

References

Bell, Daniel (1973) *The Coming of Post-Industrial Society: A Venture into Social Forecasting* (New York: Peregrine Books).

Edvardsson, Ingi Runar (ed.) (1998) *Byggdastefna til nyrrar aldar* (Reykjavík: The Institute of Regional Development and the University of Akureyri Research Institute).

Gunnarsson, Gisli Agust (1993) 'Population and Regional Development 1880–1990', in Halfdansson and Kristjansson (eds.) *Islensk thjodfelagsthroun 1880–1990* (Reykjavík: The Social Research Institute and The Historical Institute).

Halfdansson, Gudmundur and Kristjansson, Svanur (eds.) (1993) *Islensk thjod-felagsthroun 1880–1990* (Reykjavík: The Social Research Institute and The Historial Research Institute).

Iceland (1996) *Statistical Yearbook of Iceland 1996* (Reykjavík: The Icelandic Bureau of Statistics).

Iceland (1997) *Statistical Yearbook of Iceland 1997* (Reykjavík: The Icelandic Bureau of Statistics).

Johannesdottir, Gudrun Agusta (1997) *Tengsl Haskolans a Akureyri og Akureyrarboejar vio nyskopun i atvinnulifi* (Akureyri: Nyskopunarsjodsverkefni).

Ministry of Education (1996) *Statistical Manual on Education and Culture* (Reykjavík: Ministry of Education).

Olafsdottir, Gudrun and Persson, Lars Olof (1995) 'Lansbygdens uttunning pa Island', in Persson (ed.) *Balanserad uttunning* (Stockholm: NordRefo 1995: 1).

Parliamentary Reports, 16 March 1988, debate at the 110th Assembly (Reykjavík: Athingi, the Icelandic Parliament).

Parliamentary Reports, 22 March 1988, debate at the 110th Assembly (Reykjavík: Athingi, the Icelandic Parliament).

Parliamentary Reports, 26 April 1988, debate at the 110th Assembly (Reykjavík: Athingi, the Icelandic Parliament).

Persson, Lars Olof (ed.) (1995) *Balanserad uttunning* (Stockholm: NordRefo 1995: 1).

The University of Akureyri (1987–92) *The Yearbook of the University of Akureyri* (Akureyri, 1–3).

The University of Iceland, Faculty of Social Sciences (1997) *The Icelandic Living Standard* (Reykjavík: The University of Iceland).

Weller, Geoffrey R. (1998) *Universities in Northern Canada*. A paper presented at the 37th annual meeting of the Western Regional Science Association, Monterey, California, 18–21 February 1998.

Yearbook of Nordic Statistics 1996 (Copenhagen: Nord 1996: 1).

6
Greenland and the University of Greenland

Per Langgård

Introduction

Ilisimatusarfik is a Greenlandic word which means 'an institution to promote wisdom' but which is now commonly understood to mean 'the university'. Ilisimatusarfik does not look at all like one's idea of a modern
university. It is a very small and a very young institution with extremely
limited resources, placed in a little old house next to the sea, in a very
small society. In comparison with other universities, with their masses of
students and highly specialised Faculties, Ilisimatusarfik seems to be in a
weak position. With a total of 130 students and about a dozen faculty
members to cover all subjects in four departments with four different
profiles Ilisimatusarfik can hardly be expected to produce quantities of
scientific data and academic breakthroughs.

However, as the only university in the young Greenlandic society,
Ilisimatusarfik, in spite of its smallness, is the national centre for higher
education in Greenland. Thus it has enormous symbolic importance
in addition to its obvious significance as the producer of academically
trained Greenlandic-speaking Greenlanders. Furthermore, Ilisimatusarfik
is not only the only Greenlandic university, it is the only university with
MA and PhD programmes in the Inuit language in the whole Inuit area of
the circumpolar north. Moreover, Ilisimatusarfik is fully controlled and
and financed by the indigenous Greenlandic government, which makes it
the only fully-fledged, indigenous-controlled university in the world.

The story of Ilisimatusarfik is unique, as unique as the history of Greenland itself and its Inuit language and culture. This chapter provides a brief
general introduction to Greenland and tells the story of Ilisimatusarfik. It

also outlines how a series of fortuitous developments synergetically paved the way for the smallest university in the world to survive and prosper.

An introduction to Greenland

Greenland is the biggest island in the world. It has an area of more than 2 million square kilometres, 85 per cent of which is covered by the ice cap. The distance from the north (some 700 kilometres from the North Pole) to the south (60 degrees north) is 2,670 kilometres, and from east to west is more than 1,000 kilometres. Despite the enormous size of the island the Greenlandic climate is comparatively uniform, with summer temperatures ranging between +5° C and +10° C and winter temperatures ranging between –30° C and –5° C. All of Greenland is north of the timber line. Greenland is a mountainous country with almost no arable land. Attempts to exploit non-renewable resources have to date been largely unprofitable. However, prospects and prospectors are many, at least during the summer. It is the sea that was and is the source of livelihood in Greenland. A comparatively rich marine fauna was the basis of the small traditional seal-hunting societies and nowadays it is the basis of a modern deep-sea fishing industry.

About 4,000 years ago the first waves of paleoeskimo cultures emigrated to Greenland. The neo-eskimos arrived in the northern parts of Greenland just before the turn of the millennium, around the same time as the Norse settlers arrived in the southern part of the country. The Inuit culture has survived to the present day, whereas the Norse culture perished after a period of some 500 years. But the Norse settlers left one important fingerprint on the history of Greenland, an agreement between the Norsemen and the Norwegian king signed in 1261. This is the foundation of Greenland's present constitutional status as part of the Danish kingdom.

The next very important stepping-stone in the history of Greenland came in 1721 when the first missionary and a trading company arrived. This was the start of a paternalistic and protectionist colonial period that lasted for some 250 years. Greenland was effectively closed and the only contact with the surrounding world was via the Royal Greenlandic Trade Department (RGTD). In 1953 the Danish constitution was changed, Greenland's status as a colony ceased and it formally became an integral part of Denmark. Finally, in 1978, the Home Rule Act was passed by the Danish Parliament, and in 1979 Home Rule was introduced in Greenland.

On 1 January 1997, 55,971 persons were living in Greenland. Of this total, 23 per cent were living in the capital, Nuuk, 58 per cent in the other 17 towns, 17 per cent in villages and 2 per cent outside municipalities in places such as remote communications posts and military airfields. In 1960 the total population was around 30,000 and the corresponding percentages were 9 per cent, 49 per cent, 40 per cent, and 3 per cent, thus reflecting a rapid population growth and a tendency towards concentration in recent decades. This tendency towards concentration is not a recent feature even though the process was somewhat higher during the so-called Danisation years. As far back as the records go, there has been a tendency for people from smaller places to move to the next biggest dwelling places, ultimately depopulating the smallest villages and increasing the number of inhabitants in the capital dramatically.

At the beginning of the nineteenth century some 6,000 Inuit lived in Greenland. By 1950 that number had increased to about 25,000, giving an annual average growth rate of a little less than 1.5 per cent. Between 1950 and 1964 the growth rate rocketed to an average of 3.6 per cent resulting in the total number of Inuit in Greenland increasing to 35,000 in 1964. Since then the growth rate has stabilised at around 1 per cent per year, resulting in a total Inuit population today of approximately 49,000.

In the colonial period only a very few Danes, approximately 2 per cent, lived in Greenland. During the Danisation years the number of Danes increased considerably reaching a peak in 1975 of 10,000 Danes, comprising almost 20 per cent of the total population. Many of them were construction workers who left Greenland after a few years. However, quite a number settled, often marrying Greenlandic women and thus producing a considerable group of people with mixed ancestry (about one-third of the young generation in the towns). After a few years the number of Danes coming to Greenland started to decrease and has been steadily decreasing since then. Today about 12 per cent of the population are Danes.

Interaction between Danes and Greenlanders is remarkably smooth. Even though awareness of ethnicity is high among Greenlanders, as well as among Danes, it is almost always addressed in a pragmatic, non-racist manner. Some racism at the individual level was and is common, of course. But at the official level, and as a general trend, Greenland has always followed a policy of integration and equality of rights. Consequently, even though ethnic mix is an issue in Greenlandic realities, it is not as important as many outsiders seem to think. However, the germ of a multifaceted split in Greenlandic society is very obvious today. This is because the society is split vertically and horizontally on a wide range of parameters, including ethnic background, language, politics and education.

Public expenditures in Greenland in 1995 accounted for some US$794 million. About 95 per cent was administered by Greenland's Home Rule government and by the Greenlandic municipalities. The rest, some

US$89.4 million, was administered by the Danish authorities. These large figures for public expenditures are primarily the consequence of a government that is deeply involved in a wide range of enterprises, such as fishing and housing, which in a different political system would be private. In short, Greenland is a welfare state deeply influenced by Nordic social democratic traditions. This is clearly seen when one notes the sources of revenue for about Canadian $289 million is received via taxation, around Canadian $344 million from a general contribution from Denmark to the Home Rule government, and around Canadian $41.3 million from the European Union. The rest is income from other sources, including expenditures in Greenland handled by the Danish ministries via Danish grants.

Except for limited sheep-breeding in the southernmost part of the country there is little agriculture in Greenland. Ever since prehistoric times subsistence in Greenland has been based on the resources in the sea; sea mammals in the older hunting culture and currently fish. During the late 1800s climatic change took place in Greenland. Partly for this reason the number of seals decreased thus producing major problems for the kayak-hunting economy. Nowadays seal-hunting is the livelihood of only a limited group living mainly in remote parts of Greenland. Nevertheless, the symbolic value of seal hunting is very high. Large shoals of cod showed up in the Greenlandic waters after the loss of the seals. During the early twentieth century the Danish colonial authorities took the initiative and started a small-scale fishing industry. Greenlanders were given the opportunity to purchase, on quite easy terms, small boats and other necessary equipment. In addition, a number of state-owned and state-run salting-houses were built.

With the new constitution of 1953 Denmark opened up the previously closed-off island. As a consequence flotillas of foreign fishing vessels entered the rich waters around Greenland. Exact figures for the value of the catch are hard to come by, but they are no doubt enormous. The Greenlandic fishing fleet and the Greenlandic fish processing industry were unable to compete with the technologically and economically much stronger foreigners. Gradually the Royal Greenlandic Trading Company (RGTC) entered into large-scale fishing in spite of the fact that it had originally been the political intention to encourage Greenlanders to undertake private initiatives in the fishing sector. The drift towards public control of fishing was continued and even strengthened with the introduction of Home Rule. The effect of this public, large-scale approach has been an enormous increase in the value of Greenlandic fish exports. In the 1960s the overall value of Greenlandic enterprises' sale of fish was less than Canadian $8.25 million whereas nowadays it is in the area of Canadian $282 million.

The situation in the Greenlandic labour market differs radically in a number of respects from most countries in the Western World. The vast majority of the total labour force in Greenland is employed by the government, either the Home Rule government (including Home Rule-controlled corporations) and the municipal councils, or the Danish state. This situation makes it possible to use conditions of employment as a political tool, and employment has always been used this way in Greenland.

To understand this situation one must go back to the phase when Greenland was entirely cut off from the surrounding world, a period that lasted for more than 200 years. The colonial power, Denmark, had very few representatives in Greenland, just a handful of Danes in the district centres and none at all in the small villages. It is important to keep in mind that, in contrast to the siuation in arctic Canada, the few outsiders were neither private entrepreneurs, such as Hudson Bay Company workers, trappers and private missionaries, nor men-of-arms like the Royal Canadian Mounted Police. The Danes were government officials, doctors and representatives of the National Church. They were normally well prepared before arriving in Greenland. Preparations included courses in the Greenlandic language and, frequently, a period with people experienced an working in Greenland, for example, in the Danish department of the Royal Greenland Trading Company (RGTC).

The stated policy during this period was to keep development at a pace fitting with the so-called 'Greenlandic circumstances', that is, at a level where 'the natives' themselves could manage the society without imported workers. Consequently, for a long time there was little progress. Well into the twentieth century the majority of Greenlanders were still living off the land, first as hunters then as fishermen. However, more and more of the skilled and semi-skilled jobs developed in the RGTC or in the churches and their schools. Increasingly, native Greenlanders worked as caretakers, handymen, sunday school teachers, clerks, foremen and even as managers of the RGTC shops. Throughout the colonial period tuberculosis was widespread. To combat the disease effectively a whole series of policies was needed relating to hospitals, population relocations, the construction of adequate housing and the provision of modern education. These policies had the effect of undermining the old colonial form of rule.

With the coming of the new constitution in 1953 the old order changed dramatically. In order to achieve health, educational and other goals, the whole infrastructure in Greenland had to be upgraded to a high technological level. As a consequence Danish workers and engineers had to be brought in. At the same time it was necessary to recruit many professionals including doctors, teachers and administrators to take care of duties in the now modern society. However, the traditional philosophy that Greenlanders should take care of Greenlandic affairs was not altered, at least, not in theory. The whole modernisation phase was seen as an interlude. The Danish workers went to Greenland to build roads, houses, airfields, harbours and factories as well as to educate a limited number of Greenlanders to take over and run the new society. Once this phase was over, the intention was that the Danes would return home. However, it did not work out that way. Innovation and change seemed to require further innovation and change. Consequently, the large-scale importation of Danes continued until the mid-1970s, and the Inuit were increasingly put in the position of passive spectators. Despite this throughout the period of modernisation, Greenland, was regarded as Inuit land, not only by the Inuit themselves but also by the outside world.

The situation became untenable as ethnic and political awareness grew among the Inuit and the importation of Danes was steadily reduced. Reflecting this trend, a regulation was passed that stated that a worker could only be brought in from the outside if the position cannot be filled by a local person. As a consequence, the importation of low and semi-skilled Danes almost ceased. However, the introduction of Home Rule in 1979, and the transfer of resources from Denmark to Greenland, meant that there was a growing need for highly skilled workers.

Traditional Greenlandic culture has at all times been held in high esteem by Greenlanders as well as by Danes. In the early 1800s Danish missionaries started to collect the old tales and as early as 1859 a bilingual four-volume collection of the oral tradition was published at government expense. As a consequence of this high esteem, carvers and painters have always had strong public support. One example of this is the RGTC's free-of-charge sale and distribution of arts and handicrafts. The general respect for traditional culture is still a striking feature of Greenlandic society. Institutions, associations and Home Rule enterprises all have logos bearing motifs from the traditional culture. Kayaks, semilunar knives (*ulu*), harpoons, game symbols, drums and the like are found everywhere, confirming the high esteem in which traditional culture is held. A closer inspection does not change this basic assumption. Publishing activity in Greenland until recently has been carried out by public means and the vast majority of novels deal with great kayakers. It is also a fact that investment in musuems, folklore, historical and archeological exhibits, and private associations and clubs dealing with the traditional culture, such as kayakers' unions and old dance clubs, are considerable. Such high esteem holds true for modern Greenlandic society. The public awareness of, as well as moral and economic support for, Greenlandic studios, theatre groups and exhibitions dealing with the old culture is high.

But it is an open question whether it is enough. Greenland is for better or for worse a part of the international cultural mainstream and the Greenlandic culture now competes with the video industry, international publishers, American cartoons, French movies, and the like. This competition is especially and directly felt by better educated Greenlanders who speak Danish and/or English. While Greenlandic culture, in theory as well as in practice, is the official culture of Greenland the question is whether or not Greenlanders in the years to come will venerate the symbolic value of the traditional culture sufficiently to maintain its high status or adapt the traditional culture to modern forms and standards, thereby making it possible for the local and international cultures to coexist. The latter approach is precisely what the younger generations and the better educated are crying out for and a number of very promising attempts have been made and, the prospects for cultural survival seem promising.

While all other minorily languages of the world struggle for survival, Greenland has established the daring political goal of developing a monolingual Greenlandic society. This is a most unusual state of affairs and many scholars believe Greenland's situation is unique. Since it is not possible to understand the University of Greenland outside the language context I shall deal with it at some length.

Greenlandic is the principal dialect of the Eastern Eskimo language, not radically diferent from Inuktitut in Canada or Inuupiaq in Alaska, but very different from the Western dialects spoken south of the Norton Bay region in Alaska or in Siberia. Greenlandic has always been held in high esteem, not only by Greenlanders but also by representatives of the Danish colonial administration. Therefore Greenlandic never went into decline whereas almost all other indigenous languages did. Greenland has had its own newspaper in Greenlandic since 1861, and the radio braodcasting system, which was established during the Second World War and renewed in 1958, now broadcasts some 2,500 hours yearly in

Greenlandic as compared to around 1,400 hours in Danish and around 1,400 hours of music. It should also be mentioned that written, as opposed to oral tradition, Greenlandic literature has been produced for about 100 years with a full-fledged network of publishers, printing houses, libraries, book shops and authors' unions. Original novels and poems, together with non-fiction, in Greenlandic cover many metres of book shelves. In addition, a large number of titles were translated into Greenlandic throughout the twentieth century. Finally, it should be mentioned that the very newest media have also found their way to Greenland. During recent decades a number of recording studios and video production companies have had a steady output of records and videos in Greenlandic.

This is not to imply that Greenlandic has not been perceived to be threatened; it definitely has been and still is. During the Danisation period, in the period of rapid modernisation, it was a very generally believed that Greenlandic was doomed. There can be no doubt that there was an actual threat to the language during this period. First, there was a desire to be very Danish in the first hectic years after the new constitution came into force. This desire was characterised, in part, by a general wish to be fluent in Danish. Second, modernisation had the effect of producing a large number of people of mixed race who were generaly monolingual in Danish. Third, there were so many innovations, and therefore so many new concepts and new items, to be labelled in Greenlandic, that the language was unable to keep up with it. The result was a massive importation of loan words from other languages. Yet despite all these developments Greenlandic survived. Recent research by Langaard and others has documented that with the greater emphasis on 'Greenlanderness' in the 1970s, the status of the Greenlandic language rose considerably and positive attitudes toward everything Danish more or less disappeared. 'Greenlandic good, Danish bad' summed up the new attitude. Concomitant with the change in general attitudes parents of mixed-race children began to choose a bilingual model for their children instead of the earlier monolingual Danish model. In addition, the Danish government before 1979 and the Home Rule government after 1979 began to invest money and energy in the production of teaching materials in Greenlandic to provide and secure a Greenlandic terminology in all the new fields. Finally, an official body, The Greenlandic Language Board, was created in 1980 as a parliamentary committee. As a consequence, Danish influence is diminishing, while the use of Greenlandic is expanding dramatically.

Education in Greenland and the place of the university

Schooling was introduced in Greenland almost at the very beginning of the colonial period. In an 1825 report it was stated that almost all Greenlanders could read, but that few could write. Whether this was actually the case is questionable. However, it is a fair estimate that illiteracy by and large was eliminated after 1847, for in that year two teacher training colleges were established in Greenland. One closed in 1875, but the other has been functioning now for over 150 years.

Schooling was general but limited, and in the 1905 Educational Act, reinforced in the 1925 Act, the teacher training college was reformed and the first high school curricula were introduced. Vocational training in Greenland goes back a long way. Even a hundred years ago Greenlanders were trained to be midwives, carpenters, typesetters and clerks. As early as 1879 the first 'Greenlanders' House' was established in Copenhagen as a dormitory and a centre for Greenlanders studying in Denmark. But it was not until the Modernisation Act of 1950 that vocational training became widely available.

During the Danisation period instruction was carried out in Danish, in accordance with the general political climate of the time, and quite a number of young Greenlanders were sent to Denmark for secondary and tertiary education. From 1970 this policy increasingly became criticised, and during the next fifteen years, the Greenlandisation period, the Danish language and Danish eduational values were held in very low esteem. 'The special Greenlandic circumstances' was a popular phrase and summed up the desire for an educational system especially designed for Greenland, with little or no attention paid to whether or not the education would be of use outside Greenland.

A whole series of new educational approaches especially tailored for Greenland were introduced, including the founding of an Inuit Institute in 1983. It was believed that Inuit control of Inuit education in itself would solve the problems. Part of the new approach was to lower standards and to place more emphasis on pre-colonial values, the rationale being that Greenland, compared to Denmark, was a country with a lower level of technology, a different language and a different tradition.

Greenlandisation was needed and much valuable experience was gained from the process. On the other hand, it is being acknowledged that the rejection of the European focus on technology and positivism and 'European materialism' has its price. Even before 1979 Greenland was deeply involved in this 'European materialism' for its fishing fleet was heavily dependent on technology, its trading partners did not speak

Greenlandic, and its population was accustomed to high standards of housing, public services and communications. The new educational approach based on the old ideals could not meet such demands. As a consequence the tide turned again. It is now a very widely held opinion among the younger generation that compromises in the educational system are unacceptable, Greenlandic educational levels and standards must be appropriate to modern society and that modern society should be a mixture of Greenlandic and imported cultures. It might even be said that in recent years a vanguard Greenlandic yuppie generation has emerged, that is, a generation of Greenlandic-speaking young people with a footing in the hunters' culture but with their hands and heads full of everything that is 'hot' in Greenland as well as in the wider world.

Whereas the traditions of compulsory schooling and of college education go back a long way in Greenlandic history, university education has been entirely unknown in Greenland and very few Greenlanders have received a university education outside Greenland. As late as 1965 there were only eight Greenlanders attending university in Denmark.

Until recently university life and jobs requiring university-level training have been exclusively a Danish preserve. However, this picture changed in 1970 and the number of Greenlanders in the Danish university system increased dramatically. Over the last few years the number has been stable at around 250 students.

The founding of Ilisimatusarfik

Early developments

At the autumn 1974 session of Greenland's Provincial Council, two proposals concerning academic affairs were voiced (Greenlandic Provincial Council, 1974: 205ff). Mr Jonathan Motzfeldt, who later became Greenland's premier, suggested that a new institution dealing with the Greenlandic language and the native Greenlandic culture be established. Another member of the Council suggested that the Institute of Eskimology be transferred from the University of Copenhagen to Greenland. Later the two proposals were merged in one common proposal that a university-like institution named the 'Inuit Institute' be established. When Mr Motzfeldt introduced the proposal he suggested that the Greenlandic Provincial Council needed top-level Greenlandic advice on questions such as the development of Greenlandic society, culture and language, as well as the environmental protection associated with the mining industries. Motzfeldt also suggested that Greenlanders should constitute a majority on the Board of Directors of the new institute and that researchers should be Greenlanders. He even went to the extent of arguing that Greenalnders who did not meet professional qualifications should be part of the staff. Finally he suggested that the Inuit Institute should be located in Nuuk.

The proposal was well received by the Council and a commission was set up, but for various reasons never convened. However, with the introduction of Home Rule in 1979 things changed. In April 1980 the Minister for Education and Cultural Affairs appointed three Greenlanders to prepare a report on the proposed 'Inuit Institute'. The commission completed its work in November 1980 and in the autumn 1981 session the minister was ready to present a proposal for an Act concerning the Inuit Institute to Parliament. He stated in this presentation:

> In the mandate I asked the commission to give further suggestions as to how the Inuit Institute can organise studies on our cultural inheritance including language, history and our present situation. And I fully agree with the commission's proposal that the Institute during its first years of existence should attempt to look at our cultural inheritance as a whole and so avoid being split up in single, isolated subjects. In a time when conditions for life change that rapidly, it is of vital importance that we can compare our present situation to the one that our forefathers had to live in. To avoid misunderstandings I shall stress that this is not to be perceived as a nostalgic attempt to return to a period long gone. The fact is that any society wanting to know itself needs to know its history as well as its present to ensure that future innovations rest on a firm foundation.
>
> (Motzfeldt, 1974: 205)

The Inuit Institute Act was passed unanimously on 16 October 1981. The official name of the Act is 'Act No. 8 regarding Ilisimatusarfik (Inuit Institute)'. The Act's objectives clause states: 'Greenland's Home Rule creates an institution, Ilisimatusarfik, which is to pursue research and education in the Grenlandic culture and language, history, and present conditions.'

In the summer of 1983 a small building was ready for occupation and the Inuit Institute began functioning. As the first step. Professor Robert Petersen was appointed as Rector of the Institute. Professor Petersen is a native Greenlander who at the time held a chair at the University of Copenhagen. He remained Rector until his retirement in 1995. Shortly after his appointment four Associate Professors were engaged, including the author, two of whom were Greenlanders, one a Greenlandic-speaking Dane and one a 'typical southerner', that is a Dane who did not speak Greenlandic. The first curriculum, which painstakingly fulfilled the intention of the founding Act, was finished before Christmas 1983. On 1 February 1994 the first students began their education.

The Inuit Institute

The 1984 curriculum certainly looked at 'Our [Greenlandic] cultural inheritance as a whole', to quote the Minister's introduction. Admission to the Institute was granted to Greenlandic-speaking students who passed the 'GU' examination (that is, Danish 'studnentereksamen' or grade 14/15 in Canada) with average or above-average marks. Subjects taught included Greenlandic grammer, Greenlandic literature, Greenlandic history and a Greenlandic framework in political science. Furthermore, effort was invested in politically and/or culturally 'hot' Greenlandic items, such as the Inuit Circumpolar Conference, Inuit dialectology and folklore. The curriculum aimed at producing a BA level degree after two years of study and at ensuring a qualification that would lead to transfer to Danish universities. Thus, originally, the Inuit Institute was a near-classic example of a community college or local university teaching local subjects to local students in accordance with the intentions of the local politicians.

However, it was soon realised that there were significant problems in at least two major areas. First, as scholars and social scientists striving for objectivity the Faculty soon found themselves in conflict with public opinion and some local political aims. Furthermore, they began to realise that their students had trouble fulfilling the expectations placed on them. They seemed to lack basic academic abilities. After a rather painful period of introspection it was concluded that the problem was partly rooted in the curriculum and partly in the students' background of compulsory and secondary schooling. As a consequence the very holistic approach to local culture had to be abandoned and a much more traditional, discipline-by-discipline approach adopted. In addition, the traditional academic basics had to be introduced as the very kernel of the curriculum. These included general phonetics, morphology and syntax to students of Greenlandic grammar; general economic and political models to students of Greenlandic society; source material analysis and general historical methodology to students of Greenlandic history, and so on. This remedial programme to redress students' inadequate backgrounds meant that the courses had to be lengthened. As a consequence the Inuit Institute Act was repealed on 9 May 1989 and a new Act, 'Act No. 3 1989 regarding Ilisimatusarfik [University of Greenland]' was passed on the same date. In the objectives clause of the new Act it is stated that 'Ilisimatusarfik is to carry out research and offer academic education. Ilisimatusarfik is to promote knowledge regarding scientific methods and results.'

The University of Greenland

Quite a number of innovations resulted from the Act and its new objectives. In fact, the original organisation of the Inuit Institute as well as the 1984 curriculum have been totally abandoned. Instead, features which to a considerable degree resemble those of the Nordic universities have been introduced. The University of Greenland is a branch of the Home Rule Government's Ministry of Education and all its activities are financed by public funds. In the fiscal year 1998 the total grant from the government amounted to about 9.1 million Danish kroner (approximately $US1.38 million). The University of Greenland no longer has an appointed leader. In order to secure the university's independence from political interests the activities now are managed by the Rector and the Prorector, who are democratically elected members of Faculty. All Full and Associate Professors are eligible for these offices. The Rector is elected for a period of three years and the Prorector is elected for one year. The Rector is responsible for all political and fiscal matters. As a counterbalance to the Rector's position there is a democratically elected University Board, which comprises one faculty member and one student per Department, one representative of the administrative staff, the Rector, the Prorector and two politically appointed representatives. Only Greenlandic-speaking students who pass the 'GU' examination with good results and who have good marks in Danish and English are accepted as students.

At present four Departments carry out academic programmes and research. The Department of Theology has two professors. It offers a BD programme which, if complemented with one year of practical theology at a theological college, entitles the students to hold positions as ministers in the National Church of Greenland. It also offers a BA degree aimed at providing teaching qualifications in religion at the 'GU' level. The Department of Greenlandic Language and Literature has a staff of four professors. This Department offers BA and MA degrees in language and literature for teachers at the 'GU' level or other academic positions involving Greenlandic or general literature and linguistics. The Department of Cultural and Social History also has four professors. This Department offers BA and MA degrees leading to positions as teachers at the 'GU' level or other academic positions requiring professional knowledge in history or anthropology. Finally, the Department of Public Administration offers BA and MA degrees in administrative science which entitle the candidates to hold professional positions in the public and private sectors. Postgraduate studies (PhD) are carried out in collaboration with Danish universities.

The impact of Ilisimatusarfik

Practical or symbolic?

The great differences in the objectives clauses of the 1981 Act and the 1989 Act make it clear that they were two fundamentally different Acts with two fundamentally different purposes. What happened between 1981 and 1989?

First and foremost, the 1981 Act reflected the intense nation-building process that was taking place during the 1970s as a reaction to what was perceived as an imposed, Danish modernisation. This process culminated in 1979 with the introduction of Home Rule in Greenland. The creation of a very overt nationalism usually requires symbols, and symbols for such a purpose are typically taken from history, and typically from those features of the old culture that are as far removed as possible from the culture the new nationalism is in opposition to. As might be expected, the Greenlandic language, old hunting tools and old family patterns became prime symbols in Greenland. In addition, old tales flourished. The concept of 'Greenlanders' respect for their elders was contrasted with the European and American concept of the 'gap between the generations'. Modern novels dealt with old skilled hunters. Art turned its back on the present and portrayed the past. The supranational Inuit institution, the ICC, acquired a very high status, and positive connations were accorded to the words 'Greenlander', 'Greenlandic', 'hunter' and 'kinsmen', the last term meaning the Inuit in Canada, Alaska and Siberia. By the same token having one's own university is an ideal symbol for a new nation. Even though some 'conservative' scholars did frown upon it because they feared it was too restricted in the range of topics taught and its world-view, quite a number of advisers were fully in favour of the concept of a community university. Small wonder then that an Act creating a national university, dealing with national symbols, was unanimously passed in 1981.

After the establishment of the Inuit Institute, two very different developments took place which pulled it in a different direction and changed its status. First, Home Rule matured and proved to be a success. Consequently the younger generations no longer needed the rather militant nationalism and its concomitant symbols. Thus, at about the time of the tenth anniversary of Home Rule, nationalism seemed to put on its working clothes. The concept of 'Greenlanderness' being in itself a qualification was questioned. Whether Greenlander or not, the officer at the Department of Economics needs to know his field. Mistakes simply cannot be countenanced. As parents Greenlanders were not willing to let their children pay the price of falling behind because of such things as outdated teaching methods. They want the best for their children and thus they now pay less attention to questions of ethnicity. So in almost all respects modern Greenlandic society gives priority to professional skills then, if skills are equal, Greenlanders are preferred to non-Greenlanders living in Greenland.

The second development was that the staff of the Inuit Institute began to realise that 'looking at our cultural inheritance as a whole' left the students with too much superficial knowledge of academic craftsmanship. The students' level of sophistication prior to graduation, that is the BA level according to the curriculum of 1984, and their ability to find their own way in academic matters were substandard. Or, to put it another way, they were simply unable to certify that their own students had the necessary qualifications for positions as highly skilled teachers and officials.

There were two aspects to the problem of standards. First, the very basics of scholarship are by necessity international. They are not and cannot be purely local. Logic, the ability to retrieve new information from a vast mass of existing information, concepts of verifiability and refutability, muscular activity in speech, validity in statistics and thousands of other prerequisites to academic work form a common core with only minor national variations. So it was realised that much more emphaisis would have to be placed on general activities than was originally planned, and that the price for doing so had to be the abandonment of the very holistic approach initially taken. It was also realised that the importation of internationally accepted methods of teaching such skills was needed. In sum, it meant that there had to be a return to the well-known discipline-by-discipline approach.

The second aspect of the problem of standards was that in the modern information society local affairs can be properly understood only by interrelating with trends outside the local consciousness. It might be part of the local consciousness to understand how shrimps are caught, but it is surely part of one's international consciousness to decide the optimal time for selling the catch as prices, among thousands of factors, depend upon fluctuating foreign exchange quotations. In addition, it is part of the local conciousness to know the local literary system in detail, but when it comes to questions of the public's lack of interest in local literary productions because international satellite television stations seem more attractive, then one must resort to international consciousness to understand the overall situation of the local editors. So in teaching such subjects at an advanced level there has to be reliance on professors who have an understanding of such international trends as well as of local affairs.

Thus the differences in the objectives clauses of the 1981 and 1989 Acts clearly mirror a radical change of focus. While the Inuit Institute was a pure instance of a 'community university' with a very restricted scope, the University of Greenland is basically a general university which deals with specific local empirical data in ways that are not specific to the concept of localness. The task of the University of Greenland is to produce highly-skilled local people who are able to compete professionally with imported southerners for positions in the local society.

A high price has been paid to achieve this objective. Whereas at the Inuit Institute four out of five professors taught in Greenlandic, only three out of fourteen professors speak Greenlandic at the University of Greenland. The demands on the students have increased dramatically, resulting in a much higher drop-out rate. In monetary terms the University of Greenland is a much heavier burden on taxpayers than the Inuit Institute was.

There can be no doubt that the University of Greenland is on a rather perilous voyage between Scylla and Charybdis. If it is not, in everything that it does, fully aware of its basic nature as a local Greenlandic institution (which from a certain point of view might be the only *raison d'être* for the university) it is in danger of becoming a third-rank southern university mistakenly placed in Ultima Thule. If, on the other hand, it pays too little attention to the universal nature of knowledge it is likely to be reduced to a hollow symbol with very restricted practical importance.

The independent university and the surrounding society

The topic of the relationship between the university and its surrounding society can be analysed from two different perspectives, the first dealing with finances and the second with public opinion. As we shall see, these two points of view are sometimes interwoven.

As mentioned earlier, the activities of the university are supported by grants from the local government. Thus, there is always the possibility that grants might be reduced in periods of financial constraint. And, although it is unlikely in modern Greenlandic democracy, there is also the possibility that grants could be reduced if the university deviates too far from current political goals. In the very stable Greenlandic political system, no one really fears that finances might act as a constraint on the university's independence. However, financial factors could indirectly affect the university, especially in an era when public expenditures are under great stress and have to be reduced generally. A reduction in public expenditure is stated university policy which very few people question, including the university's staff. There is at least one way in which the university might help the government save money while at the same time avoiding cuts in its own budget. The government often hires consulting firms from outside at great public expense, and the advice that such firms supply is often not sufficiently grounded in local circumstances. However, the university has highly skilled professionals equal to or better than the ones that are brought in. Moreover, the university's staff are better able to situate its know-how in the local context. Thus a certain amount of money could be transferred from the public account for consultation to the public account for the university. This would provide the government with better advisers and simultaneously enhance the financial resources of the university. At first glance everybody should be happy with such an arrangement. However, this might have the effect of favouring applied subjects over the theoretical or those of no immediate practical application. The University of Greenland is very aware of the fact that refusing such practical tasks might create problems, not in the form of dubious political or administrative pressure, but in the form of the need to make hard choices concerning areas of study. Clearly the university is able to contribute much that is of value to the local society, and society is small enough so that this is very evident to both the faculty members and members of the public. However, if these immediate practical matters are addressed, then many others which need fundamental and very time-consuming investigation are likely to be left for lack of resources.

An even greater danger to the university's independence lies in public opinion, or rather, in the staff's self-censorship caused by sensitivity to public opinion. Myriad cases can occur and do occur when the viewpoints of the scholar differ radically from those of the layman in small, closed, conservative societies. The great esteem in which the old culture is held, together with an unwillingness to accept traits of cultural renewal, has been mentioned as one example. As another example one should mention the conflicts that stem fom the layman's aptness to focus on surface appearances while the scholar generally looks for structures below the surface appearances in order to explain and possibly change things.

A very specific problem exists in all small societies, and it is certainly evident in the small Greenlandic communities. In Greenland's capital the problem is not as grave as in the small villages, but it still exists. This is the concept of conflict avoidance (Langgård, 1986). Conflict avoidance is as far removed as can be imagined from the basic values inherent in academic thinking. The very *raison d'être* of a university is the basically unlimited struggle for new knowledge, whether the new knowledge is in accordance with current tastes and values or not, or whether it is popular or not. Another characteristic trait of most traditional cultures all over the world is the contentedness with, or resignation to, the established structures guiding life, a belief that they are stable and that things are 'good enough as they are'. During the nation-building years of the 1970s the expression 'Greenlandic conditions' implying 'traditional ways' lost almost all negative connotations and gained very positive connotations. However, the implications of the expressions 'good enough' and 'static society' are anethema to most scholars.

In a closed society quite a number of opinions are apt to become canonised through constant repetition. Examples of such opinions are 'youngsters ought to be ashamed of not speaking their mother tongue the way their forefathers did', and 'pupils must read and write more to learn their language and culture'. Such opinions number in the thousands. As a scholar, one realises that it is impossible to fight all such instances of a narrow outlook, and that it is wearsome even to maintain a different point of view. If you try you are apt to be harshly criticised or ostracised, especially since all your countrymen know you and your opinions in a small society like Greenland. In extreme situations, you are likely to withdraw to subjects of lesser sensitivity, even when you are convinced that the sensitive matters are the more important ones. And in all situations you are forced to refrain from dealing with very many questions because of the fact that a person who a priori is regarded as a nay-sayer loses influence. As a consequence the public loses interest in your negative comments even in those situations where, according to your conviction, saying 'no' is crucial. Thus the situation calls for circumspection. Whether self-censorship springs from strategic considerations or from fear, any degree of suppressing opinions, be it rare instances of lying low or the ultimate retirement from matters of importance, must be reflected upon seriously and honestly by those concerned.

Problems related to size

The University of Greenland suffers from several problems that affect all small universities. However, it is a very small university and the greater smallness the more glaring the problems. The first problem is that it is difficult to cover many fields or to develop many specialisations.

Whatever the subject field, many different aspects are interwoven into a core. Within a large department a high degree of specialisation is likely to take place and the core's network is made up of several individuals. This holds true whether seen through the eyes of the students or in connection with research projects. Within a small department just a few teachers and researchers have to cover many aspects of their field. A small staff, willing to deal with general approaches in a professional field, have no particularly negative connotation. Indeed, a wider perspective very often helps faculty members develop new insights into questions that could not have been well understood with a narrower perspective. However, the opposite is also surely the case.

Within the extremely small departments of Greenland's very small university, things are extreme with respect to coverage. All professors cover quite wide areas in teaching, as well as in research. An example of this is the Department of Greenlandic which has a staff of only four professors. These four teach linguistics (Greenlandic and general) and literature (Greenlandic and general) in undergraduate as well as graduate programmes. In an extreme case this could mean, and unfortunately sometimes does mean, that a professor will simultaneously have to teach bilingual education, contemporary Greenlandic poetry and general phonetics, while at the same time functioning as a tutor to a student writing a dissertation on computers in linguistic statistics. Though examples as extreme as this are rare, they nevertheless actually occur – the example given reflects the author's own timetable during the spring term of 1989. It should be obvious from this that any attempt to keep pace with new literature in a field as wide as the one outlined above is impossible, and with the few colleagues (who share the problem) at hand one cannot expect much help or professional progress through informal, everyday conversation.

The second problem related to small size is that it results in a very expensive student–teacher ratio. No single person can cover a whole professional field. Even in situations where each of the staff members covers quite a wide field, a number of people are needed to cover even the absolute minimum of essential topics. Therefore, the university faces another problem. Given the small number of students the bare necessities of professionalism generate a very expensive teacher: student ratio.

The third problem related to size concerns the reaction of staff to this reality. Two very different reactions are likely to occur with individuals who are able to live with lesser professional depth but with greater professional-width as a compensatory skill. A few of them are likely to develop a sense of inferiority vis-à-vis colleagues in bigger universities. At the other extreme a few are likely to develop feelings of superiority. The outcomes are equally unfortunate. Therefore, it is necessary to develop means to avoid or control the development of such attitudes.

The fourth problem related to small size is specific to the University of Greenland and other dedicated community universities. As stated above, it is a cardinal assumption of such universities that two very different approaches, each with its own specific demands upon the researcher, must be in force to ensure that a local university deals with local affairs in an acceptable way. This imperative poses a huge problem when recruiting for the professors' chairs. Ideally, a professor at the University of Greenland should have the insider's innate feeling for the society while at the same time have the outsider's ability to generalise beyond that society. Only Greenlandic scholars could meet such demands, and Greenlandic scholars are very few. Accordingly, quite a number of professors have been employed in spite of the fact that they do not speak Greenlandic, but because their academic qualifications have been beyond dispute.

Non-Greenlandic faculty members were hired in the belief that an academic staff member with a strong basis in theory and methodology would quickly adapt to an unfamilir situation and to unfamiliar subjects. Fifteen years' experience at the University of Greenland point to the correctness of this assumption. The staff members seem to have been able to apply their theoretical knowledge to the local context. Note that the belief that non-Greenlanders could adapt is directly opposite to the opinion aired by Mr Motzfeldt in 1974. Note also that the University of Greenland in this respect differs radically from many Arctic and northern institutions. It is worth mentioning that during this period of choice between theoretical skill and nativeness, the University of Greenland's leader was a native Greenlander and that the Minister of Education of course was, and is, a native Greenlander.

However, fifteen years' experience at the University of Greenland also point in another direction. That is, it has been difficult to make outsiders work at the University of Greenland long enough for them to acquire a knowledge of Greenland sound enough to base research upon. So, even though the staff at the University of Greenland are very stable in comparison with other workplaces in Greenland, about half of the professors' chairs did not have the same occupant for more than a few years at a time. Even in the cyber-space century Greenland is a remote place. For the mainstream academic Greenlandic lifestyle is too different, career possibilities too limited, colleagues too few and demands too high. It is hard to recruit staff and even harder to keep them.

After the first few hectic years of building up the university, it has reached a watershed that calls for some rethinking. Problems such as the ones outlined in the preceding pages have not yet become overwhelming because the very process of building up has been a strong compensatory factor for staff. Still problems must be foreseen and actions to minimise them must be taken. However, the basic duality of the University of Greenland cannot be abandoned. It is this very duality that is, and must be, the trademark of the university. Within this obligatory framework several things need to be done. First, the workplace must be made attractive enough to recruit the individuals required. Second, the university must ensure that the academic milieu provides opportunities for the staff to keep their knowledge up to date, as factually outdated know-how means poor teaching and poor research. Moreover, it can generate 'false kings', that is, professors who are not willing to enter into professional dialectics for fear of their shortcomings. Third, the university must ensure that the students, and the local society as well, are given the opportunity to hear opinions that differ from those of the local academic specialists' opinions. That is, the university should give students a thorough professional education on the local premises, and yet at the same time provide an outlook that goes beyond 'the parish pump'.

The task might look impossible at first glance, yet it can be accomplished. The staff at the University of Greenland have a strong belief that exchange programmes can help ensure that the university develops appropriately. By virtue of letters of cooperation with Danish and Canadian universities, students have the opportunity to spend one or two terms outside Greenland and return home with credits applicable to their local education. Since 1989 Greenland has been a member of the Nordic summer camps programmes. This is based on the concept of the transfer of credits among all the Nordic countries. Since 1991 Greenland has also cooperated with the Nordic universities under the Nordic Council's Nordplus programme. All in all the University of Greenland has a constant flow of teachers and students (especially graduate students) leaving for a term or two to foreign universities and a constant input of guest-students and guest-professors.

Not that this is unique to the University of Greenland, but the impact on a very little university is greater than on a larger one. A final observation about cooperation is that it is a widely held view among scholars and scientists that small universities should cooperate with each other in order to better understand and deal with common problems. However, the problems should be shared and essential parts of Ilisimatusarfik's problems are not experienced at other small universities. This is because

Ilisimatusarfik, as the only national university in the state of Greenland, is unique among the small universities.

*

It was mentioned earlier that Ilisimatusarfik means 'a wisdom-generating institution'. For a number of years the enormous challenges encountered in establishing an academic institution in a culture with no academic traditions have been so demanding that the amount of wisdom generated might be a little too limited. Ilisimatusarfik has had problems just generating itself. However, circumstances are normalising with every passing year and Ilisimatusarfik is developing into a university rather than simply an ethnic experiment. Ilisimatusarfik now has a steady production of badly needed Greenlandic BA and PhD candidates and an increased productivity in the years to come is expected. Faculty members are slowly but increasingly finding their way as specialists and analysts and being appointed to permanent boards and political committees. Scientific activities in Greenland are no longer exclusively controlled from Denmark. Ilisimatusarfik now holds a number of chairs in the major Danish research boards and funds, as well as Greenlandic influence, are rapidly growing. A number of successful research projects, some of which have dealt with sensitive and controversial subjects, have been carried out in the local society by local scientists. This, of course, has led to a number of political storms and much public debate, but there can be no doubt that a stable process has been initiated. Attitudes have changed to such a degree that one can now deal with sensitive subjects in public locally and professionally.

These new trends are not only here to stay but will no doubt escalate in the years to come. With more and more academically trained Greenlanders in policy, administrative and media positions the basic academic way of dealing with problems and debates, together with some characteristic academic attitudes, will spread in to the local society. With such developments the traditional conflict between local decision-making based primarily on age and consensus versus foreigner's imposed institutionalised decision-making will cease being the only dichotomy. A modern tradition based on local professionalism has already begun to overwrite both old tradition and imported decision-making.

Conclusion

It is far from a simple task to build a university on bare rock in a society with no academic tradition whatsoever. However, the staff of the University of Greenland understood the task. After a period of troublesome irresolution concerning questions of local values versus academic values, ethnicity and nationality versus the basic internationality of science, and the like, they have come to the conclusion that in relation to methods, theories and basic academic ethics they have to base research on both local data and internationally accepted values and standards.

This does not imply that there is any disagreement with the political intention behind Minister Motzfeldt's stated purpose for introductions the university in 1981. It is certainly true that any culture needs to know its past to understand its present. But it is just as true that the elements of a contemporary culture are part of the culture even if they are not reflected in the old culture. Within that perspective video-horror, a Mahler symphony and Coca Cola all form part of Greenlandic culture today. Such a multifaceted culture can be properly understood only in terms of the sum of local tradition and full-fledged internationalism.

After all, a general process leading to near-universal uniformity is ongoing. Satellites and computers leave their imprint on every culture, including the Greenlandic. Cultural differences are diminishing. For a small and fragile culture like Greenland's it is crucial to grasp this fact fully. A too uncritical cultural permissiveness is just as dangerous as a too conservative eagerness to preserve the old culture. Both attitudes will contribute another step towards the little culture's ruin.

References

Greenlandic Provincial Council (1974) *Landsraadsreferat* (Proceedings in the Provincial Council).

Langgård, Per (1986) 'Modernisation and Traditional Interpersonal Relations in a Small Greenlandic Community', in *Arctic Anthropology* vol. 23 (1–2), pp. 299ff.

Motzfeldt, Jonathan (1974) *Landsraadsreferat* (Proceedings in the Provincial Council). Nuuk: Greenlandic Provincial Council.

7
Universities in Northern Canada
Geoffrey R. Weller

Introduction

Fifty-one new universities and independent degree-granting institutions have been established in Canada since the end of the Second World War. Most of them were located in southern Canada. However, six were built in the northern regions of three provinces. These were Lakehead, Laurentian and Nipissing Universities in northern Ontario, the two branches of the University of Quebec in Chicoutimi and Abitibi-Temiscaming in northern Quebec, and the University of Northern British Columbia. Another university was located in northern Alberta, the University of Athabasca, but it is not discussed here because it has no special northern mission and is an open, distance education institution that offers its courses in home study format across the entire country.

This chapter begins by detailing the northern regional contexts within which these universities were established and the opportunities and difficulties that these contexts present. This is followed by an analysis of the educational context within which the northern universities exist. The chapter then details the original expectations of the the northern Canadian universities and the manner in which they were founded. This is followed by four sections that analyse the degree of success the northern Canadian universities have had in their four major roles of enhancing access, enhancing economic development and diversification, enhancing social and cultural development, and enhancing communication with other regions and nations both in reality and symbolically. The chapter concludes by arguing that the northern Canadian universities have had a significant effect in each of these roles, but that much more could have been accomplished if they had been initially regarded by provincial governments more as tools of regional development than as largely northern regional access points.

The context: northern Canada

Canada is the second largest nation in the world in terms of land area. It is a federal nation in which only 55 per cent of the territory has been organised into provinces. The other 45 per cent is organised into three federal territories, the Yukon, the Northwest Territories and Nunavut, which are allowed a certain amount of self-government. Northern Canada is usually regarded as having two components. One is the territorial north of the Yukon and the Northwest Territories; The other is the provincial north, which consists of the northern portions of the provinces of British Columbia, Alberta, Saskatchewan, Manitoba, Ontario, Quebec and Newfoundland (Labrador). The provincial northern regions are huge and between them constitute about 33 per cent of Canada's total land area. Canada's northern universities have been established in the provincial northern regions of just three of the six provinces that have extensive northern regions.

All universities have to be assessed in their own particular context and the provincial northern contexts of Canada's northern universities have many characteristics in common. The regions in which the northern universities are located all cover huge land areas. In some instances the very coming of the university defined the 'north' in a particular jurisdiction. For example, there was no generally accepted definition of a region called 'northern British Columbia' before the passage of the Act of the legislature that established the university (British Columbia, 1990a). In fact, the northern universities cover areas that constitute the majority of the total land mass of their respective provinces and these areas all tend to contain many different land forms and climatic zones.

The populations of these regions are very small, and in all cases amount to no more than 10 per cent of the total for the province. Moreover, these populations are usually widely scattered with the largest centres being relatively small in comparison with southern centres. In addition, the populations are almost all very variegated ethnically and racially. Often relatively large percentages of the total regional populations are comprised of indigenous peoples. The non-indigenous populations are relatively young, often recently located in the north, and quite transient.

The economies and the societies of the political jurisdictions of which these northern regions are a part are deeply divided. Usually, they are characterised as having two economies. The British Columbia economy, for example, is deeply divided between that of the greater Vancouver and Victoria area and that of the rest of the province (Davis and Hutton, 1989). The economies of the southern regions tend to be urban-based, service-oriented and expanding. The economies of the north tend to be small town-based, resource-oriented and, in some instances, declining. Many of these northern regions tend to have a third economy, that of the indigenous peoples, which in most cases is doing very poorly indeed. The northern economies are heavily dependent upon natural resources, especially forestry, mineral extraction, power generation and tourism. The sub-economies of the indigenous northern populations are usually heavily dependent upon a mixture of jobs related to the resource economy, the 'second economy' of hunting, fishing and trapping, and jobs linked to government service. In each case, there is little or no manufacturing outside the forest sector and the service economies of virtually all three of these regions are relatively poorly developed. The three regions are resource hinterlands of the southern regions of their particular provinces. This is clearly revealed in the nature of their transportation systems, which are designed to facilitate the movement of bulk commodities out of the regions but not for intra-regional purposes.

Like so many of the resource hinterland regions these three northern ones exhibit relatively poor social status indicators. Health status indicators such as mortality and morbidity rates, as well as the relative numbers of health personnel per capita, tend to be worse than for their respective provinces as a whole (see, for example, British Columbia, 1990b). Economic status indicators are worse as well (see, for example, British Columbia 1991; Horne and Penner, 1992). Educational status indicators are often particularly poor and tend to be much lower than for the political jurisdictions as a whole. UNBC's region provides a good example of this, as the university participation rate was only 8 per cent, half that of the provincial average (16 per cent), and nearly one-third that of the rate for the Vancouver and Victoria areas (21 per cent) before UNBC was established. As in other northern regions there tends to be substantial variation in the participation rates between the sub regions of the north, and in the case of northern British Columbia the lowest is in its northeastern sub-region, where it is a very low 4 per cent (British Columbia, 1991).

The three provincial northern regions are regarded, and tend to regard themselves, as hinterlands. The British Columbia phrase 'beyond Hope' (the last town in the Fraser Valley in which Vancouver is situated) and the Ontario phrase 'beyond the 401' (the 401 being Toronto's northern bypass highway) encapsulate the southern attitude to the north. The strength of the concept of region varies fairly widely among the three northern regions. In Ontario it is quite strong, but the region is so large that many identify with either the northeast or the northwest. It is quite weak in northern British Columbia. The fact that UNBC was established thirty years after many of the other new northern Canadian universities is partly an indication of this fact. It is also reflected in the fact that British Columbia is the only province with a northern region not to have had a ministry or special bureacratic agency devoted to the interests of the north (Weller, 1995). In fact, the campaign for the university was one of the first major indications of an increasing consciousness of region in the area. Yet outside the small circle of key promoters there was little idea of the role a university could play in regional development, let alone a knowledge of the specific examples provided by the circumpolar universities, some of which had been in existence thirty years (Interior University Society, 1988). Even so, the key reason for wanting a university in northern British Columbia was much the same as in the other jurisdictions that had established them earlier. In each of the nations in which they were established the overarching element was a desire to change the hinterland status of these regions, or at least to mitigate some of the effects of hinterland status.

A final point of note regarding the provincial northern regions is how relatively recently their resources have been exploited and, consequently, how recently a population of European origin has moved into them. With the exception of Ontario, the resource frontier began to move into the provincial norths only after the Second World War. In Ontario the resource frontier began to have a marked effect on northern Ontario at the beginning of the twentieth century. For example, the pulp and paper industry began in northern Ontario in 1918, but the first pulp and paper mill was not built in northern British Columbia until 1959. Many of the major cities and towns in the Canadian provincial north, such as Thompson in Manitoba, did not even exist until after the Second World War and many others were tiny villages or towns before the war.

The context: the Canadian system of higher education

Just as Canada's northern universities need to be understood in terms of the regional context in which they exist, so they have to be understood in terms of their place within the wider system of higher education in Canada. Thus it is important to note that at the time that Canada's founding legislative document (the British North America Act) came into force in 1867, education, especially higher education, was regarded as a matter of local concern. Consequently, the provinces were assigned exclusive jurisdiction over education in Article 93 of the British North America Act. As a result, Canada has never had a federal Ministry of Education and the only means for the coordination of education across the country are essentially informal ones. Moreover, Canada has no federally sponsored national university that deals with federally related issues or the federal territories, such as Australia has in the Australian National University.

Canada's northern universities constitute only six of the over 80 independent degree-granting institutions across the country. Moreover, they are all very small and account for only 3 per cent of the total number of students enrolled in universities across Canada. Laurentian, Lakehead and the University of Quebec in Chicoutimi each has between 4,000 and 5,000 full-time students, UNBC has about 2,000, Nipissing about 1,400, and the branch of the University of Quebec in Abitibi-Temiscaming has approximately 1,000.

Canada's northern universities are also very new ones, with the first having been opened in 1960. Higher education in Canada began almost 300 years earlier in New France (now the province of Quebec) with the establishment of the Seminaire de Quebec (now Laval University) in 1663. Various religious groups established universities in subsequent years, especially in the early part of the nineteenth century. What is now Canada's largest university, the University of Toronto, begun as an Anglican institution in 1827. There were three major expansionary periods thereafter. The first occurred at the beginning of the twentieth century in western Canada as the western provinces were created. The second occurred in the 1960s and 1970s and affected most of the country. This coincided with a massive increase in enrolments that not only resulted in new universities but in huge growth among those that already existed. The third occurred in the 1990s in British Columbia when that province increased the number of independent degree granting institutions from four to sixteen in the space of five years.

Canada's northern universities exist in a system where virtually all universities are very heavily dependent upon public funding. Despite a recent rapid rise in student fees and an almost desperate search for private funding most Canadian universities are still approximately 75–80 per cent dependent upon government funding. Even large, well-endowed, research-intensive and commercially inclined universities, such as the University of British Columbia, are about 60 per cent dependent upon public funding. Public funding began to become significant to Canadian universities just after the Second World War as part of an effort to increase enrolments to accommodate demobilised soldiers. As this type of funding increased, and since it went only to secular institutions, most universities with religious affiliations either shed them or became constituent colleges of secular universities. Public funding increased phenomenally in the 1960s as both the federal government (via transfer payments to the provinces for university education) and the provincial governments sought to expand access to education. University participation rates did increase very rapidly during and after the 1960s, so much so that they are now triple what they were when the process began. Canada's northern universities also exist in the context of a university system deeply divided between a large number of small universities with limited programming and which conduct relatively little research, and a small number of large institutions with a full range of programming and which conduct a great deal of research. About half of Canada's universities have enrolments of 5,000 full-time students or fewer and there are a lot more that have 10,000 or fewer. There are only sixteen large universities that have a full range of programming, i.e. that include Faculties such as Medicine and Law. It is only a few of even these few large universities that account for the vast majority of the research monies granted by Canada's major research granting agencies. Canada's northern universities are all small and have a limited range of programming. None of them has Faculties of Medicine, Dentistry, Pharmacy, Law and the like. Some have professional Faculties related to their region, such as Forestry, Engineering, Nursing and Social Work, but even in these cases they are small Faculties and some, such as Engineering, offer only a limited range of specialties within them. Canada's northern universities also conduct relatively little research. Their success rate in acquiring grants in the social sciences and humanities is especially low.

Canada's northern universities also exist in a university system where several large southern universities insist that they serve their respective provincial northern regions (and the territorial north) and that they do, or should, conduct most of the significant research undertaken on the north. Indeed, many of the southern universities do serve their respective provincial northern regions. They have to, as none of the northern universities has a full range of professional Faculties. Thus, for example, the southern universities with Faculties of Medicine nearly all have northern outreach programmes. No province has yet built a northern university with a Faculty of Medicine and, given the current economic climate, is unlikely to do so in the foreseeable future. It is also undoubtedly the case that there are more northern experts at Canada's southern universities than at Canada's northern ones, although most study the far north of the territories rather than the near north of the provinces. All of this leads to the suspicion that the northern universities were built in periods of rapidly expanding student numbers merely as northern access points, that is, universities *in* the north, rather than as universities intended to help in economic, social and cultural development, that is, universities *for* the north.

Canada's northern universities also exist in a university system that is becoming increasingly competitive, increasing reliant on higher student fees, private sector donations and the profits of commercial enterprises undertaken in cooperation with local industry. The northern universities suffer from several disadvantages in this increasingly competitive environment. They are not only small, with a limited range of programming and research, they are also geographically remote and thus expensive to attend for both those from the south and those from the more remote parts of the north. Since they exist in hinterland regions with very few corporate headquarters they have greater difficulty raising private sector donations than do more centrally located universities. Since they also exist in regions that are not very diversified economically, they are restricted in the range of industry/university commercial links that they can establish. Moreover, the costs of their operations are greater than for southern institutions. Not only do they suffer from the diseconomies of scale that affect all small universities but they also suffer from very high travel costs, both for travel within their huge regions and between their regions and the southern centres of economic and political power. The costs of heating, snow clearing and the like are also much greater.

The founding of Canada's northern universities

Universities began to be established in the provincial northern regions only after the resource frontier expanded to reach them in the years after the Second World War. The new migrants to these regions put considerable pressure on their respective provincial governments to establish universities in the north so that their sons and daughters had an equal chance of getting a university education, for many of them could not afford the expense of sending their children to live in the south in order to get a university education. Little might have happened had not the pressure from these new migrants not occurred at much the same time as the provincial governments decided on a rapid and massive expansion of access to university education generally. The original two northern universities in Ontario were established at the same time as many new universities were established and old ones expanded in that province in the 1960s. What is now Nipissing University was then a constituent college of Laurentian University. The two branches of the University of Quebec were established in the 1970s when Quebec was rapidly establishing new, and expanding old, universities. The University of Northern British

Columbia was established in the early 1990s when the provincial government increased the size of the existing universities and increased the number of independent degree-granting institutions from three to fifteen.

In 1960 Ontario became the first province to established a university in a northern region. It created Laurentian University, the main campus of which was located in Sudbury, the largest city (160,000) in the northeastern part of Ontario. This huge region had a total of approximately 500,000 people. Laurentian has a complicated structure in that it consists of one constitutent college, Laurentian University College, and three federated universities: Huntington University (United Church), the University of Sudbury (Catholic) and Thorneloe University (Anglican). It also has two affiliated colleges: Algoma Unversity College in Sault Ste Marie, and Le College Universitaire de Hearst. Laurentian was established in large part as the result of a lot of local pressure applied by the citizens of the northeast and by a few key local citizens in Sudbury. The idea of a university was sold largely on the basis of the claim that it would have a positive impact on northern access to university education by making it cheaper and easier for residents of the northeast to attend. Local boosters also sold the idea of a university on the basis that it would have a positive effect on virtually every aspect of the society and the economy of the northeast as well as upon virtually every community in the region. It was argued that it would increase the regional population, help diversify the economy and induce a social and cultural flowering within the region. In short, the university was expected to be a panacea for most of the region's perceived problems and the source of much of its hope for the future (Hallsworth, 1995). This rather exaggerated promotion of the benefits of a university meant that support was gained for the concept in the region, but it caused a crisis of expectations later when it was realised that the university would not have the same range of programming as the bigger southern ones and would have relatively few students and relatively little research. This meant that the impact of the university would not be as rapid, extensive or, more particularly, as rapidly diffused throughout the region as expected – or as led to expect. Moreover, the university ran into considerable problems both internally and in relations with the various communities in the northeast as a result of its efforts to serve the entire region via its affiliated colleges (which included Nipissing originally) and via distance education.

Lakehead University was established in Thunder Bay in 1965. Thunder Bay was the largest city (120,000) in the region of northwestern Ontario. This region is also huge, about the size of France, but has a population of only approximately 250,000. It was also established largely as the consequence of considerable pressure being exerted on the provincial government by the citizens of the region and a few key residents of Thunder Bay. As with Laurentian the primary purpose of the university was seen as increasing access to university education by regional residents. However, it was also promoted by many regional boosters as the answer to some, if not all, of the region's problems. Nipissing University was created in 1994. Prior to that it had been an affiliated college of Laurentian University. It is located in North Bay, a city of 50,000.

Quebec was the second province to establish a university in its north. A branch of the University of Quebec was created in Chicoutimi (population 65,000) in 1969. It was an amalgamation of three existing institutions: the Ecole Normal Cardinal-Begin, the Ecole de Commerce et Genie and the Grand-Seminaire St-Thomas. Yet again it was a university formed largely in response to considerable local pressure and it was represented as an institution that would work wonders in the educational, cultural and economic fields in its regions. The regions in this case were those of Saguenay-Lac St Jean, Charlevoix, and Cote Nord. Another branch of the University of Quebec was also set up in northern Quebec in 1983. It began life in Rouyn (population 27,000) in 1970 as the Centres d'etudes universitaires dans l'ouest quebecois, but became the Universite du Quebec en Abitibi-Temiscaming in 1983. Yet once more this was a university established largely as a consequence of much local pressure, in this case initially in the form of a request by the management committee for northwest Quebec, which was particularly concerned with the lack of teacher training in the region. The university was also expected to have considerable educational, cultural and economic impact throughout the region of northwest Quebec.

British Columbia became the third province to establish a university in its northern region when it founded the University of Northern British Columbia in 1990. The main campus was located in Prince George which, with a population of 70,000, is the largest community in northern British Columbia, a region with a total population of approximately 300,000. The university was established after a lengthy campaign by citizens of the region for a university intended not only to reduce the costs of university education for northern residents, but one that would promote cultural development as well as economic development and diversification. The grassroots effort was spearheaded by a group from Prince George and involved not only the gathering of a petition but also the gaining of the support of every community and band council in the north. Fortunately for the advocates of the university, the province had just begun to increase rapidly the number of university places in the province. However, the expansion up to that point had consisted of enlarging the existing universities and establishing several new university-colleges that were able to offer only a limited number (6–10) of undergraduate degrees. The citizens of the north very sensibly insisted on obtaining a 'real' university that would offer a wider range of undergraduate degrees, graduate degrees at both the masters and doctoral levels, and which would conduct research. They thought that only such an institution would provide the anticipated wide range of educational, economic and cultural benefits (Weller, 1994).

None of the other provinces with extensive northern regions seems likely to establish a university in those regions in the near future. This may well be because the populations of the northern parts of the other provinces are much smaller than those in Ontario, Quebec and British Columbia. It is also unlikely that a university will be established in the federal north of the Yukon, Northwest Territories and Nunavut. Twice there have been suggestions that a university be established in the territories but neither suggestion resulted in one being created. Federal letters patent for a university in the territorial north were issued in March 1971. The University of Canada North (UCN) was the idea of Richard Rohmer, a Toronto lawyer, and 57 residents of the two northern territories. The new university did not attract much northern support and many thought of it as a carpetbagger scheme. The federal government, although it issued the letters patent, hoped that the territorial governments would not support the university. The southern universities seemed to think that the creation of such a university was premature and were in the process at the time of assessing, via the Association of Universities and Colleges of Canada, the work being done by existing universities that related to the north. Moreover, the supporters of the new institution could not agree on a unified vision of what it should be like and by 1973 the project was essentially dead, even though it maintained a legal corporate existence until 1985 (Graham, 1994). In 1977 the Science Council of Canada proposed the creation of what they termed an 'unorthodox' northern university that would be intended largely to pursue graduate and extension work. The proposal for such a university was made in the context of some suggestions by the Science Council in a report on northern development. This suggestion also received little support and no such institution was created.

The northern universities and access

One of the major roles of the northern universities, and one of the major reasons for establishing them, was to provide much enhanced access to university education in their respective northern regions. The northern regional groups pressuring for the establishment of universities in the north usually argued for them on both access and regional development grounds. However, they were rationalised by government largely because of their effect upon access. This is not to say that the provincial governments completely ignored the regional development role. A former Minister of Advanced Education in British Columbia, for example, stated that the establishment of a university in northern British Columbia could not have been justified on access grounds alone (Perry, 1992). The low participation rates in each of the three provincial northern regions evident prior to the coming of the universities were a reflection of the many and great barriers to access in those regions. These barriers were financial, educational and psychological.

The financial barrier was the most apparent and probably the most important. To send a person to university for a year costs a great deal of money, usually well beyond the means of most families. The northern universities, by their very presence in their respective regions, helped to reduce the costs of attendance significantly. This was especially the case since most of them tried to regionalise their activities in different ways, so that they could reach as many people as possible throughout their vast territories. Since northern populations tend to be widely scattered, as was earlier observed, none of the universities could sit in one place and rely entirely on students coming to them. Thus they provided as many courses and programmes throughout their regions in either the face-to-face or distance education format as is possible to enable students to complete degrees either in their home towns or at least in their particular sub-regions of the north. In those systems where it was necessary, a number of the northern universities put some effort into establishing scholarships and bursaries aimed largely at prospective northern students.

Another set of barriers to access for northern students are related to educational factors. Typically, students from smaller, northern communities do not do as well in the sciences and languages as students from the larger urban areas. This is partly because of fewer physical resources being available, partly because of a shortage of appropriately qualified teachers and partly because of a lesser focus in such schools on those subjects required for university entry because of family or peer pressure to emphasise the world of work at a relatively early age. Some of the northern universities placed less emphasis on language and other stipulated entry requirements for northern students than the other universities. However, this was done cautiously because it was feared that they would be regarded as lower quality institutions. Some also worked in cooperation with the school systems of their respective regions and established programmes such as summer science schools for senior students.

There are a number of psychological barriers to access for northern students. Among the more significant psychological barriers was, and still is in some places, the widespread belief that a university education is not needed to acquire a well-paid job. While this may have been true at one time in most of the northern regions, it is no longer the case. The number of jobs in the forest and other natural resources sectors which so dominate these regions is shrinking and those jobs that do remain require higher and higher levels of education. Another of the psychological barriers in the remoter northern regions is the problem of adjusting to going away from home, life in a big city and all its attractions, and learning to lend an independent lifestyle. A number of the northern universities tackled this problem directly and established special counselling and other services. Yet another psychological barrier was a tendency to be reluctant to enter the new northern universities at the outset because they were perceived initially as not being as 'good' as the other, older universities in the south. Those that are now the better northern universities overcame this problem by hiring high quality faculty, by establishing research and graduate programmes from the outset so that they were regarded as 'full' universities, and by paying attention to the quality of their 'products' so that they acquired fairly rapidly a good reputatation among employers. Some also emphasised that their smallness enhanced their quality rather than detracted from it because of the readier access to professors and sophisticated laboratory equipment than was the case at larger southern institutions.

Although precise statistics are hard to come by, most of the new universities located in the northern regions claim marked success in enhancing access to university education within their regions. This was partly because they attracted students from the south, which enabled them to broaden the range of programming available to students from the north, thereby increasing the 'capture rate' of students from the north going to university. The clearest case is the most recent, namely that of UNBC, where directly upon opening it attracted half of its students from outside northern British Columbia and within two years it had doubled the participation rate of northerners from a very low figure (8 per cent) to the provincial average (16 per cent).

The new northern Canadian universities that have by now been in existence for some time also had a marked effect over the course of several decades on social mobility within their regions. Many of their students were from working-class backgrounds and the training they received gave them new employment opportunities. Although many of the graduates brought up in the north migrated to jobs in the south, a great many remained adding to the skill level of the locally available labour force. The migration of students brought up in the north migrating to the south was counterbalanced by many of the students who were brought up in the south migrating to the north upon graduation for employment. This latter effect clearly illustrates the importance of regarding the new northern universities as a part of the broader university system of the political jurisdictions of which they are a part.

A key to maximising access is to have as broad a range of programmes as is possible that are attractive to students not only from the north but also from the south. This means that it is advisable to have graduate as well as undergraduate programmes and to undertake relevant research activities. This combination is probably necessary to attract the good faculty that are needed to establish the reputation of a university, which will, in turn, attract more students to the university from both the north and the south. However, the northern Canadian universities will have considerable difficulty maintaining even their current range of programming and number of southern students in the face of fiscal retrenchment, increased competition among the universities, the increasing concentration of research at the larger southern institutions and the declining numbers of university age northerners in their respective regions.

The northern universities and economic development

The economies of some of the northern parts of the three provinces under discussion are heavily resource-dependent and do not have a highly educated labour force. Consequently, they are not well positioned to withstand the economic challenges of the present and the future. The phenomenon of the growth of the global economy has meant that many low value-adding jobs are exported to countries that are poorer than most of the ones in which the circumpolar universities are located. The phenomenon of automation means that those jobs that do stay in these richer nations are increasingly done by machines not people. Moreover, the very rapid rise in the importance of information technology to economic success has put a premium on the production of scientists, engineers and managers. It has also meant that a premium has been placed on everyone being competent enough to use the new technology. Thus, if Canada's northern regions are to survive and prosper in the modern world, they must all develop educational systems capable of producing an appropriately educated labour force that will not only strengthen the existing resource industry base, but help rapidly diversify it away from a very heavy dependence upon that base.

The northern universities have been and are one of the keys to the creation of the educational system needed for northern regions to prosper in the future. By creating more educational opportunities within their regions and significantly improving participation rates, they have had and will have the effect of markedly improving the educational level of the northern labour forces. The availability of a skilled labour force is an important factor in locational decision-making in business and industry. To create an appropriately trained labour force, the northern universities will have to offer the correct mix and right type of programmes. If they were simply to offer undergraduate Arts and Science programmes the experience of some of the circumpolar universities, such as Lakehead and Laurentian in their early years, would indicate that they would be largely training the youth of the region for outmigration to jobs that do not exist within their regions. The northern universities have to offer regionally relevant professional programming at both the undergraduate and graduate level. They would also be well advised to offer as many of their programmes in the cooperative education format as possible and to target a lot of their programming at the adult student, that is, already existing members of their regional labour forces.

The universities in northern Canada have tried to do these things and, by so doing, have attracted students not only from their own regions but also from their respective southern regions. As previously noted, most of them attract up to half of their enrolments from outside their own regions. This has meant that they have been able to provide the basis for a wider range of programme choice for those students who come from the north. In addition, some of those attracted from the southern regions have stayed in the north, thereby adding to the educational level of the various northern regional populaces and, as a result, the attractiveness of the northern regions in locational terms for business and industry. However, no firm figures have been gathered to confirm this effect, and reliance has to be placed here on the impressions of those involved with the northern universities since their founding.

The creation of the northern Canadian universities has had a variety of direct and indirect benefits that promote the economic development of their respective regions. The building of the campuses, which involved fairly large expenditures for construction and equipment purchases, was one of the direct impacts. The University of Northern British Columbia had an initial capital and equipment budget of CAN $137.5 million. The regular operating funds received from the provincial government are significant in the northern regional context, amounting to, for example, CAN $55.5 million at Laurentian and CAN $21.8 million at UNBC in the fiscal year 1994/5. Some 80 per cent of the funds received by the universities go to cover salaries, most of which are spent in the north. The northern universities are among the largest employers in their respective regions. The student fees and other expenditures made by students while attending the northern universities also represents a direct impact of significance. This is partly because they involve the slowing down of the outflow of monies spent by northerners in the south. It is also partly because they involve a flow of resources to the north from those students who come from the south. As Felsenstein has remarked: 'one of the main contributions of the university in a frontier area is its ability to induce migrants to the area that would not have been attracted otherwise' (Felsenstein, 1993: 17). Also representing a direct impact is the vast majority of the money raised for scholarships, bursaries and endowments. The monies brought in for research purposes, though small by the standards of the larger southern universities, has some significance in the northern context. In addition, various other university activities, such as the organisation of conferences and convocations, bring people and their expenditures to their respective regions from the south.

Because of the nature of the peripheral regions in which they exist the northern Canadian universities suffer from a great deal of 'leakage' in their spending and strong reverse migration flows. Both of these phenomena are not well understood by many local residents and are resented. Because none of the northern communities, Rouyn, Chicoutimi, North Bay, Sudbury, Thunder Bay and Prince George, is very large or diversified, more spending is undertaken outside the university region than would be the case for universities located in larger and more diversified cities. For example, much of the scientific equipment needed has to be purchased from elsewhere, as do many basic supplies and services. Thus the multiplier effect of a northern university is less than for a southern university, and neither is as high as that of a new pulp mill. One estimate for the new University of Northern British Columbia puts it at 1.5 for salaries and student spending (Reid, Enemark and Rawbotham, 1992). Both the expenditure and employment multiplier for Laurentian (MacLennan, 1995) and Nipissing (Sarlo, 1994) are also estimated to be 1.5.

Another economic benefit to the northern regions is that some of the universities in northern Canada tried to structure themselves to provide direct assistance to regional business and industry in ways other than simply producing relevantly trained graduates. Fairly early on some provided aid to small business programmes and other related services. However, they have not conducted as much regionally appropriate research of both a pure and applied nature for local governments, social groups, business and industry within their respective regions as have the northern Scandinavian universities. Neither have they been anything like as successful as the larger Scandinavian northern universities of Oulu and Umeå in establishing 'industry incubator' facilities where new ideas and new businesses had the opportunity to be nurtured and helped to achieve self-sustaining status. Umeå and Oulu are credited with helping to stem out-migration, bolstering already existing industries and helping to create a large number of new high-technology and other jobs. The University of Oulu is again particularly notable in this latter regard and it is generally credited with the creation of a mini-Silicon Valley industry in Oulu that employs several thousand people. The key to success would appear to be not only having a much wider range of programming and more appropriate programming than the northern Canadian universities, but also having closer links with governments that have broad regional development initiatives and can conceive of a clear and large role for universities within this context.

The northern universities and social and cultural development

The northern Canadian universities helped strengthen the social and cultural infrasructure of their respective northern regions. They did this for its own sake, in terms of the inherent worth of the enterprise, but also because it added to the attractiveness of their respective regions in locational terms with industry and business, thereby assisting the economic growth and diversification of those regions. However, it has been said that while each of the new universities identified a cultural mission within the broad mandate of their educational activities, 'it is usually a subsidiary concern, left as a secondary field for activity once the "more important" issues regarding student access, professional preparation, and stimulation of the local economy have been adequately addressed' (Nord, 1997).

The direct effect occurred by means of culturally-related programming and other activities and the related facilities that were constructed. The greatest impact was made by those northern universities that had the earliest and most comprehensive capital allocations for either sports or fine and performing arts facilities and related programme based operating funds. These allocations were vital to a 'rounding out' of the institutions, and to a full performance of their regional development mandates. In many cases there was some rivalry between those who wanted fine and performing arts facilities programming before sports facilities and programming, and vice versa.

The northern universities had an indirect effect in the cultural and sports areas because they led to the injection of new talent into their respective regions and to linkages with already existing sports and cultural groups, which strengthened the financial and organisational base of those groups. For example, Lakehead University developed ties with the local symphony orchestra, which led to a mutually beneficial relationship between the two organisations.

Most of the northern Canadian universities have helped the indigenous peoples of their respective regions rediscover and strengthen their cultural traditions. The key to the survival of many of these groups of indigenous peoples is a strengthening of their language and then their culture. Most of the northern universities have at least helped in this endeavour. Some of them have also developed distinctive programming in other fields that is intended to result in the possibility of the indigenous peoples leading reasonably independent existences within the framework of the dominant Canadian culture. The latest addition to this group of universities, the University of Northern British Columbia, has followed earlier examples and established a Programme in First Nations Studies and specialised programmes in areas such as First Nations self-government.

Symbolism, representation and the northern universities

The new northern Canadian universities served a number of roles that were not always originally intended in the minds of many of the initial planners and promoters of these institutions. Some of these roles were essentially symbolic ones. For example, they provided one of the first, and certainly one of the most important, pieces of evidence that there was a unifying consciousness of region in the areas in which they were located. In addition, the establishment of universities in these northern regions was taken as an indication that the regions had come of age and had acquired a certain maturity. Since universities are institutions that are seen as almost perpetual, in the sense that they rarely die, they symbolised a transition from 'frontier' areas to settled 'homeland' areas.

Another set of originally unintended roles was what might be termed the 'representational'. One of these was the role the new northern universities played in bringing the outside world to the northern regions. They brought in new people in the form of faculty, students and staff. These new people came not only from the southern parts of their respective jurisdictions, but also often from all over the world. They brought in new ideas and new ways of doing things, and frequently a more professional way of conducting operations. Another of these representational roles was almost the reverse side of the coin in that the new northern Canadian universities represented their respective northern regions to the outside world. They did this by sending their graduates all over the world, by having the research their faculty conducted on their regions presented at conferences worldwide and published in journals read nationally and internationally.

These symbolic and representational roles gave the new northern universities a number of difficulties, especially in their early years. In most of the northern regions there had been a long history of what could be called internecine rivalry between the various major communities or sub-regions. This rivalry was largely intended to ensure that a particular place or sub-region got its fair share of the southern hand-outs. The rivalry almost became a way of life and many could not cope with, or were suspicious of, the idea of cooperation for the greater good of all. The northern universities have affected the population flows both to and within their regions. Although figures are hard to come by the universities have undoubtedly enhanced the tendency already evident in the three northern regions for population and development to concentrate on a few nodal points, mainly the university cities. The anticipation of this effect was undoubtedly behind the initial strong desire for university colleges to be located in Sault Ste Marie, North Bay and Hearst in northeastern Ontario and for the other northern universities to have branch campuses (however small) in as many of the communities within their regions as possible. The 'regional issue', meaning the spread of services around the north, has been a continuing and contentious issue at all of the northern Canadian universities.

The bringing in of a relatively large number of 'outsiders' was not always well received, especially since those outsiders were mostly of relatively high social status and changed the social rank order in the northern regions, and since they often held very different views and value systems from those who already lived in the region, especially those who arrived in the 1960s. A number of the long-time residents did not like the partial loss of the frontier image that this in-migration involved. Moreover, many of those who were brought in to the regions analysed those regions (see Thomson, Hallsworth and Bonn, 1994), often from a critical perspective, and this led to what economists call the 'inspection effect'. That is, when a particular issue in a particular area is researched, the problems are often seen to be deeper than originally thought or even to have parameters that are quite different from those originally considered to hold true. Thereby, some of the received wisdom about them is revealed to be faulty. All these processes made it difficult for the previously established residents to hold on to their concept of northern ways, northern particularism or northern exceptionalism. In short, the new northern Canadian universities brought about change, and those changes, although desired by many, were also resented by many.

Another problem was that although the coming of the northern universities induced migration into the region, those migrants were easily driven or attracted away. Even though the northern frontier regions under discussion had always had a great deal of inflow and outflow of population the same mobility in the university was regarded with suspicion and many of those who left appeared to be seen as 'disloyal' in some sense. While northern living has much to commend it to many people, many of the induced migrants were willing to stay for a while only in areas with harsh climates, a restricted range of services, where it was difficult to find spousal employment, where there were often higher pollution levels than in southern cities (contradicting the image of the pristine wilderness that many had expected) and where there was a higher cost of living. Compounding these factors were distance from family connections, the extra travelling needed for virtually all purposes and the fact that singles of both sexes, but especially females, had fewer likely partners available. Many northern residents did not realise, at least not initially, that the faculty operated in a job market that was national and international in scope and in which they might be expected to work at several universities during their career.

Conclusions

When comparing the impact of northern universities around the world it is clear that the most successful are those that established close links with regional businesses and industries and, more particularly, with governmental regional economic and social development policies. These have tended to be the Scandinavian northern universities rather than the Canadian ones. This is because they have existed in societies where regional economic and social planning has been valued and conducted, and where the role of universities in this process has been recognised and acted upon. This linkage has not been achieved to anything like the same extent in the Canadian northern context, if only because there has been a dearth of true regional planning in the Canadian provinces.

This is not to say that the northern Canadian universities should become mere tools of industry or of the state. However, it is to say that maximum results will occur only if all of those involved in northern development coordinate their efforts. A major reason that the Scandinavian northern universities have had a much greater effect in their regions than have the six northern Canadian ones was that they were regarded as being central resources in broadly conceived, long-term regional economic and social development policies (Weller, 1985). The northern Canadian universities exist in political jurisdictions without clear, long-term northern regional economic and social development policies and in ones that do not fully recognise the important role that universities could play in northern development.

In Canada, regional industries tend to be aware of some of the benefits that a university can bring to a region but not of the full range of possible benefits. The governments of those provinces that have universities in their northern regions are well aware of the disparity between the northern and the southern parts of their respective jurisdictions and of the need to do something to change the situation. Some individual ministers appear to recognise that their northern universities are potentially important parts of the solution to the problem. But a number of them seem to regard them as the functional equivalent of a transfer to a region of a government office or the building of a dam. The full potential of a university as a catalyst or as the central part of a wider scheme of development seems not always to be fully appreciated. Morever, the three provincial governments have not developed comprehensive regional development policies within which a university could play a key role. In part this is because none of them, even Ontario with its fairly large Ministry of Northern Affairs, have ever conducted comprehensive studies of their northern regions or of their potential and problems. Until now everything appears to be done piecemeal or sectorally, with the result that the interconnections are missed and the importance of interconnecting institutions, such as a university, are also missed. Thus the Canadian northern universities will have to argue their cases to governments for some time yet and to press for a policy context within which they can perform in the most beneficial manner possible.

References

British Columbia (1989) *Regional Index, 1989* (Victoria: Ministry of Regional Development).

British Columbia (1990a) *Bill 40 – 1990 University of Northern British Columbia Act* (Victoria: Queen's Printer for British Columbia).

British Columbia (1990b) *Selected Vital Statistics and Health Status Indicators: Annual Report 1990* (Victoria: Ministry of Health and Ministry Responsible for Seniors).

British Columbia (1991) *Link: 1990 Highlights* (Victoria: Ministry of Education and Ministry of Advanced Education, Training and Technology).

Davis, H. Craig, and Hutton, Thomas A. (1989) 'The Two Economies of the British Columbia', *BC Studies* vol. 82: 3–15.

Felsenstein, Daniel (1993) 'Estimating the Urban and Regional Development Impacts of a University in a Peripheral Area'. A paper presented at the international conference entitled 'Regional Development: The Challenge of the Frontier', Ein Bokek, Israel, 27–30 December.

Graham, Amanda (1994) 'Not a Perfect Solution but a Good Illustration: The Life and Times of The University of Canada North, 1970–1985', *The Northern Review*, vol. 12/13: 117–32.

Hallsworth, Gwenda (1995) *A Brief History of Laurentian University* (Sudbury: Laurentian University).

Horne, Garry, and Penner, Charlotte (1992) *British Columbia Employment Dependencies* (Victoria: Ministry of Finance and Corporate Relations).

Implementation Planning Group (1989) *A Degree Granting Institution for Northern British Columbia* (Prince George: Implementation Planning Group).

Interior University Society (1988) *Brief to the Cabinet Committee on Regional Development* (Prince George: Interior University Society).

Israelsson, Anne-Marie (1992) *A House of Technology for Prince George: A Feasibility Study* (Luleå: Teknikens Hus).

Korhonen, H. Kalevi (1991) 'How the Ivory Tower Goes to Market – Universities and Regional Development', pp. 1–4 in W. S. Morrison (ed.), *The Role of Circumpolar Universities in Northern Development* (Thunder Bay: Lakehead Centre for Northern Studies).

Lane, Jan-Erik (1983) *Creating the University of Norrland* (Umeå: C. W. Gleerup).

MacLennan, Debra (1995) *Laurentian University: Making an Impact on Sudbury* (Laurentian University).

Nord, Douglas. C. (1997) 'The Impact of the University of Northern British Columbia on the City of Prince George: How Does One Contribute to Cultural Development and Diversification?' A paper presented at the 26th annual meetings of the Western Regional Science Association, Kona, Hawaii, 23–27 February.

Perry, T. (1992) *Speech to the Western Canadian Board Chairpersons and Secretaries* (Vancouver: Ministry of Advanced Education).

Reid, Mike, Enemark, Gordon and Rawbotham, Lisa (1992) *Economic Impact of the University of Northern British Columbia on Prince George* (Prince George: College of New Caledonia).

Riepula, Esko (1991) 'The Impact of Universities on Economic and Social Development in Northern Finland', pp. 13–16 in W. S. Morrison (ed.), *The Role of Circumpolar Universities in Northern Development* (Thunder Bay: Lakehead Centre for Northern Studies).

Sarlo, Christopher A. (1994) *Nipissing University's Economic Impact: Some New Estimates* (North Bay: Nipissing University, 1994).

Thomson, Ashley, Hallsworth, Glenda and Bonn, Lionel (1994) *The Bibliography of Northern Ontario 1966–1991* (Toronto: Dundern Press).

University of Northern British Columbia (1991) *Academic Plan* (Prince George: University of Northern British Columbia).

Weller, Geoffrey R. (1985) 'Universities, Politics and Development in Northern Ontario and Northern Sweden: A Comparative Analysis', *Canadian Journal of Higher Education*, vol. XV: 51–72.

Weller, Geoffrey R. (1987) 'Universities in the Circumpolar North: A Comparative Analysis', pp. 3–17 in P. Adams and D. Parker (eds), *Canada's Subarctic Universities* (Ottawa: Association of Canadian Universities for Northern Studies).

Weller, Geoffrey R. (1994) 'Regionalism, Regionalisation and Regional Development in a University Context: The Case of the University of Northern British Columbia', *The Canadian Journal of Regional Science*, vol. XVII: 153–68.

Weller, Geoffrey R. (1995) 'Should British Columbia Create a Ministry of Northern Affairs', *BC Studies*, vol. 104: 127–48.

8
The Role of the University of Alaska in Northern Development

Diddy M. Hitchins

Introduction

At the beginning of the twenty-first century, there are four accredited universities in the State of Alaska: the University of Alaska Anchorage (UAA), the University of Alaska Fairbanks (UAF), and the University of Alaska Southeast (UAS). Together they comprise the state University of Alaska System. There is also one private university – Alaska Pacific University (APU).

The purpose of this chapter is to explore the impact of universities on Alaskan development by first describing the Alaskan context (both regional and educational) in which these universities exist, then narrating the details of their founding and development. With this narrative in place, the next section will examine the impact of Alaskan universities, both from the perspective of access to higher education and professional qualification, and contributions to economic, social and cultural development. The final section draws some conclusions about the impact of universities for Alaskan development and their potential future role.

The northern context

The name Alaska comes from the Aleut term 'Alyeska' meaning 'the great land'. The great land stands apart: unique amongst contemporary northern circumpolar regions, it is a complete federal unit that is geographically separated from the rest of its political entity by the territory of another nation-state. By far the largest of the United States in geographic terms, Alaska has an east–west span of 2,400 miles and a north–south span of 1,420 miles. Alaska's land area of 586,412 square miles is equal to one third of the land area of the 'lower 48' continental states, and its 33,000-

mile coastline is half again that of the continental United States (Kresge et al., 1997).

Alaska is comprised of four distinct geographic regions: the Pacific mountain system, southern coastal Alaska with both rain forest and grasslands, interior Alaska and the North Slope, combining coastal plains and foothills of treeless tundra. Alaska experiences extremes of both temperatures and precipitation. Alaska's human geography is a product of the interaction between the natural environment and economic and social forces indicating several distinct development stages: native Alaska, characterised by aboriginal occupation and resource use; colonial Alaska (1740–1940) with resource exploitation under both Russian and US occupation; military Alaska (1940–58) with a shift to defence activity and urban living; and the state of Alaska, from 1959 until the present with state government responsibility for development of Alaska's resources (Kresge et al., 1997).

Alaska is widely regarded as the route by which the New World became occupied, with evidence for occupation of Alaska by aboriginal peoples from 15,000 years ago. Alaska's indigenous peoples, together referred to as Alaska natives, fall into five major groupings. The earliest European contact with the indigenous peoples was by Russians with the Aleuts around 1740. Contact with Northern Eskimoes did not occur for another century (Langdon, 1987). The estimated pre-contact population of native Alaskans was 60,000–70,000 people, of whom some 46 per cent were Eskimo (Northern Inupiat and Southern Yuit), 21 per cent Aleut, 20 per cent Northwest Coast Indian (Tlingit and Haida) and 12 per cent Interior Indians (Athapascan). All these Native cultures were self-sufficient subsistence economies based on natural resources (Langdon, 1987). Despite the decline of native Alaska from its dominant position once Europeans came, native Alaska has continued to the present day as a vital element in Alaskan development.

During the eighteenth and nineteenth centuries, Alaska was invaded by non-native fur traders, whalers, miners and fishermen, who exploited (and sometimes exhausted) the resources for distant markets and interests. First to come were the Russians, but once the Russians decided that Alaska had no further economic value for them, they were willing to sell it.

When, in 1867, the United States purchased Alaska from Russia, Secretary of State William Seward was ridiculed and Alaska was dubbed 'Seward's Ice Box' or 'Seward's Folly'. Further Alaskan economic development came with salmon canneries in the late 1870s and a series of small goldrushes in the 1880s. It was the stampede touched off by the Klondike gold strike in 1896 that led to the Nome gold rush of 1900, the development of placer gold mining in the Alaskan interior, coal mining at Nenana and copper mining at Kennecott, and which established mining as the major Alaskan economic activity of the period. Mining and canneries, and to a lesser extent fur, continued to be mainstays of the Alaskan economy until the mid-1920s, when a depression set in.

During the period of Russian Alaska there was a maximum of 850 non-natives in Alaska. European contact largely disrupted or destroyed the pre-existing self-sufficient Aboriginal Alaska and disease devastated the native population (Rogers, 1970). By 1910 the native population had declined by more than half the pre-contact number, to only 25,000, while the number of non-natives had overtaken natives in the population of Alaska with the influx associated with the Klondike and Alaska gold rushes, such that in 1910 there were 39,000 non-natives in Alaska. However, the non-native population could hardly be regarded as settled or resident, associated as it was with booms and busts, overwhelmingly male, and practising seasonal out-migration.

The economic growth and attendant population growth had, however, resulted in some political development, with the First Organic Act in 1884 making Alaska a US federal Civil, Land and Judicial District, followed by the application of Homestead Laws in 1898, and the Civil Code in 1900. In 1906 Alaska was accorded a voteless delegate in the US Congress, and by the terms of the Second Organic Act of 1912, Alaska became a US territory. In 1914 the federal government authorised the creation of an Alaska railroad hoping to encourage settlement and to assist in economic development, but its start-up in 1923 failed to stimulate further economic activity. However, the Alaska railroad construction headquarters camp on the east side of Cook Inlet laid the foundations for the development of Anchorage, which had become the largest population center in Alaska by 1950.

The 1930s were as depressed in Alaska as elsewhere in the United States: the Federal Emergency Relief Administration relocated 200 farm families from the mid-west to Alaska's Matanuska Valley, hoping thereby to launch agricultural production in Alaska, if only to save having to transport provisions from the lower 48 to the government employees in the territory. It was, however, only with the major military build-up of the Second World War, and the guaranteed military market, that agriculture in Alaska began to succeed. A 1937 report, commissioned by the US Congress from the National Resources Committee, failed to foresee the military significance of Alaska in the dawning aviation era, and was far from optimistic about the development potential of Alaska (Naske and Slotnick, 1979).

The bombing of Dutch Harbor and the Japanese occupation of the remote Aleutian islands of Attu and Kiska in early June 1942 brought Alaska to the forefront of US national defence and the threshold of major development. A huge Alaska military build-up – from 500 to 152,000 military personnel – occurred during 1942 and 1943. Dutch Harbor, Sitka, Kodiak, Fairbanks and Anchorage became military centres. The Alaska–Canada Highway was constructed, and all forms of transport and communication were significantly upgraded.

After the war, successive waves of military-related construction continued in Alaska as its strategic significance continued in the Cold War nuclear age: seven major Alaskan military facilities were constructed or upgraded. A series of distant early warning, ballistic missile warning and tropospheric radio communications stations were built. Garrison forces of about 50,000 personnel were maintained in Alaska throughout the 1950s. Thus, through the decades of the 1940s and 1950s defence and military-related construction was the basic economic activity of Alaska.

In 1959 Alaska achieved statehood. With a population of some 220,000, it had a small economy dominated by military activity, but with significant commercial fishing, logging and mining components. Development was spurred in the 1960s by an embryonic private service sector, by Cook Inlet petroleum development, and by rebuilding after the huge 1964 earthquake centred in Anchorage (Goldsmith and Hill, 1997). Discovery of the Prudhoe Bay Oilfield (the largest in North America) on the North Slope of Alaska in 1968 and its subsequent development, including construction of the trans-Alaska oil pipeline, caused an economic boom from 1974 to 1977. Oil production started in 1977 and by the 1980s the state government was reaping billions of dollars in oil revenues. Oil production steadily increased from the late 1970s through the early 1980s. Alaska also benefited from OPEC oil price rises between 1979 and 1981.

The state government used the revenues from the oil boom for construction, improved services and dividend payments to all Alaskans. The impact of this injection of resources was to bring Alaska's vital statistics – such as infant mortality and death rates – to a level comparable with those of the rest of the United States. A 1994 report that reviewed statistics from the late 1980s and early 1990s claimed that health status in Alaska had never been better, but pointed out that the overall rates were far better for urban, white Alaskans than for native, rural Alaskans, and did note the high level of accidental deaths and of suicides among young native men (Alaska, 1994). All levels of education received increased funding and a major effort was made to improve the quality and availability of secondary education in rural areas. The infusion of funds affected the whole economy and Alaska experienced the largest economic boom to date. Thousands of jobs were created in both the government and private sectors. Then, when world oil prices crashed in 1986, Alaska faced a severe recession: state-funded programmes had to be severely cut and painful pruning took place with many losing their jobs and significant out-migration.

Recovery began in 1988 and slow economic growth characterised the 1990s. Predictions of declining oil production combined with low oil prices have reduced state income, and state budgets have had to be constantly pruned, but overall population, jobs and income have continued to see modest growth through the 1990s.

Despite its vast size, Alaska continues to be relatively insignificant politically, ranking 49th of the 50 United States in population size (only Wyoming is smaller) with the 1998 population estimated at 650,000. According to the 1990 census, Alaska had a population of 550,043, of whom 75 per cent were white, 16 per cent native Alaskan, 4 per cent black, and 4 per cent Asian and Pacific Islanders. The 1990 census showed the proportion of females in Alaska to be slightly lower than for the US (47 per cent vs 51 per cent) and the Alaskan population was slightly younger, with a median age of 28 compared with a US median age of 32. According to the 1990 census, Alaska averaged 0.96 persons per square mile (compared with a US figure of 70.33) but 75 per cent of all Alaskans lived in the five largest census areas; Anchorage, Fairbanks, the Kenai Peninsula, Matanuska-Susitna Borough and Juneau. While 70 per cent of all Alaskans lived in nineteen urban areas of 2,500 people or more, 46 per cent of Alaska natives lived in rural areas with less than 1,000 persons. What this means is that Alaska is sparsely populated, with most of the population concentrated in a few urban areas that have services and living conditions comparable to other US urban areas, while a small number of people, of whom a high proportion are Alaska natives, live in 'bush' Alaska, with very meagre service provision and difficult living conditions.

Alaska's size, terrain and climate challenge infrastructure development and service delivery: with only 13,485 miles of road, only five of Alaska's urban centres are connected by road and many towns and villages are accessible by air or water only. Flying is the normal means of transport for most Alaskans – but it is expensive and due to climatic conditions it is also dangerous. A sizeable chunk of Canada intervenes between Alaska and the 'lower 48' United States, and Alaska shares much more in common with Canada in terms of terrain, climate and other conditions, than it does with those other 48 American states. As with Canada, Alaskan identity is conceived in terms of northernness, but whereas for Canada that northernness is a central part of the essence of the nation-state, the remoteness of Alaska and the fact that it is separated from the rest of the continental United States has meant that Alaska has long been perceived in a colonial light and both Alaska and northernness are far removed and absent from the essence of US national identity. Almost unknown to the average American until very recently, Alaska, when and if it has been considered at all, has been seen as a remote, ice-bound, resource-rich colony to be exploited for economic and security reasons for the benefit of the national interest, or latterly as a remote wilderness to be preserved for posterity.

Only with the discovery of oil on the North Slope of Alaska in 1968, and the economic impact of the Arab oil embargo of 1973, followed by the influx of people participating in oil development, did Alaska take on a permanent, real and visible significance for the American public. Only very recently, with improved transport and communications, a larger resident population and the development of American tourism, has Alaska begun to be integrated into the nation's consciousness.

The higher educational context

Alaska stands apart – not just in geopolitical terms; it has also been apart from the higher educational system of the United States. In the seventeenth century, when the first universities were being established on the East Coast of what would become the United States, Alaska was experiencing its first European contact and had not yet become a Russian colony. During the nineteenth century, as the creation of universities followed upon westward expansion, Alaska was just in transition to becoming a US territory. When Sheldon Jackson created the first institution of higher education in Alaska in 1879 (the Sitka Industrial School), it was as a mission to the Tlingit Indians, not to provide education for a resident, citizen population.

The United States has the most extensive system of university education in the world with large numbers of private institutions in addition to public institutions in every state: in 1992 more than 3,500 two- and four-year colleges served more than 14,000,000 students, mainly 20–24 year olds. In 1990 75 per cent of all US 20–24 year-olds were in higher education: with the single exception of Canada, no other country in the world has more than 50 per cent.

The system originated with eight colleges (the 'Ivy League'), founded by various Protestant denominations in the original thirteen colonies to provide a Christian education and training in religious and civic leadership for clergy and teachers in the New World. Adoption of the US Constitution endorsed the principle of local educational prerogative allowing those original colleges to continue to receive local public support while other secular state universities were founded in response to demand for trained professionals such as doctors, lawyers and teachers. What emerged was a mix of private and public institutions without any organised national system of universities.

In 1862 legislation was introduced into the US Congress to allow for the funding of colleges in every state through the grant of federal land. The intention of the Land Grant Colleges legislation (the Morrill Act) was to ensure the application of 'scientific knowledge to agriculture and the mechanic arts'. This resulted in a great expansion and popularisation of higher education. A distinction emerged between colleges with a more practical purpose and graduate research institutions.

A further popularisation of university education in the United States occurred after the Second World War, with the GI Bill of Rights legislation which afforded the opportunity for university education under government sponsorship to those who had served in the wartime armed forces. Subsequently, going to college or university after graduation from high school became the norm in the United States. Extensive access for people of many different social and economic backgrounds is now the hallmark of the American higher education system, reflecting a societal commitment to equal opportunity, rather than support for a government organised and provided system. Currently, 58 per cent of high school graduates in the United States go on to full-time higher education at universities that often combine academic, vocational and technical education. Universities in the United States are much broader and more comprehensive institutions of post-secondary education than European universities. To accommodate demand, every state in the union has created a public, state university system and in addition there are many private institutions.

The elite, academic Ivy League and research-oriented universities cream off the most qualified students by combined use of admission requirements that set up competition for places, and offering scholarship support. To be sure that they qualify for federal student funding, these institutions advertise their compliance with federal programme requirements, such as accommodating quotas of minority students, often including 'token' Alaska native students. Would-be students whose parents have had a university education, particularly if they attended an 'Ivy League' institution, are more likely to compete for the expensive, prestige places. First-generation university students are more likely to attend their state institutions which often have open admissions policies to provide access. Returning adults are now a rapidly increasing segment of the college population and many of them are engaging in higher education part-time. The US system of earning a degree by the accumulation of the required number of credits, within a system that easily accommodates transfer credits, provides the necessary portability of higher education in a highly mobile society. Such access is particularly important in Alaska, where the population is younger and even more transient than the US norm.

Standards are maintained through accreditation of programmes by regional accrediting boards which, along with compliance with federal, state and local legislation, qualifies institutions to receive public funds. Many federal funding programmes have been made available for higher education, subsequent to the Land Grants and the GI Bill, for students attending accredited institutions. These funds and programmes have been used as tools of social policy which has tended to increase the systematisation of higher education nation-wide. Universities and colleges also compete to be highly ranked in annual surveys of universities carried out by national news magazines that publish the results to guide would-be students and their parent in their college selection. Since higher education is very big business generating millions of dollars, competition is fierce.

As in most colonies, throughout the period from 1867 until 1959, and beyond, the federal government sent personnel, both military and civilian, to defend and govern Alaska. They served as if on an overseas contract, that is, people were 'posted' to Alaska for a specific period, with special 'hardship' benefits, and then they would return 'to the United States'. Frequently, those who were posted to Alaska did not bring their families. It was like an overseas posting where wives stayed at home to make sure that children were not deprived of a good education. Certainly, most of those in Alaska who had had university education themselves and wanted their children also to receive such benefit, sent them to their own alma mater or to other established universities 'outside' in the United States. Serving in Alaska was like being sent overseas in that it was an exciting challenge and potential career-builder for young government agents or military officers who had already completed their higher education, but it was not regarded as a permanent assignment. If one needed either education or medical care, one went 'home' for it. Some young pioneers chose to accept the challenge of Alaska rather than going to university, but it was not until the population build-up associated with military Alaska (1940–58) and the post-Second World

War popularisation of university education amongst Americans resulting from the GI Bill, that there was significant demand for general university programmes in Alaska. In this, Alaska was a classic colonial situation and it was only with statehood in 1959 that the question of access to higher education for the resident population really became an issue.

By then, the University of Alaska, located just outside Fairbanks, had been in existence offering courses, both practical and academic, that were specially adapted to the Alaskan environment, since 1922. During the 1950s the university began to deliver higher education statewide by creating community colleges in three urban centres. The Constitution of the State of Alaska, implemented with statehood in 1959, identified the University of Alaska as the state university, to be governed by a ten member Board of Regents (increased to eleven in 1974 with the addition of a student member), appointed by the governor and confirmed by the legislature for eight-year, staggered terms. The Board of Regents reviews and approves educational policy, degree programmes, campus development and budget requests. The Board also appoints the president, who is responsible for the administration of the Statewide System and serves as the executive officer of the Board (University of Alaska, 1996)

Even after statehood and up to the present, there have been significant voices in the debates in the Alaska legislature on university funding, that argue that it made no sense to offer general university education in Alaska, that the costs are too high and the numbers too low to achieve an acceptable standard of quality. They have generally felt that it would make more sense for the state to subsidise Alaskans to go 'outside' for general university education (while offering specialised, 'Alaskan' subjects at the University of Alaska in Fairbanks). This view might well have prevailed were it not for the financial resources that became available to the state with the oil boom beginning in the late 1970s. The situation was also affected by a 1976 Alaska Supreme Court case that ruled that all Alaskans had the right to secondary (high school) education in their own home community and should not have to attend a distant residential (boarding school) programme to receive preparation for high school graduation. Following from this, there was a growing assumption that it was the responsibility of the University of Alaska System to respond to growing demand to accommodate needs for university education statewide.

University education in Alaska

The University of Alaska originated from the Alaska Agricultural College and School of Mines (AACSM), created in 1915 by the US Congress under Land Grant College legislation. The AACSM, located just outside Fairbanks, then the richest mining district in interior Alaska, was able to admit its first students in September 1922, having obtained appropriations from the Alaska Territorial legislature to construct and equip a college building.

What the Alaskan media called 'Farthest North College' was a very practical venture, intended to bring federal funding to Alaska while offering training in 'scientific methods of mining and agriculture', that might lead to stabilisation of the economy. At its opening, AACSM had six faculty and offered five fields of study: Agriculture, Mining Engineering, Civil Engineering, General Science and Home Economics. Certainly, the college could not have been justified in terms of community need or local demand for university education – only fifteen students enrolled the first year – but from its inception the college became an important element in the economy of Fairbanks.

In 1935, a year after the Northwest Association of Secondary Schools, Colleges and Universities granted the AASCM full accreditation as a four-year university institution, the Alaska legislature officially changed its name to the University of Alaska. Since opening, the AASCM had steadily grown so that by 1935 it was attracting more than 150 students each year, and many more students participated in the practical non-credit short courses, such as the ten-week, winter, miners' short course. Keeping the college going was difficult since the annual federal government appropriation of $US50,000 only covered about half the costs and revenue from the land grant was non-existent because the land was unsurveyed, so the college depended on appropriations by the Alaska legislature. To this day, the University of Alaska has not benefited from the land grant that it should have received and that would have gone a long way towards meeting operating expenses.

The new University of Alaska had great prospects: it had outgrown its previously limited curricula and had now expanded into the sciences, liberal arts, languages and social sciences. Although the School of Mines continued to be the largest, most professional and best-equipped department through the 1930s, the new university offered degree programmes in ten disciplines. These included Arts and Letters, two-year pre-law, pre-journalism, pre-medicine, forestry, aeronautical engineering and architectural engineering programmes in response to the vocational training needs of the territory (Cole, 1994). Programme development was spurred by incorporation of the US Department of Agriculture's Agricultural Experimental Station, the US Biological Survey, as well as by development of the University of Alaska Museum, and research on the aurora borealis funded by the Rockefeller Foundation. Recognition of the enhanced status of the institution by the Alaska Legislature resulted in funding for a library, which would later, with the acquisition of several important collections, become the most comprehensive collection on Alaska and the major US collection on the north.

By 1940, the University of Alaska consisted of important research institutes and programmes and was attracting an enrolment of more than 300 full-time students each year, but it was evident that the campus lacked adequate funding. When the Second World War intervened, the university nearly closed, but, in the new aviation age, Alaska was no longer remote and unknown, but of key strategic importance and in the front-line of American defence. Record breaking post-war enrolment due to the GI Bill resulted in a financial crisis indicative of the rickety financial structure of both the university and the Territory. But even as the crisis was taking place, the US Congress appropriated $US975,000 for creation of a Geophysical Institute at the University of Alaska, reflecting recognition that arctic geophysical research was now a vital element in national security. The addition of the Geophysical Institute to the University of Alaska marked its transition from a pioneer to an atomic age institution and the Geophysical Institute became the core of the university's research and graduate programmes (Cole, 1994). The transition demonstrated the need for thorough modernisation, with better long-range planning and budgeting, and a strategy for positively and successfully representing the University to the legislature. This modernisation took place between 1950 and 1960, with increasing numbers of faculty and students, and an improved campus. In 1955–56, the University of Alaska hosted Alaska's Constitutional Convention, which drafted the statehood constitution in which the University of Alaska was identified as the state university. Enthusiasm surrounding statehood also resulted in the founding of Alaska's only private university, Alaska Methodist University, chartered in 1957, to provide a religious-based, university education option in Anchorage.

The 1960s was a period of tremendous development for the University of Alaska with student enrolment increasing from 1,000 students a year to more than 3,500, and equivalent development in research. The University of Alaska continued its commitment to arctic research and northern studies, and by taking over the operation of the Naval Arctic Research Laboratory from the US navy in 1954, the University of Alaska gained the pre-eminent role among American universities in polar research. Creation of many new research institutes and programmes followed: the Institute of Marine Science, the Institute of Social, Economic and Governmental

Research, the Instititute of Arctic Biology, the Mineral Industry Research Laboratory, the Institute for Water Resources, the Institute for Arctic Environmental Engineering, the Poker Flat Research Range (the world's largest land-based rocket range) and the Atomic Energy Commission's 'Project Chariot'. Taking advantage of these new research institutes, during the 1960s, two dozen new graduate programmes were added, but finding the funding for new facilities continued to be a struggle.

With statehood, a new type of financing became possible: from 1960 the issue of bonds that required voter approval could be used to finance university construction. Bonding was used successfully to fund university construction and until 1975 the voters approved every UA bond issue. The business community supported the bond issues since they felt that this investment would bring federal dollars to Alaska (Cole, 1994).

In 1951, the Board of Regents first began to consider the need to deliver higher education programmes statewide. By then Anchorage was the biggest community in the state and unserved by higher education. The first community colleges – in Anchorage, Ketchikan, Juneau-Douglas and Palmer – came out of this initiative. In 1958, the university launched a long-range planning initiative to anticipate how it could take up its statewide mission and cope with burgeoning student demand.

The new Master Plan proposed a new Division of Statewide Services to supervise continuing education, a network of community colleges offering associate degrees and lower division courses, and a senior college in Anchorage. It perpetuated the special role of the University of Alaska in Fairbanks in providing a highly unusual mix of programmes, many of a practical nature and specially adapted to its northern location, while the other institutions in the system were created to respond to the needs of the largely urban, in-migrant population only for general or vocational higher education. The plan was implemented between 1960 and 1975 and resulted in the creation of three new and separate universities: the University of Alaska Anchorage, the University of Alaska Fairbanks, and the University of Alaska Juneau (later Southeast). The plan did not anticipate the 1972 request from the Alaska Federation of Natives (AFN) for locally controlled community colleges in northern and western Alaska to teach the skills necessary for natives to successfully run the corporations created by the 1971 Alaska Native Claims Settlement Act, which had made oil development on the North Slope possible. Providing higher education access for Alaska Natives had not previously been identified as part of the mission of the University of Alaska and had certainly not figured in the reasons for its founding. The University denied AFN's request, arguing that Natives could take advantage of existing Cooperative

Extension programmes. This led native legislators to use their power in the university budget process to create community colleges that were not part of the statewide University System budget requests, in Bethel in 1972, Nome in 1975 and Kotzebue in 1976. It also led the North Slope Borough to create its own Inuit Ilisagviat-Inupiat University of the Arctic in 1975, which represented a break with western thinking about university education and resulted in a very different institution from anything that the University of Alaska System provided.

These developments occurred against the backdrop of the first failed university bond issue (1976) and followed by a financial crisis. The university system was saved from bankruptcy in 1977 only by a reluctant and highly critical state legislature, which blamed the crisis on too rapid expansion. The crisis continued for two years and was put to rest only with a new president in 1979. The new president realised that to be funded and to fulfil its statewide mission, the university would have to develop its various institutions to meet demands in their respective communities and would also need to embrace specialisation and programme rationalisation and become a leader in distance delivery through utilisation of the most modern technology. But at least in 1979, with oil beginning to flow, the financial prospects for doing so looked very good.

The new state universities in Anchorage and Juneau struggled to become established. They were not comprehensive universities and faced public scepticism. It was difficult for them to obtain an adequate share of funding within the system since they were fighting against UAF, which was well established and had political support and was thus able to guard its share of the funds and thereby protect its status. Being incomplete and precariously funded, UAA and UAJ failed to command the respect of the public. Parents and high school counsellors regarded them as a last resort for high school graduates who could not afford to go outside or to UAF. What they did, was meet the demand for continuing education for professionals already employed in Anchorage or Juneau, offer the opportunity for spouses and dependants of those employed in Anchorage or Juneau to obtain a degree while posted there, or offer those who had not gone to university from high school and now decided they wanted a degree, to obtain one in Anchorage or Juneau. They both met the needs of a growing element in US higher education: returning older and mature students, often female and studying part-time. Alaska Methodist University, which had closed its doors for one academic year as a result of a financial crisis, also took advantage of the economic boom and the demand for higher education in Anchorage, reopening its doors as Alaska Pacific University in 1978. Having undergone major reorganisation, it managed to get national recognition as 'one of America's best small colleges', and embarked on a successful private endowment campaign.

In 1986, the University of Alaska System faced the need for drastic budget cuts in the face of the collapse of oil prices. The rapid growth funded by the oil revenues of the early 1980s had to be checked. Since by 1986 the State of Alaska was dependent for 85 per cent of its income on oil, all state-funded programmes were severely affected. Without any comprehensive planning to respond to the crisis, the University of Alaska System only narrowly avoided financial exigency. Faced with the need to cut back its annual budget drastically, a major reorganisation of the university sytem was undertaken. Eleven community colleges were abolished and fifteen administrative units were consolidated into the three regional universities (the University of Alaska, Anchorage, Juneau, now renamed the University of Alaska Southeast). Operating costs were slashed, but this eroded responsiveness to local demands and narrowed the range of offerings. Much of the projected savings from this administrative reorganisation turned out to be illusory and the reorganisation was bitterly contested, not least by the unionised faculty of the community colleges.

Faced with annual decrements in both operating and overall budgets, the statewide University System has struggled from 1986 to the present to maintain and expand physical facilities, to respond to programme needs and to try to preserve the reputation of the University of Alaska Fairbanks as a centre for world-class circumpolar research. Within the system, a constant battle has been enjoined between units and within units to try to find a satisfactory formula to streamline programmes while at the same time responding to the needs of the state in the face of annual budget cutbacks. Each of the state universities has embarked on private fundraising initiatives. Over the years there has been little innovative thinking and only some minor rationalisations have occurred, while attempts to eliminate programme duplication have been largely resisted in favour of constant across-the-board erosion. In the late 1980s low salaries led to a brain-drain of top science and engineering faculty from UAF's research institutes, the demoralisation of the faculty and to faculty unionisation in the late 1990s. Across-the-board retirement incentive programmes continue to be used to cull expensive senior faculty and administrators with little thought for the adverse effect this might have on programmes.

Thus the current system comprises three regional universities, each headed by a chancellor who reports to the president. The president is the chief executive officer of the Board of Regents with responsibility for running the University of Alaska System. The University of Alaska Fairbanks is the most comprehensive institution in the system, offering degrees at all levels and serving over 9,000 students at its main campus in Fairbanks and six other campuses. UAF is affiliated with Ilisagvik College, an autonomous institution created in 1986, and funded by the North Slope Borough. The college 'serves the residents of the North Slope Borough by providing quality post-secondary academic, vocational and technical education in a learning environment that perpetuates and strengthens Inupiat culture, language, values and traditions' (Ilisagvik College Catalog 1998–99).

UAF is a land, sea and space grant institution and is the system's major research and only doctoral degree-granting institution. It is classified as a Doctoral 11 institution by the Carnegie Foundation. With its cluster of seventeen research institutes, centres, laboratories and programmes, the University of Alaska Fairbanks is the United States' major centre for research on Alaska, and the circumpolar north. Its recently funded Arctic Research Center, attached to the Geophysical Institute, will be the centre for cooperative international research on global climate change, earthquake prediction and auroral activity, and it will make use of a super-computer provided by Congressional funding.

The University of Alaska Anchorage, with an annual student enrolment of 19,000, serves the largest number of students. As an open enrolment university, UAA offers pre-college through Masters-level degree programmes. With campuses in Anchorage and four other locations, it is described as a public comprehensive university which strives to meet the higher and continuing education needs of the residents of Anchorage and Southcentral Alaska (Board of Regents, 1997). With its location in the population, commercial and service centre of Alaska UAA is the lead unit in the statewide system for the areas of health and biomedical sciences, business and international trade, public policy and administration, vocational and technical education and special education. It also offers academic programmes in the liberal arts, the sciences, and professional and technical fields. UAA also has responsibility for statewide delivery of military education programmes. Organised research and training units at UAA complement the academic programmes and reflect the special character of UAA's mission: they include the Institute for Circumpolar Health Studies, the Environment & Natural Resources Institute, the Institute for Social & Economic Research, the American Russian Center, the Center for Alcohol & Addiction Studies, the Center for Economic Education, the Justice Center, and the

Aviation Training Center and Mining & Petroleum Training Service (University Advancement, 1997). The amount of grant-funded research conducted at UAA is tiny by comparison with UAF.

The University of Alaska Southeast, with its main campus in Juneau, Alaska's state capital, and branch campuses in Ketchikan and Sitka, serves some 5,000 students. It has three academic units: the School of Business and Public Administration, the School of Education and the School of Career Education. UAS offers certificate, associate, baccalaureate and Masters degrees and credential endorsement programmes. Through a cooperative agreement with Yukon College in Whitehorse, UAS delivers Masters of Education degrees in Canada, and provides the AAS in business administration, BBA and MPA to military personnel in Southeast Alaska. In response to local needs, UAS campuses offer programmes in welding, diesel, marine technology and marine training; environmental technology; public management, law enforcement, health information management, physician assistant and nurse practitioner training; visitor industry and visitor industry for native Alaskans; and also conducts recruitment and retention programmes for Alaska native students (University of Alaska, 1996).

Alaska Pacific University (APU) was also affected by the 1986 oil price slump that hit Alaska's economy. Some general liberal arts, international and social science programmes were cut and so were sports programmes. APU has now carved out a niche for itself in higher education in Alaska by responding to very specific areas of professional need. It offers eleven undergraduate majors and five graduate programmes. The undergraduate majors are in Business Administration, Education, Environmental Science, Liberal Studies, and Psychology and Human Services. APU also offers a very popular degree completion programme in Organisational Management. APU offers a Master of Arts in Teaching, an MBA and MBA in Telecommunication Management, a Master of Science in Environmental Science, and a Master of Science in Couselling Psychology. All of APU's programmes provide professional training in Alaska for high-need occupations, indicating that it has become more responsive to specifics of the Alaskan economy and less a general liberal arts college. APU is the host for two international initiatives, namely the Secretariat for the Northern Forum and the Institute of the North. Hosting these ventures generated some ongoing revenue for the university and a positive link with Alaska's international development business sector. With the slow growth of the Alaskan economy in the 1990s, APU has continued to seek to build its student body through high-profile advertising and has also vigorously pursued expansion of its private endowment.

The impact of universities on and in Alaska

The earliest introduction of post-secondary education in Alaska was not in response to any demand for access to university education. It was missionary in that it was intended to bring Christianity to the native people, in an attempt to assimilate them into the dominant culture. Not until the resident population built up to more than 100,000 after the Second World War, and non-natives outnumbered natives in the population by at least 3 to 1, was there enough demand to warrant the creation of institutions of higher education to meet local needs. That demand was from non-native American residents who wanted the same educational opportunities for themselves and their children in Alaska that they would find anywhere else in the United States. Particularly with statehood in 1959, Alaskan pride demanded that Alaska offer the same educational opportunities as any other state, and that included university education, since going to college after high school graduation had by then become the American norm.

During the colonial and territorial periods in Alaskan history, there were too few permanent residents desiring to fulfil their need for higher education in Alaska to warrant the availability of a traditional four-year, liberal arts, university curriculum. Clearly, the University of Alaska was founded to contribute to economic development, not to access, but its creation did make some university education available. Alaska's special development requirements, as the United States' only northern circumpolar region, generated the need for specialized research and education which was satisfied to some degree with the creation of the Alaska Agricultural College and School of Mines in 1922 and its evolution inot the University of Alaska with its special Mission and focus on the north. The University of Alaska gradually developed a range of traditional university programmes alongside its specialised Alaskan and northeren focused prgrammes, but with the major shift of population from the interior to south central Alaska, many Alaskans wanted higher education elsewhere than just in Fairbanks.

The problem was that the full range of university programmes were in Fairbanks which was not where they were needed! The first attempt to respond to demand for access was contained in the modernisation plan developed at the end of the 1940s that created the Division for Statewide Services and twelve community colleges. These began to address statewide needs for lower-division university course work, vocational and continuing education. The creation of the Senior College in Anchorage in 1971 indicated recognition of the need for traditional university baccalaureate programmes in the major population centre of the state. The failure of the University of Alaska administration to respond to the request from the Alaska Federation of Natives for Community Colleges that would offer a specialised curriculum to meet Alaska natives new need for financial and managerial skills, grounded in a programme that respected and incorporated their cultural traditions, is reflective of the administration's lack of imagination and failure to appreciate the new Alaskan political and social realities or to anticipate the slowly growing national and international re-evaluation of aboriginal cultures and support for indigenous people's rights.

The two new universities in the University of Alaska System created in the mid-1970s came into existence in response to population and political pressure for by then Alaskans wanted to be able to pursue university programmes where they lived and worked. The potential availability of millions of dollars of oil money made this feasible. Since the early 1970s, on average, most Alaska residents have more post-secondary education than people nationally, although the reverse is true for Alaska natives (Western Interstate Commission on Higher Education, 1996). People with post-secondary education usually encourage their children to pursue higher education. Although the median age of Alaskans is younger than that for the United States, the median age of students at Alaskan universities is older and a higher proportion of Alaskan high school graduates pursue first degrees out-of-state than is the norm for other western states. Students at Alaskan universities are generally older and there is a higher proportion of women than is the national norm. Much of the initial demand for Alaskan in-state university programmes came from military and government personnel and teachers, who needed university courses for career development, and who also wanted university education available for their spouses and children. Many spouses of government and military personnel wanted to seize the opportunity of their posting to Alaska to earn a baccalaureate or a Master's degree, especially since there was no suitable employment for them. In response to this demand, and given the well-known and longstanding regional rivalries that permeate Alaskan politics, the Board of Regents created three separate institutions with two different missions, that of maintaining the circumpolar research focus at UAF while meeting local demand for access at UAA and UAJ. Alaska Pacific University has also evolved by offering programmes in response to demand.

The oil price crash of 1986 and the state's drastic cut in university funding, created a difficult dilemma. Having previously responded to demand (and to federal funding requirements to equally serve minority populations by creating new institutions, programmes and retention support) the budget was no longer sufficient to keep them all going. The choice made by the Board and the administration was to cut administrative costs immediately by cutting back to three major administrative units which would deliver programmes statewide while at the same time maintaining Fairbanks special research role and trying to increase grant and private financial support for the institutions. Cutting back to three units undermined what little autonomy and local responsiveness existed. Oil wealth accruing to the North Slope Borough permitted that community to develop an autonomous college to meet their own specific needs, but the University of Alaska eliminated those community colleges that had been funded by native legislative action. Since reorganisation, and despite special programme efforts at each of the three universities, the University of Alaska has been singularly unsuccessful at meeting the post-secondary education needs of Alaska Natives.

Subsequent rounds of programme assessments, intended to rationalise and eliminate duplication for cost-saving purposes, have further limited programmes and offerings. Restricted budgets have meant that UAA has had to cut course offerings quite drastically and the Alaskan universities have witnessed declines in enrolment. The decline in state appropriations to higher education means that the university system is not able to provide access either in terms of programmes or places for all those who want them. Alaska has one third fewer programmes than other western states, and whereas on average 58 per cent of US high school graduates attend college full-time (and of those 81 per cent enrol in-state), only 45 per cent of Alaskans enrol at Alaskan universities.

The effect of the University of Alaska on local and regional economic development is more positive than on access. The University of Alaska started out to help develop Alaskan agriculture and mining and the University in Fairbanks has, throughout its existence, concentrated on research and programmes related to its northern location. It should be noted, however, that this impact is within the framework of the US pattern of free market economic development which is essentially based on individual initiative and which is unplanned. As the narrative relating the creation and development of the University of Alaska system above makes clear, the existence of the university came about as a result of individual initiative and was almost accidental. Its development has been 'like Topsy', consisting of reactions to, and the taking advantage of, circumstances rather than of being carefully planned to have the maximum potential impact. In the United States planning is regarded with suspicion. Alaska has historically had a boom-and-bust economy based on resource development and, despite the passage of time and hugely increased population, there has been little diversification of the economy. So much so that Alaska is now more dependent on a single commodity, oil, than it was in the past and consequently continues to be subject to boom and bust. Rather than having the state take advantage of university expertise to plan a coordinated approach to stabilising the economy, as originally anticipated, the University of Alaska is subject to the boom-and-bust cycle just like any other state service. That is, the university budget is cut after a bust so that it contributes to unemployment and is less able to offer the programmes for retraining that those who have lost their jobs have time for and need during the bust period. Then the university budget is increased during a boom, just when plenty of jobs are available and people do not have the need or the time for higher education!

The University of Alaska Fairbanks is the leading research centre on the circumpolar north and has trained many of the scientists who engage in this research. It has attracted millions of dollars in federal research funds to Alaska and has been a significant contributor to the Alaskan and Fairbank's economy in terms of the employment it generates, the students it attracts and the services that it requires. The university is the major economic unit in Fairbanks. The various research institutes at UAF have been devoted to Alaskan research and have been responsive to both federal and state needs. Thus it has contributed significantly to such economic activities as Engineering, Fisheries, Forestry, Petroleum Development, Wildlife Management, as well as Agriculture and Mining. It has also provided training in Alaska at all levels for such needed occupations as teachers, miners, engineers, business people, managers, and public administrators, quite apart from historians, anthropologists, ethnographers, biologists and all those other products of a traditional university education.

The universities in Anchorage and Southeast (Juneau) also provide economic benefits to their locations and train needed personnel. Neither of them has extensive northern research institutes that contribute to Alaskan economic development, but each specialises in programmes that respond to local needs for training. UAA specialises in service-delivery occupations, since it is the service centre for Alaska, notably health, aviation, tourism, telecommunications, environmental services, and oil and gas. UAS serves the needs of state government by giving training in public administration and teaching.

The various extended campuses, while now offering mainly the lower division courses of baccalaureate programmes, do offer some locally needed vocational and certification programmes, thus providing training for the occupations offered by their local economies. The recentralisation of the system that occurred in 1986 limited their scope, autonomy and ability to respond to local economic development needs. This occurred at a time in the United States when a national reappraisal of education was taking place. This concluded that the weakness of the US higher education system was that it had too many general liberal arts degree programmes and not enough vocational and technical programmes. The outcome of this debate nationally was to lead to the creation of more community colleges, at just the same time that Alaska eliminated them! This indicates that the University of Alaska runs quite contrary to US thinking concerning how best to improve the system of higher education.

During the colonial period there was a tendency to look outside Alaska for expertise. To some extent this is still the case for, when a report is needed, outside experts (often from prestigious or Ivy League institutions or from the alma mater of the person commissioning the report) are called in rather than making use of the University of Alaska System's capabilites. Even within Alaska, there has been a tendency to assume that the necessary expertise would only be available at the university of Alaska Fairbanks. To some extent this inhibits the ability of the university system to contribute all of its potential to development of the state, but in many fields university expertise is now recognised. This has been especially so since the post-1986 developments made it clearer to the state government, the public and the business community just what expertise the university has and where it was located within the system. The scientific institutes at UAF are constantly engaged in both federal and state research projects, many of which are tied to the economic development of the state. The Institute for Social and Economic Research and the Environmental and Natural Resources Institute, both at UAA, are also continuously engaged on research projects commissioned by state government agencies that contribute to economic development. From the early 1980s through 1997, the Alaska Center for International Business at UAA worked closely with the state Office of International Trade and the World Trade Center to assist would-be Alaskan exporters and to develop Alaska's export markets, with significant impact in Japan, South Korea and the Russian Far East. Unfortunately, the legislature has ceased to fund the ACIB and it is now defunct. UAA's American Russian Center, however, continues to play a significant role in developing Alaska's links with the Russian Far East, including operating Small Business Development Centers in three different regions of the Russian Far East, thus contributing to development of the north outside of Alaska. UAA provides considerable training for personnel from the Russian Far East, not just business and government, but, for example, courses in English language for air traffic controllers. The existence of universities in Alaska means that the state is now able to 'grow its own' professionals in many fields. However, there are still some gaps for there is no medical school, no law school in Alaska and no school of architecture. Alaska continues to be a medically underserved area with only 151 physicians per 100,000 population compared with a national figure of 255 per 100,000. Over 91 per cent of Alaska's private physicians practise in the seven largest urban centres. Consequently, there are very few practising in vast rural areas. Since the Alaskan environment is entirely different from any other part of the United States, the medical problems and conditions are also different. However, there is no medical school in the state to address topics unique to Alaska. It is generally accepted that Alaska's population is too small to support the critical mass of students necessary for an in-state medical school. An in-state medical school to serve just the population of Alaska would not be a feasible or an economic proposition. Accepting this reality, Alaska participates in WAMI – the Washington, Alaska, Montana and Idaho Medical Science Program. This is a cooperative venture between the participating states and universities that supports students who wish to take their pre-medical science courses at their home-state university before proceeding to medical school at the University of Washington in Seattle. The WAMI programme is one of the few instances of rationalisation and elimination of duplication that has taken place since the reorganisation of 1986. It is no longer offered by UAF, but only by UAA, which is the lead unit in the system for health education. However, even funding even for this purpose is in peril. Although the universities in Alaska do not provide programmes for medical doctors, UAA has had a School of Nursing since the early 1980s and various UA system units provide training for health workers such as village health aides, dental hygienists and nurse practitioners. UAA also provides both baccalaureate and Master's programmes in Social Work and in Psychology, responding to the community need for these professions. All three regional universities have Schools of Education providing programmes to certify teachers for Alaska and providing programme for school administrators. Both UAA and UAF have Schools of Engineering and all three state univesities have Schools of Business, providing professional training in these high-demand fields.

Perhaps the area of most significant impact of universities in Alaska is on the social and cultural development of the state. Almost from the first day of its existence, the AACSM in Fairbanks began to exercise a civilising influence on the mining camp. The college's social, cultural and sports functions became the focal point for the community. Not only at UAF, but wherever in Alaska there has been a university institution, it has become a focus for the cultural and artistic life of the community. Even in Anchorage, with a much larger population and established cultural institutions before the university existed, the university has had a major impact, stimulating and contributing to theatre, music and the arts as well as to sports events. There is not a community political, cultural or sporting endeavour that does not have UAA people – faculty, students and staff – involved, by serving on the board, participating or performing, or providing an audience. Rural extension centres often serve as the cultural centre of rural Alaskan places. University faculty and staff, like the students whom they educate, share with others who have higher education, the interest, the background and the resources to play leading roles in the cultural development of community. They lend their professional expertise in community service with every community organisation from the Anchorage Arts Council to the Anchorage Zoo.

Conclusions

One might expect to find universities created purposely to play a role in bringing about desired economic development. In Alaska that has certainly not been the case. In Alaska economic development has been left to market forces and it is generally true to observe that universities have come about more by default than by design. There is in Alaska, as in the rest of the United States, an abhorrence of planning: planning is thought to smack of socialism, while the US economy is thought to be a free market. Economic development, like the creation of universities and their development, results from individual initiative, is piecemeal rather than systematic, and is quite informal and unconstrained by regulation. Like Topsy, it just grows!

Universities in Alaska have had a significant impact on development: they have assisted the economic development of the state; they have provided access to higher education, they have trained and certified professionals to serve in Alaska, and they have provided appropriate vocational and technical education for Alaskans to to be able to perform the jobs that the economy proffers. In addition, the universities have contributed immeasurably to the social and cultural development of Alaska.

Amongst the universities in Alaska, the original University of Alaska in Fairbanks has undoubtedly contributed most to the economic development of the state because of its focus on Alaskan and northern programmes and research. Although its origins were opportunistic – to bring federal dollars to Alaska – in its original conception and in its evolution, it has always operated to contribute to the development and transmission of scientific knowledge about Alaska, for Alaskans to use in the development of the state. In addition, the location of the original college certainly had a major impact on Fairbanks which, with the decline in mining activity, might have disappeared. Instead it became a centre for university education and research, in receipt of millions of dollars of federal grant monies, itself a source of development. One cannot but conclude that the University of Alaska Fairbanks has contributed significantly and successfully to many aspects of Alaskan development, partly because it has been conceived as truly a university for the north, and the United States' only dedicated northern university. The clarity of its mission and the single minded dedication of a sucession of administrators to that mission, has helped UAF to have significant impact.

The other university institutions in Alaska have also had an impact on development: they have brought economic benefits to their locations, contributed to social and cultural development, provided access to higher education for Alaskans, been somewhat responsive to special professional, vocational and technical needs, and (to a lesser extent than UAF) engaged in research related to Alaskan development. However, they have been more limited in their impact than UAF because they have been universities in Alaska providing access, rather than universities specially designed for Alaska.

While the creation of university institutions in Alaska after 1950 was in response to demands for access, it would be unrealistic to expect Alaskan high school graduates proceeding immediately to college to study in-state in the same proportion as is the case nationally, because this is their opportunity to experience somewhere other than Alaska. The task for the University of Alaska is to meet the programme demands of those who either choose, or have, to study in Alaska, and to prepare people adequately to participate in the Alaskan workforce.

It is still the case that some professional education is not available in Alaska, even though the need, in the case of the medical professions, calls for relevant, northern training. Since the sparse population makes it unlikely that there will ever be the numbers for sufficient economic justification for the creation of a medical school in any one northern region, this would seem to be the ideal project for cooperative effort amongst northern regions, to create a medical school that would serve the special needs of the whole circumpolar north.

One aspect of providing access to university education that is not yet satisfactorily being addressed in Alaska is the provision of higher education that is appropriate for, and in response to, the needs of Alaska natives. The University of Alaska system is seeking to provide traditional, western, university degree programmes as extensively as possible using the least expensive distance delivery extension programmes, but this is not what Alaska natives want. This is not just a problem in Alaska: throughout the United States and elsewhere, indigenous peoples are not succeeding in the dominant cultures' education systems and are demanding higher education that incorporates traditional indigenous cultural heritage. Since the University of Alaska has not satisfactorily addressed this need, at least on the North Slope of Alaska, Alaska natives have created and funded their own university institution and are about to seek accreditation for it.

An observation: it seems to be the case that the universities in Alaska have made the most significant contributions to Alaskan development, when they have been run by administrators who have broadly conceived the responsibility of their institutions to contribute to Alaskan development, and have been, or have made themselves, knowledgeable about Alaska. When top administrators have been brought in from outside, often to resolve a crisis, because of their general university management skills, and do not have intimate knowlege of Alaska and its circumstances, they have rarely succeeded in advancing the interests of the university in the political arena on which the system financially depends. By contrast, when led by able administrators who are well informed about Alaska, the university fares better.

Finally, in times of boom when money is readily available, the university has been able to obtain the funding to respond to both access and development needs, whereas in times of bust, the University, like other services, is cut back. However, it is in times of bust that the university could potentially contribute most to stabilising Alaskan development, which is exactly how the University of Alaska system started!

References

Alaska, State of (1994) *Healthy Alaskans 2000* (Department of Health and Social Services).

Atwood, E. (1979) *Frontier Politics: Alaska's James Wickersham* (Portland: Binford and Mort).

Board of Regents (1996) *Report to the Legislature 1994–1995* (University of Alaska).

Board of Regents (1997) *Report to the Legislature 1995–1996* (University of Alaska).

Cole, T. (1994) *The Cornerstone on College Hill* (Fairbanks: University of Alaska Press).

Goldsmith, S. and A. Hill (1997) *Alaska's Economy and Population, 1959–2020* (Institute of Social and Economic Research, University of Alaska Anchorage).

Jennings, M. and C. Shepro (1998) 'Local Control of Postsecondary Education', pp. 285–307 in A. Blunt et al., *Education and Development* (Calgary, Alberta: Detselig).

Kresge, D., T. Morehouse and G. Rogers (1997) *Issues in Alaska Development* (Seattle: University of Washington Press).

Langdon, S. (1987) *The Native People of Alaska* (Anchorage: Greatland Graphics).

Naske, C. and H. Slotnick (1979) *Alaska: A History of the 49th State* (Grand Rapids: Eerdmans).

Rogers, G. (1970) *Change in Alaska* (College, Alaska: University of Alaska Press).

University Advancement (1997) *Cultivating Friends and Funds* (University of Alaska, Anchorage).

University of Alaska (1996) *UA in Review* (University of Alaska).

Western Interstate Commission on Higher Education (1996) *Regional Fact Book for Higher Education in the West.*

9
Universities in the European North of Russia

Victor Vasiliev and Nicolai Toivonen

Introduction

The functions performed by universities in the social and economic development of Russia are rapidly evolving due to major changes that are occurring in the political and economic life of the country. Many of the structures and processes that existed in the Soviet period are being replaced. The traditional role of the Russian university as a stronghold of basic education and of scientific research is also evolving in response to new priorities and demands emanating from various sectors of the society.

The universities of the Northern Economic Region of Russian Federation are experiencing many of these new changes and pressures on post-secondary education. They confront a number of common problems and crises found by universities across this vast country. Yet there are also some unique challenges and opportunities that distinguish their condition from other institutions of advanced education in Russia. A harsh climate, a dispersed population base and continuing limited public investment in facilities and infrastructure create major barriers to the future growth and development of these northern universities. On the other hand, their proximity to vast natural resources, their established working relationship with international networks and the willingness of their administrative leaders to make major innovations in their development roles all point to the possibility that these post-secondary institutions will eventually bring significant change to the Russian north.

The current situation in Russia and, in particular, its peripheral regions suggests that the universities are likely to play a key role in the future development of the country. They will have an essential part to play in educating the new generation of personnel that will contribute to this development process. They will also be the sites of major scientific research that will support the social and economic development of their communities as well as contributing new technology to the economy. In this sense, it is difficult to overestimate the future impact that Russian universities will have in providing the whole country with a democratic society and a market economy. This is particularly true for the roles to be played by the post-secondary institutions of the European north of Russia.

In this chapter, the authors seek to analyse the environment of change in which university education and research are taking place in Russia today. The focus of inquiry is the special case of the post-secondary institutions of the European north of the country. Their challenges and opportunities are detailed. Their unique roles in shaping and directing the process of economic and social development in their regions are outlined. Special attention is given to their contributory roles of conducting regionally relevant research promoting new technology in business and ordinary life and in educating the key personnel required for such efforts.

The Northern Economic Region of Russia

The Northern Economic Region of Russia (hereinafter the Region), includes the Republics of Karelia and Komi and the counties of Arkhangelsk, Vologda and Murmansk. It is one of ten economic regions within the Russian Federation and is located in the northwestern portion of the country. The total area occupied by the Region is about 1.47 million square kilometres, making it the third largest among all the economic regions of Russia. Its population is about six million (Luzin, 1992).

The Region possesses a unique combination of favourable factors that may contribute to its future economic growth and development. Its physical location places it at the crossroads of the Baltic and Barents regions. It has established good working relationships with its Nordic neighbours – some of the most technologically advanced societies in the world in the fields of democratic practice and technological development. It has become an active participant in a variety of regional and international development assistance projects. The lands of the European Russian north possess enormous stocks of natural resources. They suffer little in the way of ethnic or religious rivalries that have plagued other parts of the country.

The Region is characterised by many unfavourable natural and climatic features. These include low temperatures, strong winds and a long winter caused by the far northern location of the Region. The vast territory of the Region accounts for some significant climatic differences between its various areas. On the Kola Peninsula winter may last for 240–280 days and the ground remains frozen for 9.5–10.5 months. In the southern territories of the Region, by contrast, climatic conditions are far less severe.

The Region has a very favourable geopolitical position in at least two respects. First, its only foreign border is with the Nordic countries of the northern Europe. This facilitates the development of various cooperative endeavours with Norway, Sweden and Finland. The Region today actively participates in several Nordic-sponsored development programmes directed towards the Barents and Baltic areas (Kozyrev, 1997). Equally important, however, is that the geographic position of the Region historically has allowed the creation of strong cultural, ethnic and economic relations between its various populations and the neighbouring societies of the Nordic region. The historic Pomor trade between the inhabitants of Norway and the Arkhangelsk area, along with the traditional contacts between the inhabitants of Russian Karelia and Finland and Sweden, create the backdrop for ongoing regional cooperation (Nielsen, 1994). The territory of modern Russian Karelia has traditionally served as a meeting place for Slavonic and Finnish-Ugric peoples. For example, the runes of the national epic 'Kalevala' were collected by the Finnish scholar Lennrot in his travels from the northern part of Lake Ladoga to the Kola Peninsula.

The population of the Region is characterised by four features. The first is the diversity of its ethnic structure. There are indigenous peoples – mainly from the Finno-Ugric language group – as well as other nationalities from all the republics of the former Soviet Union. Second, the region suffers little from the ethnic and religious rivalries that have plagued other parts of the country. Third, population figures from the Region reflect an overall very low density of settlement – some 2–10 persons per square kilometre. Finally, in recent years, there has been both strong internal migration within the area as well as external migration from it (Heleniak, 1999).

The diversity of the population base of the Region provides a series of challenges and opportunities. An important problem for the Region has been the preservation of the cultures, languages and traditional handicrafts of the indigenous peoples. At the same time, the near-absence of any national, ethnic or religious conflicts in the area provides an attractive setting for foreign investment from northern Europe and elsewhere.

The Region is one of the richest of Russia in the diversity and stocks of natural resources. For example, in the Murmansk area there are deposits of natural gas in the adjacent Barents Sea. Some of these are among the largest in Europe. There is also a wide variety of mineral deposits. In

Arkhangelsk area there are gold and diamond deposits. Oil fields are found in the Nenets Autonomous District. Throughout the Northern Economic Region of Russia there are huge stocks of timber, fish and other renewable resources (Republic of Karelia, 1999; Lausala and Valkonen, 1999).

The western neighbours of the Region – the Nordic countries – possess a similar set of natural resources. This coincidence determines a similar structure for the economies and industries of the two adjoining areas. Priority is given to the development of forestry and the pulp-and-paper industry, as well as fishing and mining enterprises. Second, it predetermines the spheres of international cooperation developing in the European North (Jalonen, 1996).

Three of the five members of the Region – Arkhangelsk, the Murmansk counties and Russian Karelia – all have priority status within the development programmes of important foreign organisations. These include: The European Commission, the Barents Euro-Arctic Region, the Nordic Council of Ministers, the CIMO (Finland), the Swedish Institute and the Research Council of Norway. Each of these bodies has contributed significant resources to assisting post-secondary education, training and research in the Russian North. The priority status accorded the Region within the framework of the European Commission's TACIS Programme is reflected in the following figures. In 1996 the Region received more than 26 million ECUs for the realisation of various project – which is twice what Ukraine received, three times more than was secured by Belarus, and five times more than Moldova received (Svensson, 1998).

This external development assistance has also served as a lever to secure additional resources from the national government in Moscow. Russian Karelia, for example, while representing only a small fraction of the land mass and population of the country, has, none the less, secured nearly a tenth of the Russian national redevelopment budget by linking its efforts to external assistance projects. These international cooperative projects have been of significant assistance in providing new economic and educational opportunities in the Region (Sergouinin, 1999).

Some other international organisations are also actively working in the Region. These include: the Council of the Baltic Sea States, the Arctic Council, the Northern Forum and the North Calotte. Their activities are directed in a number of fields related to programme development and personnel training. This wide list of organisations and programmes indicates the unique opportunities for the Region in developing international social and economic cooperation with foreign partners (Lassinantti, 1994).

Higher education in Russia

In the Russian Federation two ministries are directly charged with responsibility for higher education and research. The Ministry of General and Professional Education of Russian Federation (hereafter the Ministry of Education) is responsible for primary, secondary, technical and vocational training, as well as advanced education in the form of instruction and research at the classical, technical and teacher training universities. The Ministry of Science and Technical Policy of the Russian Federation (hereafter the Ministry of Science) is responsible for the support of research and the development of national policy in the field of science. It also supervises and funds various research institutes.

A number of specialised schools are also directly linked to other particular ministries – a continuation of earlier Soviet practice. For example, in the Region there are a number of agricultural colleges (such as Vereschagins Vologada State Dairy Academy) which are run by the Ministry of Agriculture of the Russian Federation. However, most applied teaching and research facilities within Russian universities are supervised by the Ministry of Education.

The responsibilities of the Ministry of Education with respect to higher education are extensive. They include the issuing and cancellation of university licences to train specialists as well as the determination of what fields of study may be offered. The certification of universities and their curricula takes place every five years. The Ministry also provides the resources for the salaries of university administrators, instructors and support staff. It also furnishes most student grants and is responsible for the payment of everyday expenses associated with university building maintenance and support services.

The Russian system of higher education is similar to the German one. Most universities offer a five-year educational programme. Students receive a diploma of higher education in a specified field. In addition, Bachelor's and Master's degree programmes modelled on North American practice are gradually being introduced.

The universities of Russia are independent educational institutions. Teaching is conducted according to the curriculum recommendations made by educational and methodical associations and authorised by the Ministry of Education. At the same time, each post-secondary institution has the right to vary the list of subjects in its own curricula from national guidelines by some 20 per cent.

According to the Constitution of Russian Federation higher education in Russia is free of charge, and is to be provided by a network of federal higher educational institutions. The reforms in the educational system that were introduced in the 1990s resulted in greater democratisation of the higher education system. New institutions were created. These included the establishment of commercial educational institutions at various levels. An example of this for-profit type of post-secondary institution within the Northern Economic Region is the Murmansk Humanities Institute, which offers courses and degrees in the humanities and social sciences.

The supreme managerial body of a university is the Conference of its staff members. The Scientific Council of the university is elected from the leading scholars and instructors. It is the executive body of the institution and gets together once a month to solve current problems. The administration of a university is headed by a rector. The principal directions of activity for the university, such as educational work, research and international cooperation, are coordinated by a number of vice-rectors.

The main structural subdivision of a university responsible for organising advanced education is the department. They can be of two types. The first is a graduate department. It has responsibilities for training specialists and for offering diplomas in specific fields. The second type of department is a general one. It supplies a number of courses to the graduate departments, but does not normally offer its own diploma.

Several departments specialising in a certain educational and research field form a Faculty. Usually, the Faculty consists of three or more departments. A department in a specific scientific or educational field can be established if there are at least five specialists in this field among its staff. Three or four of these must have a scientific degree at PhD level or higher.

Each year, state universities select students from a group of applicants through a system of entrance examinations. The number of overall admissions is determined and financed by the Ministry of Education. Funding is supplied to the universities and institutes according to the guidelines established by the Ministry – currently at a ratio of one instructor per ten students. A university has the right to increase its enrolment beyond these guidelines. However, it is obliged to do so on a commercial, cost-recovery basis by means of additional fees paid by students. The new private universities often admit students on a simple interview basis. Their student fees are quite high and provide a significant portion of the funds necessary to operate such institutions.

The academic year in Russia begins on 1 September and ends on 30 June. There are two examination periods at most universities – one in January and the other in June. Students who have successfully passed examinations receive a small monthly grant to cover some of the expenses of attending the university. Increasingly, the cost of going to university is beyond the means of many Russian students and their families.

Professors and instructors of a university are chosen publicly on the basis of competition among all applicants. The competition for the position of a Professor and Associate Professor within a certain department is announced every five years in the leading local mass media. At the department meeting an applicant is required to present a brief report on the results of his or her previous work and their plans for additional activities in the new position. According to the results of the presentations, the department staff vote and recommend to the Faculty Council the best nominee. The decision of the Faculty Council is final. During the Soviet era renewal of faculty contracts was made every five years. However, at the present, and in accordance with new regulations, the rector of a university has to sign an annual contract with each employee of a university.

Like their students, the faculty at Russian universities face a number of challenges Due to the economic crisis in the country, many lack the necessary teaching materials and equipment. Faculty members teach a large number of courses. Classrooms and laboratories sometimes lack though space for the number of students desiring to take courses that are in high demand. In recent years, the salaries of university staff have not been paid regularly. Often, skilled instructors are lured away from the university by higher-paying jobs in private business.

In the present crisis, the federal budget cannot ensure the complete financing of universities. Financing of their current expenses, including purchase of equipment, materials and the repair of premises, has been curtailed. In 1994–7 the financial resources provided by the Ministry of Education did not exceed 50 per cent of the required amounts. This has forced Russian universities to look for additional sources of financing. These include charging additional cost-recovery fees for students enrolled over the limit set by the Ministry or in specialised programmes like Business. Applied research efforts, the conduct of various entrepreneurial activities and the leasing of university premises and equipment have all been turned to overcome budget deficits. Certain features of Russian legislation also provide opportunities for local authorities to support regional universities. For example, the government of the Republic of Karelia has granted Petrozavodsk State University the right to harvest and sell certain timber resources within the area.

Regional higher education in Russia – the case of the Northern Economic Region

At present, these are some 992 federal higher educational institutions in Russia, of which 331 are non-governmental, commercial ones. In the Northern Economic Region there are twenty institutions (Tomsk Polytechnic University, 1997). This is very low compared to other areas of the country.

The majority of higher educational institutions in the Northern Economic Region were founded in the 1930s and 1940s by the Soviet government with the dual purpose of personnel training and the cultural development of the population. These higher educational institutions have become centres of culture and education. They provide important access to advanced training and world cultural values for both indigenous and settler populations (Kauppala, 1998).

Regional post-secondary schools in Russia have undergone dramatic changes in recent years caused by social, economic and political change in the country. They are being forced to work in unstable and unpredictable conditions. Some of the major challenges confronting universities in the Region include: a low student participation rate; a shift in enrolment patterns from technical fields to the social sciences and humanities; the need to improve the qualifications of staff; and the necessity of securing adequate and stable funding for their operation.

Beyond responding to these immediate problems, the Russian universities of the north are considering their future development. They are discussing the desirability of establishing new research centres and branches, initiating information-sharing and telecommunication projects, and promoting international educational cooperation. They are also looking at ways to make their universities more flexible and response to the labour and service needs within the new market economy. They also wish to see their universities contribute more to regional growth and development (Gurtov and Vasiliev, 2000).

Higher education in the Northern Economic Region of Russia has been characterised by extremely low student participation rate. In the Region the number of residents who go on to some form of post-secondary education is about 115 per 10,000 inhabitants. In the neighbouring North-West Region of Russia – which includes the metropolitan centres of St. Petersburg, Novgorod, Pskov and Kaliningrad – the participation rate is close to three times that of the Northern Economic Region. In Russia as a whole, the participation rate has risen from 170 per 10,000 in 1994 to 190 per 10,000 in 1998. This is still considerably lower than comparable rates in the Nordic countries (225/10,000) or in Germany (250/10,000) or in the United States (340/10,000). The continuing inability of the Region to match overall Russian student participation rates – let alone those of the West – is a less than promising result. It points to one of the continuing barriers to regional development: the lack of a highly educated workforce.

The number of student places at public universities in the Russian north have not expanded significantly in recent years. Limited budgetary allocations have made it difficult to sustain existing academic programmes. It has been a major challenge to launch new programmes of study, such as in business administration and political science. Equally difficult has been the training of additional staff to teach in these new areas. Some of this expansion of offerings and training of specialists has been accomplished through the establishment the new, non-governmental universities.

The number of students studying today at northern regional universities fluctuates somewhat according to the changing social and economic conditions. At Petrozavodsk State University some 6,500 students take day courses in a single academic year. Another 2,000–3,000 students are enrolled in evening and/or distance education courses. The retention rate tends to be quite high given the economic uncertainties of the day. However, approximately 10–20 per cent of students leave or are sent down during their five-year academic programme.

One feature of the Northern Russian provincial universities is that they accumulate a significant part of the well-educated and highly skilled specialists within the region. This is caused, in the first place, by the absence of alternative institutes of applied and fundamental research that might offer employment to such individuals. In the second instance, the northern regional universities have attracted staff by virtue of the libraries, theatres and cultural centres they house. In recent years, however, it has become difficult to fund and maintain the latter facilities.

While the northern universities have been able, in the past, to attract talented instructors and researchers, there are increasing examples of such institutions losing such staff to other employers in the private sector. At the same time there is a significant shortage of experts in a wide spectrum of fields – especially those that have been newly added to the academic offerings of the institutions. In the Soviet era, it was much easier to select and retain academic staff. In those times, it was also possible for instructors to improve and upgrade their qualifications and receive special federal funding for this. Unfortunately, in our day, neither the northern Russian universities nor the Ministry of Education have money to send their faculty for further specialised education or training for any substantial period of time.

Northern regional universities during the Soviet period tended to specialise in the training of instructors and researchers in the fields of the science and technology. The staff were to work on practical problems of applied study. They also taught courses and trained new generations of educators. The transition of Russia to a democratic society and market economy has created a growing demand for curriculum and instruction in business, the social sciences and health sciences. At the moment, the most popular fields of study among students at Northern Russian universities are Economics, Law, Political Science, Sociology and Medicine. These universities are endeavouring to respond to changes in the labour market and student interest by adding new programmes and by furthering their scientific and technical training activities.

One of the possible ways of solving the problem of providing a wider scope of educational services for the population in the Northern Region is the establishment of new universities and branches. For example, in the last three years Petrozavodsk State University has founded three branches of the institution in larger cities of the Region: Apatity, Belomorsk, Sortavala and Kostamuksha (Republic of Karelia). It is possible that in the future an additional branch will be opened in Segezha.

These attempts to expand higher education in the region have also been stimulated by new outreach programmes on the part of the metropolitan universities in Moscow and St. Petersburg. Through their various regional research centres and institutes in the Region, the latter are organizing short-term instruction and retraining courses. Several of these offerings are in areas of high demand – including business, legal and social service fields.

Many regional universities in the Russian North experience certain difficulties when they compete with these metropolitan institutions in marketing educational services in the region. They often lack the necessary staff, support materials and library resources to deliver new curricula. Also, they tend to be less experienced in organising new training courses. Frequently, because of severe underfunding of their central operations, the regional universities have only the most modest of resources to deliver distance education courses.

Because of the changing economic and social conditions in Russia, the regional universities in the north are attempting to develop a certain degree of flexibility and mobility in their delivery of curricula. They are also trying to keep an eye on the changing market demand for labour and services. They are trying to be responsive to both short- and long-term needs in these areas. The growth of public and private universities in the Northern Economic Region may be critical to solving the 'brain drain' problem. Youth and highly skilled staff are less likely to leave the Region if they can receive adequate training for employment in the area. As such, universities are becoming community-forming enterprises.

Despite the severe economic and social challenges faced by the Region – and the drastic underfunding confronted by its universities – slow progress is being achieved. The regional institutions of higher education in the Russian north still aim to provide adequate personnel and scientific support for the economic development of their communities. This is illustrated by their recent efforts to provide training for specialists in natural resource fields such as forestry, fishing and mining. For example, a number of new specialists are now being trained in reorganised regional educational centres such as the Murmansk State Technical University (formerly the Academy of Fishery Sciences) and the Arkhangelsk State Technical University (formerly the Institute of Forest Engineering).

At the same time, many of the Region's universities are providing new educational services across a wide spectrum of specialisations. For example, Petrozavodsk State University trains students in the humanities, natural sciences and the polytechnic disciplines. New courses in business, law and social services allow the institution to respond to new societal needs and employment opportunities. Such a wide scope of offerings allows it to satisfy the diversifying labour needs of its region to the maximum extent.

Research carried out in regional universities in the Region has traditionally had an applied character. It has been aimed at the solution of specific problems confronting the major natural resource industries of the region. This continues to be a strong feature of the universities of the Northern Economic Region. In addition to this form of research, new initiatives designed to help solve applied problems of social and economic life are being implemented.

A distinctive feature of all the research programmes implemented in the Region are their international character. This is brought about by the close international connections being established between northern Russia and foreign universities. For example, Petrozavodsk State University participates in over sixty joint scientific, educational and innovative projects with foreign researchers each year. Many of these are in cooperation with universities from the Nordic countries, but they also include projects with other European and North American institutions.

Several of the post-secondary institutions in the Region have made major infrastructure and administrative investments to promote international education and cooperation. A number have signed formal exchange agreements to send and receive students, teachers and research staff. Though more distantly located than the metropolitan institutions in Moscow and St. Petersburg, the northern universities of Russia have being very successful in establishing for themselves an international profile.

The broad contributions of northern Russian universities to regional development

The contributions which Russian universities can make to overall regional development is determined in large part by the training of their staff, their material and technical facilities, and their ability to market its research, services and innovative activity. As noted above, having a university within its territory is a boon to any region. However, being able to establish a mutually beneficial relationship – one in which the community and university both grow – is a difficult target to meet. At the moment, the funding problems confronting both regions and universities are quite severe. Opportunities for Russian universities to earn additional income by rendering services to their regions are dependent upon the economic health of the regions and their ability to deliver services which are in demand.

This reality can clearly be seen in the Northern Economic Region of Russian Federation and its university system. As was mentioned earlier, the Region has a large potential for economic growth and development. It also faces hard economic times. Industry is not working because there is no new investment. New investments are not made because investors have doubts about the security of their money and wonder when industry will begin to work. It is a vicious cycle which harms the health of the Region and its institutions – including its post-secondary institutions (Daviddi, 1999).

New economic thinking and policy formulation must take place. A favourable investment climate must be established. Public investment in necessary infrastructure and technology must take place. Expanded education and training of specialists in applied and general fields of knowledge must come about.

The majority of the aforementioned needs should be addressed by national political authorities and, therefore, is beyond the scope of the consideration of the present essay. At the same time, however, the question of expanded education and training should be solved in the regions through the efforts of local authorities and institutions – including universities. There are a number of areas in which the latter can have a significant impact.

One of the most obvious areas for activity is in the fostering of links between technological research and the development of new industries. Today, there is almost a complete absence in the Northern Region of a distributed network of innovative research centres and technology parks. The creation of such bodies – as seen in the Nordic countries – ensures that there is an integration of scientific research with industry.

Universities in the north of Russia can take the lead in developing such activities. They should expand the training and retraining of their staff. They need to develop new applied research programmes. They need to introduce new technologies in their instruction and research. They need to encourage innovation. They need to promote international collaboration and joint research. They need to encourage free enquiry that builds entrepreneurial activity and democratic practice.

This list of university tasks also conforms to the funding priorities of various international development assistance programmes that are aimed at the Region. This coincidence is extremely important since without such outside funding most of these initiative cannot be started. In today's Russia, reform and development must be a partnership between regional, national and international actors.

The universities of the Region will also contribute to regional development in other ways. They will continue to serve as the major providers of both general and specialised instruction for post-secondary students who will probably find their future employment in the area. This requires that the universities update their curricula and instruction methods. It means that universities will continue to focus their teaching and research efforts in fields of important regional significance such as forestry and fishing technology. It also means, however, that the universities will be offering new areas of instruction such as in business and the social sciences – which are in high demand – but were not provided during the Soviet era.

The universities of the Region will also have an impact on regional development by means of their retraining initiatives. The post-secondary schools of northern Russia will be in the forefront of assisting workers to make a successful transition from the old economic system to the new market-oriented system. They will provide both new training opportunities as well as the ability for workers to expand and upgrade their education qualifications. They will also provide counselling and advice on how workers can best adapt to the new market economy.

The universities of the Russian north will be active in addressing pressing concerns of the community in the coming decades. They are developing new instructional and research programmes focusing on the various environmental threats to the land, animals and peoples of the region. Some of these programmes are being facilitated by generous grants from foreign governments and international agencies (Sigurdsson, 1999). The regional universities are also undertaking a concerted effort to protect and promote the native languages, histories and cultures of their indigenous populations. Such initiatives can also have a positive impact on the future tourism potential of the area. Finally, the universities of the Region are actively involved in teaching the languages and cultures of the neighbouring countries. There has been a rapid expansion in instruction in the Nordic languages and the history of Scandinavia. This bodes well for the ability of the community to develop further economic and commercial ties with their immediate Western European neighbours.

Conclusions

The northern universities of Russia are continuing to play a major role in the social, economic and cultural development of the Region. Clearly, the major economic and social challenges that have confronted the country over the past decade have also had a significant impact on these institutions. Their responsibilities and working environments have been significantly altered from those which existed during the Soviet era. It has become somewhat more difficult to provide necessary instruction and conduct research. None the less, it is possible to assert that these universities of the Russian north have managed to weather the storm and adapt to new circumstances. In fact, they have learned to become more flexible and responsive to the changing development needs of their communities.

If one looks at the various activities of the northern universities today, one can see new efforts in a variety of fields. They are educating students and specialists with knowledge of the market economy and foreign languages. They are exposing these same groups to new methods of learning, advanced technologies as well as opportunities to participate in international activities. They are helping workers and community residents to seek new employment opportunities, both in the traditional natural resources sectors of the economy as well as in new fields. As such, the Russian universities of the north occupy the front edge position in assisting the process of societal change and in restructuring industry and employment in the area.

The ability of contemporary Russia to continue to make significant social and economic progress in the coming decades will be largely dependent on important decisions taken at the national level. However, it is equally clear that change in a positive direction can be facilitated at the regional level through effective cooperation between political, economic and educational leaders. The universities of the Russian north will make their contributions to such endeavours in a variety of ways. They will continue to serve as major forces for regional development.

References

Daviddi, Renzo (1999) 'The August Economic Crisis and Its Aftermath', pp. 11–21, in Douglas C. Nord, *Pax Nordica 1999: Preconditions for Security in Russia* (Umeå: Umeå University Press).

Gurtov, Valery A. and Victor Vasiliev (2000) 'Education in the European North of the Russian Federation – Regional Features and Trends in Development', pp. 605–12 in Hakan Myrland and Lars Carlsson (eds), *Circumpolar Change: Building a Future on Experiences from the Past* (Luleå: Luleå University Press).

Heininen, Lassi and Richard Langlais (eds) (1997) *Europe's Northern Dimension: the Bear Meets the South* (Rovaniemi: University of Lapland Press).

Heininen, Lassi and Gunnar Lassinantti (eds) (1999) *Security in the European North: From 'Hard' to 'Soft'* (Stockholm: Olof Palme International Centre).

Heleniak, Timothy (1999) 'Out-Migration and Depopulation of the Russian North during the 1990s', *Post-Soviet Geography and Economics*, vol. 40 (3): 155–205.

Jalonen, Olli-Pekka (1996) 'Conversion, Economic Integration, and Development in the Russian Calotte', pp. 122–44 in Jyrki Kakonen (ed.), *Dreaming of the Barents Region: Interpreting Cooperation in the Euro-Arctic Region* (Tampere: Tampere Peace Research Institute).

Käkönen, Jyrki, (ed.) (1996) *Dreaming of the Barents Region: Interpreting Cooperation in the Euro-Arctic Region* (Tampere: Tampere Peace Research Institute).

Kauppala, Pekka (1998) *The Russian North: The Rise, Evolution and Current Condition of State Settlement Policy* (Helsinki: Finnish Institute for Russian and East European Studies).

Kozyrev, Andrei (1997) 'Euro-Arctic Region Cooperation – Past and Future', pp. 45–52 in Lassi Heininen and Richard Langlais (eds), *Europe's Northern Dimension: The Bear Meets the South* (Rovaniemi: University of Lapland Press).

Lassinantti, Gunnar (ed.) (1994) *Common Security in Northern Europe after the Cold War* (Stockholm: Olof Palme International Centre).

Lausala, Tero and Valkonen, Leila (eds) (1999) *Economic Geography and Structure of the Russian Federation* (Rovaniemi: Arctic Centre of the University of Lapland).

Luzin, Gennady P. (1992) *The Northern Economic Region – Problems, Tendencies and Perspectives in Development* (St. Petersburg: Nauka).

Myrlund, Håkan and Lars Carlsson (eds) (2000) *Circumpolar Change: Building a Future on Experiences from the Past* (Luleå: Luleå University of Technology Press).

Nielsen, Jens P. (1994) 'The Barents Region in Historical Perspective', pp. 88–100 in Olav Schram Stokke and Ola Tunander (eds), *The Barents Region: Cooperation in Arctic Europe* (London: Sage).

Nord, Douglas C. (ed.) (1999) *Pax Nordica 1999: Preconditions for Security in Russia* (Umeå: Umeå University Press).

Republic of Karelia (1999) *Republic of Karelia 2000* (Petrozavodsk: Republic of Karelia, Ministry of Foreign Relations).

Sergouinin, Alexander A. (1999) 'Russian Policy Towards the BEAR: From "Hard" to "Soft" Security', pp. 175–96 in Lassi Heininen and Gunnar Lassinantti (eds), *Security in the European North: From 'Hard' to 'Soft'* (Stockholm: Olof Palme International Centre).

Sigurdsson, Jon (1999) 'The Environment of the Barents Region and the Role of the Nordic Investment Bank', pp. 129–35 in Lassi Heininen and Richard Langlais (eds), *Europe's Northern Dimension: The Bear Meets the South* (Rovaniemi: University of Lapland Press).

Stokke, Olav Schram and Tunander, Ola (eds) (1994) *The Barents Region: Cooperation in Arctic Europe* (London: Sage).

Svensson, Bo (1998) *Politics and Business in the Barents Region* (Stockholm: SIR).

Tomsk Polytechnic University (1997) *Principles of the Current in Social, Economic and Organisational Reform of Higher Schools in the Russian Federation* (Tomsk: Tomsk Polytechnic University).

10
Universities in Northern Japan

Shigeo Aramata

Introduction

Japan is usually regarded as a southern nation not a northern or circumpolar one. After all, the Japanese islands are strung on a line from the Ryuku islands near Taiwan, and near the Tropic of Cancer, to the Kuriles, near the Kamchatka peninsula. The northern limit of Japan is only about latitude 45 degrees north. However, Hokkaido, the northernmost of the larger islands does have many sub-arctic characteristics and a number of institutions on Hokkaido, including some of its universities, do have circumpolar connections.

Japan consists of four main islands, one of which is Hokkaido, and another 3,900 smaller islands. Japan's total land area is about 370,000 square kilometres – excluding the four islands in the north, the possession of which is disputed with the Russians. The island of Hokkaido has a total area of 78,400 square kilometres, or about 21 per cent of Japan's total land area. Hokkaido has a population of 5.64 million or about 4.6 per cent of Japan's total population. The population density of Hokkaido is 72 per square kilometre compared with 332 per square kilometre for all of Japan.

The island of Hokkaido has some sub-arctic climatic characteristics. This is because the climate is influenced by the seas and ocean currents that wash its shores. The Tsushima Current affects southwestern Hokkaido, and the cold Kurile Current the southeastern part of the island. The Sea of Okhotsk influences the climate of the northwestern part of Hokkaido. Fresh water from the Amur river on the border of China and Russia flows into this sea reducing its salt content somewhat and this, along with the cold winds that blow across the sea from Siberia, result in its being ice-covered in the winter. Temperatures can often get quite cold, with communities in northern Hokkaido, such as Moshiri, recording some as low as minus 40 degrees centigrade. Hokkaido also gets quite a lot of snow, so skiing conditions can be good. The northern climatic conditions are indicated by the fact that Sapporo, the largest city on Hokkaido, was the site of the Olympic winter games in 1972 Hokkaido is referred to by those who live in the more southerly islands as the 'North Land' or the 'Snow Land'.

Hokkaido was originally known as Ezo and was the homeland of the Ainu people. 'Ainu' means 'human'. There are various theories concerning the origins of the Ainu, but most maintain that they migrated across the ocean from what is now northern China and southern Russia. Beginning in the mid-1400s the Japanese began to settle in the southern part of Ezo (Hokkaido) and then slowly to expand their area of control. The Ainu fought several battles against the Japanese, notably the battles of Kosyamain (1457), Syaksyain (1669) and Kunasiri-Menasi (1789). After the battle of Kunasiri-Menasi the Ainu became effectively controlled by the Japanese. The Ainu have remained a disadvantaged, 'indigenous' population to this day. They were treated in much the same way as indigenous peoples in North America in that they were given a separate status, that of 'former aboriginals', and were dealt with by means of separate legislation, the 'Hokkaido Aborigine Protection Act', and generally discriminated against. A census of the Ainu began in 1807 and at that time the Ainu population was 26,256. The population decreased thereafter in the face of the effect of multiple infectious diseases and forced labour. However, it has recovered somewhat in recent years and is now estimated to be about 25,000.

The modern development of Hokkaido began after the Meiji Restoration, that is the transfer of power from the Shogunate to the Emporer. The new government was very interested in developing what was then regarded as a 'frontier' land. In 1869 the name of the island was changed from Ezo to Hokkaido, a Development Commission (Kaitakushi) was established, and Japanese settlement or colonisation of the island began to be encouraged on a relatively large scale. Farmers from Honshu were encouraged to emigrate to the new world of Hokkaido. In 1882 the Development Commission was abolished and in 1886 Hokkaido Prefecture was established. The development of Hokkaido at this time was partly because of a desire to exploit the regions many natural resources, partly to strengthen Japan's northern frontier against an expanding Russian empire, and partly to provide land grants for 'Shizoku', descendants of the Samurai, who became unemployed in some numbers with the Meiji Restoration.

Initially, Hokkaido developed as an agricultural, forestry and mining area. Rice cultivation was not easy to sustain even in southern Hokkaido and other types of farming had to be started and other food sources found. Agriculture developed well and Hokkaido became in time the biggest agricultural production area in Japan. The new sources of food included salmon, sardines and other fish from the nearby seas. However, Hokkaido remained a relatively underdeveloped resource frontier region into modern times and had a relationship with the more southerly Japanese islands that is very similar to that between the northern and southern regions of the nations of the circumpolar north.

Hokkaido's major industries remained farming, timber, mining and tourism throughout the period after the Meiji Restoration. Hokkaido's significance increased somewhat in the post-war, period especially with the creation of the Hokkaido Development Agency and the adoption of the Hokkaido Comprehensive Development Plan in 1950. This encouraged leading businesses and manufacturers on Honshu to open branches in Sapporro and Hokkaido. Significant industrial expansion resulted, along with a big increase in the island's population. By 1970 the population of Sapporo passed the one million mark and by 1983 Sapporo had reached a population of 1,483,182 making it the fifth largest city in Japan and the pivotal city in northern Japan. Sapporo currently has a population of 1.8 million and this constitutes nearly one third of Hokkaido's total population. However, the resource sector still remained relatively important so when the terms of trade moved against the resource sector the islands economy began to suffer. By the late 1980s the timber and mining sector had shrunk drastically and agriculture was in difficulty. As a consequence unemployment rates were much higher than in the rest of Japan – 7 per cent as opposed to 2.6 per cent (Thayer, 1988). The third term (1998–2007) of the Hokkaido Long-Term Comprehensive Plan is now in force (Hokkaido Prefecture, 1999) and there are plans to relocate the Hokkaido Development Agency from the Prime Minister's Office to the Ministry of National Land and Transport and reorganise it. Despite all these efforts Hokkaido has not reached parity with the rest of Japan in all respects, for example, per capita income on Hokkaido in 1999 was 94.1 per cent of the national average (Hokkaido Prefecture, 2000).

Higher education in Japan

The modern Japanese system of higher education began, as did the colonisation of Hokkaido, with the Meiji Restoration. The Meiji government decided to open up the Japanese economy to the world market. It was aware that it would have to learn about the West very rapidly and be able to compete with it on its own terms. In the field of education generally the government established a new unified, and strongly government-controlled, system encompassing all education levels from the primary to the university.

The primary schools were very regimented and the curriculum common to all pupils. Thereafter, pupils were divided and passed on to academic middle schools or vocational middle schools. From the middle schools student passed on to general schools that taught students basic skills or to grammar schools that prepared students for university. The higher educational system consisted of universities, which were heavily influenced by the German model, and specialised colleges in agriculture, technology, fisheries, commerce and other such practical subjects. Thus a hierarchy of establishments was created that became connected to social status and to pay scales.

A major restructuring of the Japanese system education took place after the Second World War and reflected a change of outside influences from the European to the American. This resulted in the adoption of a system whereby students had six years of elementary education, three of junior high school, three of senior high school and four of university undergraduate education. In addition, the system was democratised somewhat, specialised technical institutes were incorporated into the universities, and the universities began to combine both general education of the American sort and highly specialised education. A somewhat puzzling mixture of German and American models of higher education resulted.

In the post-war years government control of the universities decreased somewhat with the introduction of Faculty Boards and there was a massive expansion in the number of student places connected with the expansion of the Japanese economy. The total number of students in the system grew from 220,000 in 1950 to 2,547,000 in 1995 (Ministry of Education, 1999). By 1995 32.1 per cent of senior high school students were going on to the universities. Given the hierarchical nature of Japanese society and the consequent strong desire of parents to give their children a university education, there was a big demand for university places. This, in turn, attracted much private activity in the sector. Consequently, there are now three types of universities in Japan: the state universities funded by the central government, the public universities funded by local governments and private universities funded by fee-paying students and, recently, some small government subsidies. In 1995 the state universities had 599,000 students, the public universities 84,000 and the private universities 1,864,000. These different types of universities, and the fact that government research money is distributed selectively, has resulted in a continuation of a hierarchical division in the system, but now between different types of university and within each type.

More recently the demand for university education has declined somewhat as a result of a declining birth rate. This problem has arisen just at a time when all universities in Japan are trying to adjust to the adoption of new technologies, the need for life-long learning, a demand for more occupational training relative to basic scientific education, a demand for greater transferability of credits between universities, and an increasing deregulaton of the system combined with a greater scarcity of public monies (Ministry of Education, 1995).

Higher education on Hokkaido

Higher education began on Hokkaido somewhat earlier than one might expect. The Sapporo Agricultural College, which later became the University of Hokkaido, was founded in 1876 – one year before Tokyo University. The Meiji governments purpose in establishing a university on Hokkaido was both to further education in the region and to assist in the colonisation of a new territory by advancing agriculture. Since the type of agriculture appropriate to the island was not familiar to most Japanese Dr William S. Clarke, the President of the Massachusetts Agricultural College, was invited to be the Vice-President of the College in 1876. Other Americans were also invited to Hokkaido at much the same time, including a former US Agriculture Secretary, Dr H. Kapron, to advise on how best to proceed. There was also substantial foreign influence in the forestry and mining industries that were opened up in the last part of the eighteenth century on Hokkaido.

Sapporo Agricultural College became incorporated into Tohoku Imperial University, which was established in Sendai in 1907. Then in 1918 both institutions were incorporated into the newly formed Hokkaido Imperial University. This university established a medical school in 1919 and began offering doctoral degrees in 1922. During the period of Japanese imperial expansion the Japanese central government became increasingly interested in supporting research activities at the university, especially in connnection with regionally relevant subjects. Thus, in 1941, the Research Institute of Low Temperature Science was established within Hokkaido Imperial University. One of its most remarkable research results was the making of the artificial snow crystals by Dr Ukichiro Nakaya. Hokkaido Imperial University had a special interest in northern studies and for fifteen years prior to the end of the Second World War it had published a journal entitled *Northern Cultural Studies*. From its very beginning Hokkaido Imperial University graduated a number of prominent Japanese leaders as well as a significant number of people who entered all fields of development upon Hokkaido. Many of the graduates became local leaders and Hokkaido Imperial University retained a pre-eminent role in this respect at least until the end of the Second World War. In 1947 the university's name was changed from the Hokkaido Imperial University to Hokkaido University and it expanded over the subsequent decades become to the largest university in Hokkaido Prefecture.

As business and industry developed on Hokkaido new needs in the field of higher education became apparant. The Japanese central government, therefore, established specialised vocational higher educational institutions on Hokkaido. One of these was the Otaru University of Commerce, established in 1910, which was intended to train local business leaders. Another example is the Hokkaido University of Education, which was a consolidation of several previously existing teacher training colleges. Other examples are the Muroran Institute of Technology (1949) and the Obbihiro University of Agriculture and Veterinary Medicine. Hokkaido University also developed a series of institutes of technology at much the same time.

At the end of the Second World War Japanese society lacked many economic resources and also lacked individuals trained to teach at university level. One consequence was that advanced research tended to be done in the research divisions of private companies rather than in the universities, thus losing the benefit that would have resulted for graduate, and undergraduate, students. Moreover the strict state rules regarding the financing of universities, which essentially held that only the universities, and not private companies, could benefit from state financing of universities, precluded any major connections between the private companies and the universities.

In 1950, with the establishment of Sapporo Medical University, central and local government resources were combined for the first time to establish a university. The same was the case with the Kitami Institute of Technology in 1960 and the Asahikawa Medical College in 1973. The two medical schools were established largely to meet the needs of the state sickness insurance schemes that were being developed and the needs of the rapid post-war industrialisation required more and more technically trained graduates. The institutions established by this joint funding were, however, not so numerous as to markedly affect the nature of the general development of higher education on Hokkaido.

There was a rapid expansion in the number of private universities on Hokkaido, and in Japan generally, in the post-war decades. This was caused by two things. First, the rapid industrialisation of Japan after the Second World War created a huge demand not only for technically trained people but also for large numbers of university trained salaried middle managers of all types. Second, the hierarchical social system based on differences in school and university background that had existed between the Meiji restoration and the Second World War carried over into the post-war period. This led to people wanting not only a university education for their children so that they could succeed in the new economy but also to them wanting a good university education for their children. Thus there was an intense pressure on university places, especially at the better universities. In such an environment there were good business openings for people wanting to establish private universities. Indeed, such businesses were very lucrative in such circumstances. The central government controlled the standards of the private universities and so the universities tended to compete on the basis of reputation rather than standards, that is, entrants were screened for their general background as much as for their academic potential. At first a lot of students moved from Hokkaido to private universities in the large cities farther south. In reaction there was something of a feverish founding of private universities on Hokkaido to take advantage of the obvious demand. At first all these private universities were completely privately financed. The state universities charged nominal fees and got large grants from the government. The private universities, in contrast, had to charge high fees in return for what was usually a lower level of service than in the state-funded universities. Considerable public pressure eventually led the government to subsidise the private universites and increase the fees that students had to pay at state universities.

The final stage of university development on Hokkaido was the increasing involvement of local government authorities in funding both some new private and public universities. The cities of Kushiro, Hakodate, Tomakomai and Kutami have all contributed varying sums to new local universities. This expenditure is made in the expectation by the local authorities that their investment in the universities will help revitalise their local economies. Sekijuji (Kitami) Kango University, which was founded in 1997, reflects a nationwide trend to upgrade existing nursing and social welfare institutes to the university level. The end-result of all this unversity development was that currently there are seven national universities four public universities and sixteen private universities in Hokkaido Prefecture.

The rate of growth in university student numbers in Japan was relatively slow before the end of the Second World War. In 1900 there were only 3,000 students nationally and by 1945 this had risen to 100,000. This rate of growth increased greatly and steadily (except for the decade 1975–1985) after the Second World War, from 100,000 in 1945 to 520,000 in 1955, from 940,000 in 1965, 1,730,000 in 1975, 1,850,000 in 1985, and 2,547,000 in 1995. The participation rate increased markedly in the post-war period, from 8.2 per cent in 1960 to 32.1 per cent in 1995. The participation rate for women over the same period rose from 2.5 per cent to 22.9 per cent. The statistics for Hokkaido Prefecture follow exactly the same trends but always a few percentage points behind.

The universities on Hokkaido succeed in attracting varying, but significant, numbers of students from outside Hokkaido Prefecture. Hokkaido University, one of the major Japanese universities, and one receiving strong government support, regularly attracts about one half of its students from Hokkaido and the other half from all over the rest of Japan. The main market for jobs for university graduates is local, that is, on Hokkaido, however, many graduating students go to other areas of Japan, partly because Hokkaido is still seen as something of a frontier area and partly because the Hokkaido economy has consistently lagged somewhat behind that of the rest of the country. While attending university the students also contribute significantly to the local workforce, especially as part-time workers in the service sector.

The impact of Hokkaido's universities

The rapid development of universities on Hokkaido had many beneficial effects on the development of the Prefecture economically, socially and culturally. In terms of economic impact the universities rapidly changed the nature of the local labour force. This was most noticeable in the area of Sapporo, the Prefecture's largest city, but it was also noticeable throughout the island as some of the new universities located elsewhere. As a consequence the universities have been able to supply a sophisticated labour force to an increasingly sophisticated set of industries on the island. Recently the universities have also contributed to the economic development of Hokkaido by teaming up with the private sector and local governments in the establishment of research parks. For example, Hokkaido University and Hakodate Technical College are partners in Technopolis Hakodate and Hokkaido University and Tomakomai Technical College are partners in the Central Hokkaido Technopolis. It is amazing that this development is a relatively recent one in Japan. The delay was caused by the fact that the Ministry of Education, as previously mentioned, regarded research cooperation between state financed universities and private companies as improper. Universities on Hokkaido that specialise in economics and business are also reaching out to local communities and businesses. Asahikawa university is working on cooperation with the local authorities along the Ishikari river. Otaru University of Commerce has a history of cooperating with local businesses and has special state funding for the training of new entrepreneurs. Kushiro Public University of Economics recently started a new division for cooperating with business and research centres in its region.

Two individuals have been key to this growing university–industry cooperation on Hokkaido. One is Dr Nirihito Tambo, the Rector of the University of Hokkaido, and the other is Mr Kazuo Toda, the chairperson of the All Hokkaido Manager's Association. Dr Tambo is working on the establishment of a research park on the University of Hokkaido's campus and, thereby, taking advantage of the transition in Ministry of Education policy. Mr Toda, who has good connections with the city of Oulu in northern Finland (a northern success story), is contacting all sectors of business throughout Hokkaido seeking to establish numerous business clusters for Hokkaido that will better enable it to succeed in the new global economy. Business 'clusters' are associations where businessmen and university researchers can meet frequently on a friendly and informal basis in the hope that these contacts will lead to innovations that will help economic growth. These two individuals have had some influence on a number of the universities, for ones like Kushiro, Kitami and Obihiro have all established research cooperation offices on their campuses, though on a smaller scale than at the University of Hokkaido.

The rapid expansion of universities on Hokkaido since the Second World War has also had a significant impact on the island's society. They have contributed to a closing not only of the living standards between those on Honshu and Hokkaido but also the social outlook of the two. The universities have graduated significant numbers of medical personnel of all types and this has helped produce similar service levels for Hokkaido and the rest of the country. However, there remains a shortage of medical specialists in the more remote parts of Hokkaido. The universities on Hokkaido have produced so many teachers that the problem has gone from being one of an undersupply to that of an oversupply. Consequently Hokkaido's universities now export new teachers to Honshu. However, while the universities have been the source of much social change in recent decades they are currently having some difficulty convincing those in the local societies that more changes are needed in the educational system to prepare the region for the new information and newly globalising society. Some universities are offering special courses on the information society and on international topics but it really needs to become a component part of nearly all courses.

The cultural impact of Hokkaido's universities has also been significant in recent decades. They have helped preserve something of the traditional culture while, at the same time, pursuading local people of the value of the modern, European-based, culture. Some of Hokkaido's universities, such as Sappora Gakuin University, have paid special attention to cultural matters. Sapporo Gakuin University became a university in 1968 and began as Sapporo Junior College in 1946. It has always had extensive cultural programming and activities. It hosts numerous public lectures and publishes a series of books related to cultural matters. It has been helped by the fact that one of the local newspapers, the Hokkaido Shinbun has also had a strong interest in cultural matters.

However, this having been said, relatively little is offered by the universities on Hokkaido dealing with the traditional Ainu people and culture. Moreover, few links have been made with the Ainu people. This is partly because there is no clear territory for the Ainu as for other indigenous people's in the circumpolar north and partly because Ainu culture has, in many ways, been incorporated into the common heritage of Hokkaido's residents. However, the Association of Museums of Hokkaido has been trying to make contacts between the Ainu and the other indigenous peoples of the circumpolar north.

Hokkaido's universities are also having a cultural effect on the population because of their increasing international links, especially their northern links. Hokkaido University of Education has a good cooperative relationship with the northern part of the Russian Far East, that is, places such as Magadan, Yugdino Sakhalinsk and Kamchatka. Hokkaido Tokai University has had good connections with Stockholm University in Sweden for a long while. In addition Dohto University and Kushiro University of Economics have been eager to cooperate with the Circumpolar Universities Association. Dohto University and the Kushiro Public University of Economics have connections with Canada. The latter university recently sent the first student from Japan to study at the Russian Kamchatka University of Education. There are some connections between Hokkaido's universities and the Northern regions Centre. The Centre was established in 1978 in Sapporo with the support of government (Northern Regions Centre, 1982). Other northern related initiatives have been the formation of the Hokkaido Association for Far Eastern Russian Studies in 1985 and the formation of the Kushiro-Kamchatka Association in 1997.

Conclusions

Hokkaido's universities, like those elsewhere in the world, have a vital role to play in assisting the creation of new businesses that can adapt to the newly globalising world and in connecting, and helping to adapt, their local culture to the national and international one. However, until recently, strict regulation by the central government and the universities own conservative protectionism have stifled this role. Hokkaido's universities have done much for the Prefecture but they have tended to be somewhat limited in their outlook to Hokkaido. They have helped the local population adapt to the national labour market and helped bring the standard of living much closer to the national average. Now the challenge for Hokkaido's universities is to help the Prefecture set its sights even higher so that Hokkaido can effectively take its proper place in the global arena.

References

Hokkaido Prefecture (1999) http://www.pref.hokkaido.jp/skikaku/sk-kkaku/gaiyo/p02_03.html

Hokkaido Prefecture (2000) http//www.pref.hokkaido.jp/keizai/kz-bkkry/env/env-e.html

Ministry of Education (1995) *Remaking Universities: Continuing Reform of Higher Education* http://www.monbu.go.jp/hakusyo/1995eng/contents.html

Ministry of Education (1999) http://www.monbu.go.jp/stat-en/em09010.html

Northern Regions Centre (1982) *Hoppoken Today: Toward a New International Community* (Sapporo, Northern Regions Centre).

Thayer, Richard (1988) 'Hokkaido has a Grand Scheme to Catch up with the Rest of the Nation', *Toronto Globe and Mail,* 28 November.

11
The Role of Universities in Northern Development: A Comparative Perspective
Douglas C. Nord

Introduction

Over the course of the past three decades there has been a steady expansion of opportunities for higher education within the areas of the circumpolar north. Responding in part to broad global trends associated with the growth and development of the 'new information age', the governments of the Nordic countries, Canada, the United States and Russia have all sought to provide their northern communities with the capabilities to better adapt themselves to the challenges of this new reality. In so doing, they have contributed to the creation of new institutions of advanced education, the expansion of curricula and degree offerings and the sponsorship of both applied and general research in these northern areas. Often these governments have portrayed the future development of their northern regions as being directly linked to the effective operation of these northern universities (Lipponen, 1997).

Yet the expansion of higher education opportunities across the circumpolar north has not come as quickly or as effortlessly as most government spokespersons would suggest. In many cases, the peoples of these northern regions have had to wage extended campaigns to bring the attention of government officials to their educational needs. Similarly, the eventual resource allocations that have been made by centrally located governments to expand educational opportunities in their peripheral northern regions have been far less than the residents of those areas would have expected or desired. It has required a continuing commitment on the latter's part to ensure that the original government promises of better integrating the north into this 'new information age' have been honoured (Nord and Weller, 2000).

Nevertheless, at the start of the twenty-first century, it is clear that some real progress has been made in enlarging educational opportunities for northern residents. A number of new northern universities have been established over the past thirty years. These new institutions have graduated a significant number of well-educated students who have contributed to the economic and social development of their communities. New opportunities for professional education and advanced specialised training have also been provided by many of these circumpolar universities. Likewise important research related to northern problems and concerns have been conducted by the faculty and staff of these institutions. These same individuals have also provided both energy and leadership for broader community-based efforts focused on improving the general quality of life in their regions (Palmér, 1997).

In the wake of such initiatives, it is perhaps important to assess the general patterns of higher education growth in the north and their various contributions to regional development. While it has been repeatedly stated by a number of observers that the northern universities have played significant roles in fostering community growth and development, far too little focused attention and sustained research has been devoted to investigating their actual impact. Unfortunately, what work has been done of this kind has usually not been of a comparative nature or continued over a significant amount of time. As a consequence, we tend to know a bit about the specific role played by a single northern university, in a single region, over a limited period of time. (Langlais and Snellman, 1998). Yet at the same instance, we tend to know very little about the broad patterns of university behaviour and regional development across the circumpolar north as a whole.

The nature of the inquiry

The purpose of this chapter is to provide some of this broad comparative analysis. It takes as its focus for investigation the significant patterns of influence which universities have exerted on the direction of regional development throughout the circumpolar north. An effort is made to detail the features of these several patterns and to note both changes and continuities in the manner in which they have operated over the past four decades.

The chapter begins with a discussion of the various rationales which government planners, university administrators and community leaders have provided for encouraging the growth of higher education in northern regions. These positive arguments are considered in the context of desired impacts on community and regional development. Specifically, the chapter considers how university development in the north has been traditionally been portrayed as a vital tool in promoting community economic growth and diversification.

The study then moves on to examine three alternative models for university and regional development that have been followed in different sectors of the circumpolar north over the past four decades. In broad terms, these three approaches reflect varying degrees of focused and integrated planning ideas for university and regional development. Areas of both commonality and divergency in approach are highlighted in this review.

Having outlined the main features of these alternative models for university and regional development, the chapter turns to a consideration of the accomplishments and limitations of each of these approaches. It examines the specific successes and problems that have been encountered by the northern universities in the Nordic states, North America and Russia over the past forty years. The chapter seeks to identify the various key factors which seem to have accounted for these differing results.

In reviewing the patterns of university and regional development in the circumpolar north over the past three decades, the chapter endeavours to note what seem to be continuing forces at work as well as what appear to be some new trends and directions. In considering the latter, the study discusses some of the problems and issues which are likely to confront both regional planners and university administrators in the coming years. The chapter concludes with an overview of the challenges awaiting those who would seek to broaden still further higher education opportunities in the north in the new century.

Northern universities and regional development

A considerable body of literature exists which has examined the roles that northern universities have played in responding to the development needs of their regions. Whether one is examining the case of northern Canada, Scandinavia, Russia or the United States, one discovers that there is a surprising consistency in the manner in which these postsecondary institutions have been viewed by both politicians and community leaders as being vital instruments in their effort to address regional concerns and priorities. Basically, the authors of several studies report that these northern universities have been called upon to perform four major services for their host regions. They include: providing new access for higher education, broadening professional education and training, assisting regional economic growth and diversification and fostering new social and cultural development opportunities (Morrison, 1991; Frovlov, Shabarov and Silin, 1992; Heininen, 1994; McLarnon and Nord, 1997; Myrlund and Carlsson, 2000).

With respect to access, most scholars of northern universities note that one of the basic *raison d'être* for these institutions' existence has been to facilitate greater regional participation in post-secondary education. Politicians and community planners frequently point out that advanced education participation rates in northern areas have been traditionally lower than those in communities in more southern and urban locations. As a consequence, the long-term economic and social development of these northern communities is hindered. However, it is argued that, by placing a university in the north, some of the established barriers of distance and cultural estrangement can be overcome and thus allow northern students to easily access the benefits of a university education (Weller, 1987).

A call for greater social equality is embedded in this demand for increased access to post-secondary education. Why should distantly located northern students be excluded from the broad benefits of such instruction? With this in mind, the new northern universities are seen as not only fostering a general growth of regional access to the benefits of higher education, but also as having a special outreach role in providing educational opportunities for both native peoples and isolated communities in the north (Weller and Rosehart, 1985).

Providing specialised training and professional education for the region is another commonly perceived role for universities in northern regions. Most analysts note that nearly all northern communities share the common dilemma of having an insufficient number of well-educated and experienced professionals in the fields of health, education and social service. They also lack individuals with other specialised skills and background in business and engineering that might enable the community to respond more effectively to new economic and resource opportunities. As a consequence, many regional leaders and community planners have seen as one of the primary missions of the northern university to be that of educating their own professionals. With this in mind, they have regularly argued that university planning should give a high priority to the development of professional programmes and curricula alongside the more traditional post-secondary offerings in the arts and sciences. They have spoken on behalf of the establishment of degree-granting programmes in medicine, dentistry, engineering, education, social work, forestry and the law as well as for expanded opportunities for post-degree training and enrichment. From this perspective, the northern university is seen as playing a key role in regional development by providing the educated professionals required of a modern and complex society (Korhonen, 1991; Riepula, 1991).

Contributing to community economic growth and development is another role seen as being central to the operation of the university in the eyes of most northern residents. Most community members are not at all hesitant in discussing their post-secondary institutions as being identifiable 'engines of economic expansion'. They see the university as contributing to the economic vitality of the region in several dimensions. First, they point to the actual jobs provided by the institution to workers in the area as well as its ancillary spending in the community. Second, they note the positive economic consequences of the university providing the community with a well-educated and skilled workforce in the form of its graduates. Third, they cite the potential commercial spin-offs to be derived from applied and targeted research and development on the campus. Fourth and finally, they note the promise of additional investment coming to the community as a result of outside business seeking to locate in an enlightened region. This economic dimension of the northern university tends to be given a prominent position in the minds of many community leaders (Nord and Weller, 2000).

Many proponents of northern universities also identify a social and cultural development role for these institutions. While this type of impact tends to be less clearly defined than the access, professional training or economic development contributions of the university, none the less, it is deemed to be important to the overall future health of the community. Broadly conceived, it involves the university either providing or encouraging new cultural and artistic opportunities and perspectives in the region. As such, the university would be contributing to the social capital of the area. Sometimes this role is best expressed as 'bringing the world to the region and the region to the world'. It involves building an attitude of openness and self-confidence in the region and the destruction of narrow and parochial perspectives. It can involve both promoting a more cosmopolitan vantage point and celebrating the unique cultural contributions of the peoples of the region. It is a role that is central to the nexus between university operations and regional development. Unfortunately, it tends to be underplayed in the thinking of many community planners and university administrators (Nord, 1997).

Alternative models

While each of the arguments outlined above have been incorporated into the rationale for university development across the circumpolar north, it should be noted that in each case where a new university has been proposed, the precise mixture of the four arguments has varied. Similarly, more limited rationales related to 'regional rewards' and pork-barrel politics have also been advanced as part of specific appeals (Weller, 1993). Yet it is possible to identify from the mix three broad models or approaches to university development and regional growth which underlie most of the efforts made within communities of the circumpolar north over the past four decades.

The first of these might be referred to as the Nordic Model as it has been in evidence primarily in the establishment of the new northern universities in Norway, Sweden and Finland (Tromsø University, Luleå University of Technology, Umeå University, Lapland University and the University of Oulu). This model gives almost equal emphasis to each of the four rationales outlined above. It stresses the importance of all within society having access to higher education and the beneficial results that are derived for the country as a whole. The provision of advanced education in the north is seen as a feature of a healthy social democracy rather than simply as a 'regional reward' or political payoff (Lane, 1983).

The Nordic Model suggests that in order to provide appropriate levels and forms of social and health services in northern communities a significant amount of direct investment in the education and training of professionals in the north must take place. This is a recognition of both the need to redress past imbalances between the centre and the periphery as well as the expressed desire to develop specific northern responses to northern needs. This approach manifests itself in the establishment of a wide number of highly visible professional schools within the new northern Nordic universities including those focusing on medicine, dentistry, engineering, social work and the law (Varjo and Hultenan, 1977).

While the regional economic benefits derived from university development are not in any way down played in the Nordic Model, it is important to note that these economic gains are not envisaged as temporary local spin-offs, but as long-term benefits to be derived from a broad restructuring of the northern economy. In addition to the local employment and spending that the university will give to the region, the Nordic Model argues that the most significant contribution that the university can make to the area is by providing the opportunity for true regional economic diversification and real linkage to the broader national and global markets. This takes the form, in part, of providing a new educated work-force with up to date skills and abilities. It comes as well in the form of research and development initiatives undertaken by university faculty often in cooperation with local business interests. It gives rise to an environment in which new outside industries and businesses are likely to invest in the area. Most importantly, the Nordic Model suggests that investment in advanced education in the north is a means both to remake the economic foundations of the region – which have related largely to natural resource exploitation – and to stem the outflow of young and talented workers from the area (Eskelund, 1991).

Finally, the Nordic Model sees the social and cultural dimensions of its development role as being of a central endeavour. Not only does the university assist in providing new opportunities for social and cultural opportunities in the region, but it also plays a vital role in widening the horizons and perspectives of the local residents. In a dual role, the university provides the bridgehead for cosmopolitan cultures and attitudes to enter the region from the outside as well as serving as a catalyst for the recognition and promotion of regional cultures and identities. The university becomes, in fact, an active meeting place for this two-way cultural exchange. In order to provide such a forum, the Nordic Model suggests that the university should devote significant resources to provide social and cultural venues in the region – either as part of its campus plan or in cooperation with broader community initiatives (Snellman, 1997).

The second model or approach to northern university development and community growth is the North American Model. It has operated primarily within the context of the development of the new universities in northern Canada and the United States (UNBC, Lakehead University, Laurentian University, University of Quebec at Chicoutimi and at Abitibi-Temiscaming, University of Alaska at Anchorage, and the University of Minnesota at Duluth). In this model or approach, the four arguments for university development are not given equal emphasis by any means. Clear priority is given to two – access and economic growth.

Reflecting the general pattern of expanding student populations in the second half of the twentieth century, most of the new northern universities in North America have come into existence primarily as avenues of entry to higher education for growing numbers of upwardly mobile high school graduates. The residents of both northern Canada and the United States have seen the establishment of these new universities as an effective means to provide additional education opportunities within their own communities at a relatively low cost. They have organised themselves to bring pressure to bear on their state and provincial legislatures to provide such enhanced educational opportunities in their region. Most often such institutions have been established not as part of an overall commitment by the government or the broader society to secure greater social and economic equality, but as the clear result of skilful lobbying and political tradeoffs (McCafferey, 1995).

As a consequence of the emphasis given to access, less consideration is often directed toward the particular type of academic programmes to be offered at the new northern universities in Canada and the United States. Largely missing from the North American Model is any sustained commitment to broad professional education or training. Very few of the high-profile – and often resource-demanding – professional schools such as medicine, law or engineering are incorporated into the original plans of these new northern institutions. The focus is directed, instead, to providing a curriculum of undergraduate arts and science courses that are deemed responsive to the needs of the contemporary 'educated person'. Some applied courses in business or the health services may be added to this menu. However, the dominant viewpoint expressed in many planning documents is that most professional education can be deferred until the institution is better funded and more firmly established. Required professionals – trained to meet community needs – need not be 'homegrown' but can continue to be brought in from the outside as required (Nock, 1993).

The economic rationale for creating a new northern university is the other central element of the North American Model. It is a rationale, however, that is more limited and narrowly focused than was the case with the Nordic Model. In the northern regions of Canada and the United States the economic benefit derived from university development is seen as primarily short-term in character and not linked to a broad reconstruction of the local economy. Proponents of the establishment of a new university tend to cite the new job opportunities associated a new major employer in the community. They also emphasise the impact of the multiplier effect of university spending in the region. While some notice is given to potential new enterprises that might come to the community as the result of the operation of the new university, less emphasis is given to the economic diversification effect of the university than in the Nordic Model. Instead, greater attention is given to how the university might sustain existing patterns of employment and economic activity. The university's teaching and research activities are seen assisting the maintenance of the region's natural resource-based exploitation economy – be it in mining, forestry or fishing (Reid and Enemark, 1992).

Finally, in terms of social and cultural development, the northern university is seen to play a limited role in the North American Model. As was the case with the training of professionals, the community does not feel that the new university should commit significant resources to cultural and artistic activities at the outset of its operation. Perhaps once the institution is better established and better funded. Spending on culture and the arts is to be definitely subservient to economic development and to access priorities. Overall, in the North American Model, the emphasis tends to be placed on sustaining the specific cultural identity of the northern residents rather than exposing them to new cultural influences from the outside, As a consequence, very little in the way of reciprocal cultural exchange tends to take place between the campus and the community. Instead, a form of the traditional 'town/gown' division tends to emerge (McAllister, 1997).

The third approach to northern university development and community growth that has been practised in areas of the circumpolar north over the past thirty years is that of the Soviet Model. It inspired most efforts to advance higher education opportunities in the northern regions of the former USSR (Syktyvkar University, Tuyumen University, Kemerovo University and Petrozavodsk State University). This third model shares elements of both the Nordic and North American Models in its attitude and approach to furthering higher education in the north. However, it is somewhat distinct from the other two models in its method of operation.

Like the Nordic Model, the Soviet Model spoke – at a rhetorical level – of the abilities of the new universities in the north to contribute to the social and economic equality of the citizens of the USSR. By providing new education opportunities in the north, the basis for establishing true societal equality would be extended to even the peripheral peoples of that vast state (Heleniak, 1999). However, it was clear from the outset that the new institutions that were being created would never become true rivals to the established academic centers in Moscow and Leningrad. Their budgets and staffs were much smaller than those seen in post-secondary institutions further south. These regional institutions in the north were more symbols of equality rather than true examples of it. They provided additional access opportunities to higher education for the people in the region, but the quality of instruction that was received was of necessity inferior to that received in urban locations further south (Ivandaev, 1991).

Again with respect to professional training, there was much discussion by policy-makers in Moscow of the need to provide the northern regions with their own doctors, dentists, educators and engineers. However, as was the case with much of the overall planning of these northern institutions, there was only a limited implementation of this stated plan. While the Soviet Model educated professionals in some regions that had never had access to services prior to that time, the numbers produced were consistently smaller than promised. Likewise the education and training that these professionals received in the north was less than provided in Moscow or Leningrad (Kauppala, 1998).

In terms of economic benefit, a significant portion of the interest of the Soviet Model in developing northern universities related to the ability of the Soviet state to derive a commercial benefit from the effort. Like the North American Model, near-term economic exploitation of the natural resource base of the north was a significant motivation for establishing post-secondary education in the Soviet north. Schools of mining, forestry and petroleum engineering often dominated university teaching and research. What was telling about the operation of the Soviet Model, however, was that the economic benefits derived from the existing natural resources were not necessarily to be focused on the development needs of the regions from which they came. Rather than developing or diversifying the local communities, the northern regions remained largely unchanged in their economic base long after the coming of the new universities (Peterson, 1993).

With respect to cultural and social development, the Soviet Model presents a mixed assortment of attitudes and approaches. On the one hand, the northern universities of the Soviet Union were seen as the vanguard of a modernising effort that would expose remote regions of the Soviet north to the benefits of a scientific and industrial society. As in other areas of the USSR, emphasis was given to the university assisting in the creation of a 'new Soviet Man' through its teaching and research activities. On the other hand, several of the northern universities in the Soviet Union provided significant academic programmes and research focused on local culture, traditions and languages. While important contributions to the better understanding of these native societies were advanced during the course of their operations, many of these programmes eventually took on an exclusively historical-anthropological interest in these northern societies. They tended to present their work as documenting 'cultures in decline' rather than being advocates for the native peoples (Polyakova, 1997).

Accomplishment and limitations

Each of the above models has produced a distinctive pattern of university development and community growth within the circumpolar north over the past four decades. Each has facilitated a number of significant accomplishments and each has encountered some problems and disappointments. By in large, the former have outdistanced the latter. Still it is important to look more closely at the actual end results of the operation of the models to be able to identify some of the more salient factors that have accounted for their differing results.

On the whole, it appears that the Nordic Model has produced the largest number of successes. In the space of four decades, it has brought about major change in the educational opportunities in the northern regions of Norway, Sweden and Finland. It has provided access to high-quality undergraduate and graduate instruction in this area. In so doing, it has stemmed much of the traditional outflow of young people from this region (Riepula, 1997).

Similarly, the Nordic Model has brought forth a variety of professional services that were once severely lacking in the north. The creation of professional schools in medicine, dentistry, social work, education engineering and the law has endowed the region with 'home-grown' talent that can contribute to solving the problems of a modern and complex society. These professional programmes have also attracted new talent and investment from the south.

Major economic improvements have also come as a consequence of the establishment of the new Nordic universities. The quality of the workforce has been improved through access to additional education and training. Both employment and wage levels have increased as a result of new knowledge-directed investment in the region. Most importantly, the expansion of higher education has allowed for a restructuring and diversification of the local economy. High-tech and skilled service employment are replacing many of the traditional jobs in the declining natural resource sector of the economy. The northern communities of the region are becoming more effectively linked to broader national and international markets (Arbo, 1997)

Of equal significance, has been the fact that the Nordic Model has produced vibrant social and cultural development in the region. Not only are there now greater opportunities for the residents of the region to access arts and culture from outside their community, but the new universities have also assisted in the promotion and celebration of distinctive local cultures and traditions. An effective two-way cultural communication is being established.

In comparison to the broad-scale success of the Nordic Model, the North American Model has produced far more limited results. Clearly the establishment of several new institutions in northern Canada and the United States has expanded community access to the general benefits derived from higher education. However, both the breadth and level of instruction offered at these new institutions has often been less than has been witnessed in the Nordic sector of the circumpolar north. By and large, these North American institutions have come to offer primarily an undergraduate curriculum largely focusing on the arts and sciences. They lack much in the way of offerings in the professional areas – especially at the graduate level. As a consequence, these institutions are somewhat restricted in their ability to respond to significant issues and concerns of the north. They also have been unable to produce the needed number of trained professionals in the fields of health, education and social work (Weller, 1994a, 1994b).

Equally significant, has been the failure of many the northern North American institutions, to facilitate long-term economic growth and diversification in their host communities. In general, these institutions have had only a marginal impact in reshaping the economic patterns of their regions. What influence that they have had tends to reinforce existing patterns of business activities rather than fostering innovation and change (Nord and Weller, 2000).

With respect to social and cultural development, the impact of the new northern universities in North America has also been of less consequence to their surrounding communities than in the Nordic states. The North American institutions have provided some additional venues and some encouragement for the arts in their communities. However, on the whole, they have demonstrated little sustained interest in investing in this vital form of social capital (Graham, 1997).

The Soviet Model presents, perhaps, the least successful of university development and community growth. While its initiatives to broaden access and to train required professionals in the region began in a promising fashion, there has never been the necessary follow through on the part of central decision-makers to ensure the desired results. As a consequences, the Soviet north has been endowed with a number of poorly funded and marginally sustained universities. This reality has become more clear in the wake of the collapse of the Soviet Union (Gurtov and Vasiliev, 1997).

Equally significant, however, has been the fact that the Soviet Model never really strove to bring about basic changes in the economic and social opportunities of the northern communities of the USSR. The expansion of higher education in the Soviet north was consistently treated as a means of sustaining the exploitation of the natural resources of the region for the benefit of the Soviet state – not for improving the living conditions its northern peoples (Kauppala, 1998). Likewise, what 'cultural development' activities were undertaken by the new Soviet northern institutions tended to be more in the character of imposing cultural standards and expectations from the centre rather than encouraging a two-way cultural dialogue (Roginsky, 1991).

Is it possible to identify a few key variables which might account for the relative success of the Nordic Model and the less positive results of the North American and Soviet models? Clearly three items merit attention. The first has to do with the guiding transformative philosophy which underlies the first model of university development and community growth and is evident only in reduced levels in the other two models. In the case of the Nordic approach to the development of new universities in the north, there exists a broad commitment to making a significant change to the region – economically, socially and culturally. The new universities of the region are being introduced to provide access to a condition of greater societal equality. There is a clear recognition that northerners should have the same opportunities to access health care, social services and high-wage employment as others in society. University buildings are not an end in themselves, but as a means to broader ends (Jappinen, 1991).

A similar transformative philosophy is lacking in both the North American and Soviet Models . It is missing, however, for different reasons. In the case of the former, there is an unwillingness to accept the notion that the university should take a major role in societal change. Instead, the dominant North American view has been that the new northern university should reflect the existing features of its host community. In the case of the Soviet Model, the directing belief was that the northern university would best serve its community by assisting it to conform to direction from central authority. In either case, there was only a limited notion that the university might take a creative lead in helping to shape community development.

The second variable which has contributed to the differing results of the three models relates to the existence of comprehensive and integrated planning. In the case of the Nordic Model, the coming of the new northern universities in Finland, Sweden and Norway was preceded by careful study and analysis of the problems and issues related to northern community development. Due consideration was given to the precise types of programming and instruction that might best assist the growth and transformation of the north. Much of this was done by scholars and government officials who were somewhat screened from the effects of short-term political influences and bargaining. As a consequence they were able to produce comprehensive plans which placed the new universities in the context of a broader strategy for northern regional development (Lane, 1983).

In the case of the North American Model, this commitment to reasoned, integrated planning has been largely absent. Instead it has been replaced by an appeal to skilful improvisation and short-term gain. Proponents of university development in this setting have seen their efforts as a limited lobbying effort directed at key legislators and government officials. Their goal has been to have as many resources as possible allocated to their university development project without having to be overly specific about the long-term results of such investments. As such, the new university tends to be thought of as an individual economic development enterprise that is not directly linked to any broader ongoing community development plans. The consequence of this type of behaviour is that university and community development priorities are often out of step with one another (Weller and Rosehart, 1985).

In the case of the Soviet Model, the variable of comprehensive planning may operate in two different manners. In the first instance, there existed some initial broad planning as one might expect in any command economy. However, it is to be noted how easily such planning was derailed or colored by individual and regional influence peddling. Equally significant, however, was the Soviet Model's failure to provide the requisite amount of administrative follow-up to ensure that there was a true integration of university and community planning objectives.

Finally, the third variable which seems to account for several of the differences between the Nordic Model of operation and that of the North American and Soviet Models has to do with resource allocation – or the lack thereof. In the case of the Nordic Model, the effort to integrate university planning with regional development was, in most cases, accompanied by the necessary funding from government sources. Both at the planning stage and in the implementation period, appropriate levels of resource allocations were made to build the physical plant of the university, hire its staff and fund appropriate degree and course offerings. This does not mean that northern university planners and community leaders in Sweden, Finland and Norway had ready access to all the funds they thought were required to implement from the outset their complete development visions. However, they did have the capability of securing funds for worthwhile initiatives like expanding professional education in the north by making regular reasoned appeals to government officials.

A somewhat different pattern of resource allocation has existed in North America. A characteristic feature of the North American Model has been the desire of government officials to produce a northern university 'on the cheap'. The bare minimum of resources are allocated for the development and implementation of the project. As a consequence, the university that emerges tends to be of inferior academic quality. Since there is no strong vision for the transforming role of the university in regional development – and since the appeal is based upon political or regional reward rather than comprehensive planning – the tendency exists for politicians to give only what is necessary to meet the immediate demand. Having allocated the 'required' funds, additional appeals for development monies are not welcomed. The university and the surrounding community stumble on until the next successful political attack can be orchestrated.

The Soviet Model, as noted above, has long suffered from inadequate funding and support for its northern universities. Partly this has been the consequence of institutional rivalries with the more long-established institutions of higher education in Moscow and Leningrad. Partly it has been the consequence of the attitude detailed above which suggested that these new northern universities had only a 'limited role' to play in Soviet society. In either case, under the Soviet Model northern communities and universities had only minimal resources on which to operate let alone plan or innovate. The challenge confronting contemporary Russian officials is one of securing adequate resources in a period of extreme economic uncertainty.

Continuing issues and future trends

Having reviewed the patterns of university and regional development over the past four decades, it is important that an effort be made to point to some of the continuing problems and issues that are likely to confront both regional planners and university administrators in the coming years. Clearly, there will be a continuation of some past trends. Yet there will also be some new challenges as they strive to expand, still further, the opportunities for higher education in the circumpolar north. Noted below are some of the more significant questions that they will have to address.

First and foremost of these is funding. It is clear that in the coming years the new universities of the north are going to be under intense financial pressures as they attempt to deliver their services to the community. Some of these institutions are already feeling the economic pinch – perhaps none so much as several of the northern universities in Russia. However, even in relatively well-funded regions as the Nordic states and North America there appear to be increased budget limitations confronting these post-secondary schools. In the case of the new Nordic universities, the consequences stemming from this funding restraint are focused primarily on the ability of the institutions to further expand programming and research that may be of benefit to their surrounding communities. In the case of many of the North American northern universities it has meant an actual decline in capabilities – often with cuts in staffing and services, a reduction of research funding and the deterioration of their physical plants. In each instance, the northern communities served by these northern universities are likely to suffer in terms of reduced access opportunities, professional training, economic stimulation and cultural diversification. The resource challenges confronting the northern universities of Russia are even more severe. Unless there is a major improvement in the basic economic conditions of the broader society, many may no longer be able to operate.

While other – more centrally located – universities may also be facing budgetary woes, the effect of resource restraints on northern institutions and their service communities is particularly destructive. This is because, as noted above, these institutions were only recently established and created often with the most modest of initial funding. As such, they have little ability to absorb many budget cuts and must of necessity reduce services (Nock, 1993). This is a cruel reality that northerners are unfortunately quite used to in their dealings other publicly funded institutions. Frequently their new hopes of participating in advanced education are soon dashed by shortcomings in governmental appropriations. One of the great challenges confronting both university officials and regional planners in the future is how to provide a continuing flow of resources to these new northern universities that will enable them to make an ongoing contribution to regional development.

An equally significant issue that these northern leaders must confront is the question of the changing functions and purpose of their northern universities. For some regions, the passing of considerable time has required them to focus their attention again on what should be the appropriate roles for post-secondary institutions in their communities. In the case of Russia, this review of the roles of northern universities is taking place within the context of a far broader consideration of the character and direction of the society and its institutions. What course these northern Russian universities will follow is somewhat dependent upon the outcome of these discussions. However it is clear that the traditional Soviet Model of university development and community growth is unlikely to be followed in the future. Already there are signs that the expectations of the local communities are broader than those voiced in the Soviet period. There are numerous voiced opinions that these northern universities should play more of a leading role in assisting their regions to make basic changes in the social, economic and political conditions.

In the case of the Nordic region, there is a similar search underway for new directions and objectives. Having successfully contributed to major social, economic and cultural changes in their communities, the new universities in this area are now looking for additional challenges as they approach middle age. The maturation of these 'new' institutions raises the question of whether their objectives should be broadened in scope and increased in number. Should these new northern universities aspire to become major research institutions on the par with the larger more established universities to the south? Should they significantly broaden their research and teaching agendas from their original northern base of activity? If they do so, will they be turning their back on the communities for which they were first established? Is there a way to strike an acceptable balance between being a 'research university' and a 'regional university'? These questions will continue to be vigorously discussed over the coming decade.

In the case of many of the new North American institutions, the questions for discussion do not really relate to a broadening of the agenda. Instead many northern Canadian and American universities are asking themselves how they can more adequately meet the community development challenges that have already been established for them. Many of these institutions are confronting the reality that much of the community development work that was set out for them at the time of their founding remains to be accomplished. As they search for more clear identities and purposes in the coming decade they will be debating the priorities for action in this area (UNBC, 1997). They will also be considering new methods and approaches toward meeting their goals. In so doing, the traditional North American Model of university development and community growth may well need to be revised.

Finally there is the important issue of accountability that each of the circumpolar universities will need to consider in the coming years. Simply put, each of these institutions needs to discuss the question of whether they are truly meeting the expectations of their host communities. As access to advanced education becomes more readily available to the residents of the north, each of these new universities needs to consider whether or not it is making as full a contribution to community development as can be expected. They need to review carefully their teaching, research and service roles and ponder whether or not their activities continue to facilitate positive change in their region. Similarly, they need to incorporate new methods and approaches that can foster improved responsiveness to community needs. Perhaps by further exchange of information in this and other areas, the new circumpolar universities can learn from the experiences of one another.

As one looks further into the future, it is clear that the challenge of providing effective university education for community growth and development in the circumpolar north is unlikely to become any less daunting. While important progress has been over the past thirty years, additional new and unmet needs continue to confront us on a regular basis. It is hoped that by investigating past strategies and approaches, one can arrive at a better understanding of how one can respond to current issues and problems. Only the passage of additional time will determine whether or not these lessons of the past have been properly understood and responded to in a useful fashion.

References

Arbo, Peter (1997) 'The University as a Vehicle for Economic Restructuring – Lessons from the Norwegian Periphery'. Paper presented at the conference on The Role of Universities in Regional Development, Programme on Institutional Management in Higher Education (IMHE, OECD), Edinburgh, Great Britain, 2 October.

Eskelund, Trond (1991) 'How to Maintain a High Standard of Universities in the North: The University of Tromso as a Case Study', pp. 52–4 in William Morrison (ed.) *The Role of Circumpolar Universities in Northern Development* (Thunder Bay: Lakehead University Centre for Northern Studies).

Frovlov, N. K., Shabarov, A. B. and Silin, A. N. (eds) (1992) *The Role of Universities in Northern Development: Proceedings of the Second Annual Conference of the Association of Circumpolar Universities* (Tyumen, USSR).

Graham, Amanda (1997) 'Seats of Learning/Centres of Conflict: Contradictory Expectations for Northern Universities', pp. 12–27 in Shauna McLarnon and Doug Nord (eds). *Northern Parallels*, (Prince George: UNBC Press).

Gurtov, Victor and Vasiliev, Victor (1997) 'Education in the European North of the Russian Federation: Regional Features and Trends in Development', pp. 605–11 in Hakan Myrlund and Lars Carlsson (eds), *Circumpolar Change: Building a Future of Experiences of the Past* (Luleå: Luleå University of Technology Press).

Heininen, Lassi (ed.) (1994) *The Changing Circumpolar North: Opportunities for Academic Development – Proceedings of the Third Circumpolar Universities Cooperation Conference*, (Rovaniemi, Finland).

Heleniak, Timothy, 'Out-Migration and Depopulation of the Russian North during the 1990s', *Post-Soviet Geography and Economics*, vol. 40 (3).

Ivandaev, A. I. (1991) 'The Role of Tyumen University in the Development of Northern Territiories', pp. 5–8 in William Morrison (ed.), *The Role of Circumpolar*

Universities in Northern Development (Thunder Bay: Lakehead University Centre for Northern Studies).

Jappinen, A. (1991) 'Government's Role in the Regional Development of a Higher Education Network', pp. 122–4 in William Morrison (ed.), *The Role of Circumpolar Universities in Northern Development* (Thunder Bay: Lakehead University Centre for Northern Studies).

Kauppala, Pekka (1998) *The Russian North: The Rise, Evolution and Current Condition of State Settlement Policy* (Helsinki: Finnish Institute for Russian and East European Studies).

Korhonen, L. K. (1991) 'How the Ivory Tower Goes to Market – The University and Regional Development', pp. 122–4 in William Morrison (ed.), *The Role of Circumpolar Universities in Northern Development* (Thunder Bay: Lakehead University Centre for Northern Studies).

Lane, J.-E. (1983) *Creating the University of Norrland: Goals, Structures, and Outomes* (Umeå: C. W. K. Gleerup).

Langlais, Richard and Snellman, Outi (eds) (1998) *Learning to be Circumpolar: Experiences in Arctic Academic Cooperation* (Rovaniemi: University of Lapland Press).

Lipponen, Pavo. (1997) 'The European Union Needs a Policy for the Northern Dimension', pp. 29–35 in Lassi Heininen and Richard Langlais (eds), *Europe's Northern Dimension: The Bear meets the South* (Rovaniemi: University of Lapland Press).

McAllister, Mary Louise (1997) 'Contributing to Diversity: The Role of the University of Northern British Columbia in Northern Economic Development' pp. 466–9 in Shauna McLarnon and Doug Nord (eds), *Northern Parallels* (Prince George: UNBC Press).

McCafferey, Charles J. (1995) *UNBC – A Northern Crusade* (Victoria: Morris Printing).

McLarnon, Shauna and Doug Nord (eds) (1997) *Northern Parallels – Proceedings of the Fourth Circumpolar Universities Cooperation Conference* (Prince George: UNBC Press).

Morrison, William (ed.) (1991) *The Role of Universities in Northern Development: Proceedings of the First Conference of the Circumpolar Universities* (Thunder Bay: Lakehead Centre for Northern Studies).

Myrlund, Håkan and Lars Carlsson (eds) (2000) *Circumpolar Change: Building a Future on Experiences of the Past – Proceedings of the Fifth Circumpolar Universities Cooperation Conference* (Luleå: Luleå University of Technology Press).

Nock, David (1993) 'Lakehead University As a Hinterland Institution', in Chris Southcott (ed.), *Provincial Hinterland: Social Inequality in Northwestern Ontario* (Halifax: Fernwood Press).

Nord, Douglas (1997) 'The Impact of the University of Northern British Columbia on the City of Prince George: How Does One Contribute to Cultural Development and Diversification?'. Conference Paper presented at the 26th Annual Meeting of the WRSA, Kona, Hawaii.

Nord, Douglas and Geoffrey Weller (2000) 'The Emergence and Maturation of Circumpolar Universities: Lessons From British Columbia and Ontario', pp. 583–603 in Håkan Myrlund and Lars Carlson (eds), *Circumpolar Change: Building a Future on Experiences from the Past* (Luleå: Luleå University Press).

Palmér, I. (1997) 'Serving the Needs of the North Through Modern Higher Education'. Speech to the Fifth Circumpolar Universities Cooperation Conference, Luleå, Sweden.

194   *Douglas C. Nord*

Peterson, Robert (1993) *Troubled Lands: The Legacy of Soviet Environmental Destruction* (Boulder: Westview Press).

Polyakova, Maria (1997) 'Public Response to the Perceived Decline of the Karelian Language in Karelia', pp. 242–50 in Shauna Mclarnon and Doug Nord (eds), *Northern Parallels* (Prince George: UNBC Press).

Riepula, Esko (1991) 'The Impact of Universities on the Economic and Social Development of Northern Finland', pp. 13–16 in William Morrison (ed.), *The Role of Circumpolar Universities in Northern Development* (Thunder Bay: Lakehead Centre for Northern Studies).

Riepula, Esko (1997) 'Universities in Northern Finland'. Conference Paper Presented at the Fifth Circumpolar Universities Cooperation Conference, Luleå, Sweden.

Reid, M. and G. Enemark (1992) *The Economic Impact of the University of Northern British Columbia on Prince George* (Prince George: College of New Caledonia).

Roginsky, V. M. (1991) 'Contribution of One of the Most Northern Universities of the World to the Development of the Norilsk Industrial Region', pp. 69–71 in William Morrison (ed.), *The Role of Circumpolar Universities in Northern Development* (Thunder Bay: Lakehead Centre for Northern Development).

Snellman, Outi (1997) 'Social and Cultural Impacts of the University of Lapland, Finland', pp. 28–32 in Shauna McLarnon and Doug Nord (eds), *Northern Parallels* (Prince George: UNBC Press).

UNBC (1997) *Planning for Growth: The Final Report of the University Planning Committee* (Prince George: UNBC press).

Varjo, U. and M.-L. Hultenan (1977) *The Founding of the University of Oulu and its Effect on Regional Development* (Oulu: University of Oulu).

Weller, Geoffrey (1987) 'Universities in the Circumpolar North: A Comparative Analysis', pp. 3–16 in P. Adams and D. Parker (eds) *Canada's Subarctic Universities* (Ottawa: Association of Canadian Universities for Northern Studies).

Weller, Geoffrey (1993) 'Hinterland Politics: The Case of Northwestern Ontario', in *The Canadian Journal of Political Science*, vol. 10 (4): 727–54.

Weller, Geoffrey (1994a) 'UNBC and the Development of Northern British Columbia', pp. 214–24 in Lassi Hieninen and Lars Carlsson (eds), *The Changing Circumpolar North: Opportunities for Academic Development* (Luleå: Luleå University of Technology).

Weller, Geoffrey (1994b) 'Regionalism, Regionalisation and Regional Development in a University Context: The Case of the University of Northern British Columbia', *The Canadian Journal of Regional Science*, vol. 17 (2): 153–68.

Weller, Geoffrey (1997) 'The Impact of Lakehead and Laurentian Universities on the Development of Thunder Bay and Sudbury'. Conference Paper Presented at the 26th Annual Meeting of the WRSA, Kona, Hawaii.

Weller, Geoffrey and Robert Rosehart (1985) 'Universities, Politics and the Development in Northern Ontario and Northern Sweden: A Comparative Analysis', *Canadian Journal of Higher Education*, vol. 15 (3): 51–72.

Select Bibliography

Comparative and international perspectives

Circumpolar Universities Association, *With Shared Voices: Launching the University of the Arctic* (Rovaniemi: University of Lapland, 1998)

Dahllöf, Urban, 'Faculty Structures, Enrolments and Staff Retention in Circumpolar Universities: A Comparison of Sixteen Universities in Six Countries', pp. 138–54 in W. Morrison (ed.), *The Role of Circumpolar Universities in Northern Development* (Thunder Bay: Lakehead University Centre for Northern Studies, 1991)

Dunk, Thomas, 'Taking the Locals Seriously: The Social Determinants of "Useful" Knowledge and Their Implications for Northern Development', pp. 240–43 in W. Morrison (ed.), *The Role of Circumpolar Universities in Northern Development* (Thunder Bay: Lakehead University Centre for Northern Studies, 1991)

Frolov, N. K., Silin, A. N. and Shabarov, A. B. (eds), *The Role of Universities in Northern Development: Proceedings of the Second Annual Conference of Circumpolar Universities* (Tyumen: Tyumen University, 1992)

Graham, Amanda, 'Seats of Learning/Centres of Conflict: Contradictory Expectations for Northern Universities', pp. 12–27 in S. McLarnon and D. Nord (eds), *Northern Parallels* (UNBC Press, 1997)

Heininen, Lassi (ed.), *The Changing Circumpolar North: Opportunities for Academic Development: Proceedings of the Third Circumpolar Universities Cooperation Conference* (Rovaniemi: Arctic Centre of the University of Lapland, 1994)

Heininen, Lassi, 'International Cooperation in the Barents Region – Competing and Conflicting Interests', pp. 456–464 in S. McLarnon and D. Nord (eds), *Northern Parallels* (Prince George: UNBC Press, 1997)

Kramer, Joyce, 'Advancing Post-Secondary Education in the Circumpolar Regions While Respecting Indigenous Peoples Rights to Self-Determination', pp. 203–16 in W. Morrison (ed.), *The Role of Circumpolar Universities in Northern Development* (Thunder Bay: Lakehead University Centre for Northern Studies, 1991)

Lange, Manfred, 'The Arctic in a Changing World: New Challenges for Circumpolar Universities', pp. 151–65 in L. Heininen (ed.), *The Changing Circumpolar North* (Rovaniemi: Arctic Centre of the University of Lapland, 1994)

Langlais, Richard and Snellman, Outi (eds), *Learning to be Circumpolar: Experiences in Arctic Academic Cooperation* (Rovaniemi: University of Lapland Press, 1998)

Lazin, Fred, 'Universities, Political Development and Regional Imbalance', pp. 96–101 in W. Morrison (ed.), *The Role of Circumpolar Universities in Northern Development* (Thunder Bay: Lakehead University Centre for Northern Studies, 1991)

McLarnon, Shauna and Nord, Douglas (eds.), *Northern Parallels: Proceedings of the Fourth Circumpolar Universities Cooperation Conference* (Prince George: UNBC Press, 1997)

Morrison, William (ed.), *The Role of Circumpolar Universities in Northern Development: Proceedings of the First Conference of the Association of Circumpolar Universities* (Thunder Bay: Lakehead University Centre for Northern Studies, 1991)

Myrlund, Hakan and Carlsson (eds.), *Circumpolar Change – Building a Future on the Experiences of the Past: Proceedings of the Fifth Circumpolar Universities Cooperation Conference* (Luleå: Luleå Technological University Press, 2000)

Nord, Douglas and Alworth, Royal D., 'Education Across the Northern Circle', pp. 130–7 in W. Morrison (ed.), *The Role of Circumpolar Universities in Northern Development* (Thunder Bay: Lakehead University Centre for Northern Studies, 1991)

Weller, Geoffrey R., 'Universities in the Circumpolar North: A Comparative Analysis', pp. 17–35 in P. Adams and D. Parker (eds), *Canada's Subarctic Universities* (Ottawa: Association of Canadian Universities for Northern Studies)

Weller, Geoffrey R. and Rosehart, Robert, 'Universities, Politics and Development in Northern Ontario and Northern Sweden: A Comparative Analysis', *Canadian Journal of Higher Education*, vol. xv, no. 3 (1985), 51–72.

Canada

Adams, Peter and Parker, Douglas (eds.), *Canada's Subarctic Universities* (Ottawa: Association of Canadian Universities for Northern Studies, 1987)

Belanger, Charles, 'Laurentian University's Role in the North', pp. 47–51 in W. Morrison (ed.), *The Role of Circumpolar Universities in Northern Development* (Thunder Bay: Lakehead University Centre for Northern Studies, 1991)

Blackbourn, Anthony, 'Northern Universities in Development: The Case of Nipissing University College', pp. 9–12 in W. Morrison (ed.), *The Role of Circumpolar Universities in Northern Development* (Thunder Bay: Lakehead University Centre for Northern Studies, 1991)

Graham, Amanda, 'Not a Perfect Solution but a Good Illustration: The Life and Times of the University of Canada North, 1970–1985', *The Northern Review* no. 12/13 (1994), 117–32

Hallsworth, Gwenda, *A Brief History of Laurentian University* (Sudbury: Laurentian University, 1995)

Hilyer, Gail, 'Higher Education in the Northwest Territories', in G. Jones (ed.), *Higher Education in Canada: Different Systems, Different Perspectives* (Garland Publishing, 1997)

MacLennan, Debra, *Laurentian University: Making an Impact on Sudbury* (Sudbury: Laurentian University, 1995)

McAllister, Mary Louise, 'Contributing to Diversity: The Role of the University of Northern British Columbia in Northern Economic Development', pp. 466–9 in S. McLarnon and D Nord (eds.), *Northern Parallels* (Prince George: UNBC Press, 1997)

Nord, Douglas C. and Weller, Geoffrey R. 'The Emergence and Maturation of Canada's Circumpolar Universities: Insights form Ontario and British Columbia', pp. 583–604 in H. Myrlund and L. Carlsson (eds), *Circumpolar Change* (Luleå: Luleå Technological University Press, 2000)

Reid, Mike, Enemark, Gordon and Rawbotham, Lisa (eds), *Economic Impact of the University of Northern British Columbia on Prince George* (Prince George: College of New Caledonia, 1991)

Sarlo, Christopher, *Nipissing University's Impact: Some New Estimates* (North Bay: Nipissing Universty, 1994)

Vervoort, Patricia, 'The Built Environment in the North: Arguments for a Positive Vision', pp. 115–21 in W. Morrison (ed.), *The Role of Circumpolar Universities in Northern Development* (Thunder Bay: Lakehead University Centre for Northern Development, 1991)

Weller, Geoffrey R. 'Universities, Politics and Development: The Case of Northern Ontario', pp. 210–22 in Fred Lazin, Samuel Aroni and Yehuda Gradus (eds), *The Policy Impact of Universities in Developing Regions* (New York: Macmillan, 1988)

Weller, Geoffrey R. and Rosehart, Robert, 'The Politics of Government Intervention in Higher Education: A Case for the North', pp. 48–76 in Cecily Watson (ed.), *Readings in Canadian Higher Education* (Toronto: Ontario Institute for Studies in Education, 1988)

Weller, Geoffrey R., 'UNBC and the Development of Northern British Columbia', pp. 214–24 in L. Heininen (ed.), *The Changing Circumpolar North* (Rovaniemi: Arctic Centre of the Unversity of Lapland, 1994)

Weller, Geoffrey R., 'Regionalism, Regionalisation and Regional Development in a University Context: The Case of the University of Northern British Columbia', *Canadian Journal of Regional Science,* vol. xvii, no. 2 (1994), 153–68.

Weller, Geoffrey R. and Soleau, David, 'Integrating an Academic Plan and a Campus Master Plan: The Case of the University of Northern British Columbia', *Canadian Journal of Higher Education,* vol. xxvi, no. 1 (1996), 111–34.

Weller, Geoffrey R., 'The Impact of a New Unversity in a Developing Region: The Case of the University of Northern British Columbia', *Higher Education Policy,* vol. 11, no. 4 (1998), 281–90.

Finland

Jäppinen, Arvo, 'Government's Role in the Regional Development of a Higher Education Network', pp. 122–24 in W. Morrison (ed.), *The Role of Circumpolar Universities in Northern Development* (Thunder Bay: Lakehead Centre for Northern Studies, 1991)

Julka, Liisa ja Kyosti, *Oulun yliopiston perustamisen historia* (Rovaniemi: University of Lapland, 1983)

Jussila, Hekki and Segerstahl, Boris, 'Northern Regional Development, Peripheries and Communications – The Role of the University', pp. 571–82 in H. Myrlund and L. Carlsson (eds), *Circumpolar Change* (Luleå: Luleå Technological University Press, 2000)

Korhonen, H. Kalevi. 'How the Ivory Tower Goes to Market – Universities and Regional Development', pp. 1–4 in W. Morrison (ed.), *The Role of Circumpolar Universities in Northern Development* (Thunder Bay: Lakehead University Centre for Northern Studies, 1991)

Riepula, Esko, 'The Impact of Universities on the Economic and Social Development of Northern Finland', pp. 13–16 in W. Morrison (ed.), *The Role of Circumpolar Universities in Northern Development* (Thunder Bay: Lakehead University Centre for Northern Studies, 1991)

Snellman, Outi, 'Social and Cultural Impacts of the University of Lapland, Finland', pp. 28–32 in S. McLarnon and D. Nord (eds), *Northern Parallels* (Prince George: UNBC Press, 1997)

Tovionen, Klaus, *Lapin yliopisten yhteiskunnallinen vaikuttavuus* (Rovaniemi: University of Lapland, 1995)

Greenland

Langgård, Per, 'To Be a Very Small University in a Very Small Society', pp. 27–35 in W. Morrison (ed.), *The Role of Circumpolar Universities in Northern Development* (Thunder Bay: Lakehead Centre for Northern Studies, 1991)

Lyck, Lise, 'Education and Research in Regional Development: Greenland and the Faroe Islands', pp. 64–8 in W. Morrison (ed.), *The Role of Circumpolar Universities in Northern Development* (Thunder Bay: Lakehead Centre for Northern Studies, 1991)

Iceland

Edvarsson, Ingi Runnar (ed.), *Byggdastefna til nyrrar aldar* (Akureyri: University of Akureyri Research Institute, 1998)

Johannesdottir, Gudrun Agusta, *Tengsl Haskolans a Akureyri og Akureyrarbœjar vid nyskopun i atvinnuliffi* (Nyskopunarsjodsverkefni, 1997)

Olafsdottir, Gudrun and Persson, Lars Olof, 'Landsbygdens uttuning på Island', in L.-O. Perrson (ed.), *Blanserad uttunning* (NordRefo, 1995)

University of Akureyri, *The Yearbook of the University of Akureyri* (Akureyri: University of Akureyri, 1987–92)

Japan

Ministry of Education, Japan. *Remaking Universities: Continuing Reform of Higher Education* (Tokyo: Ministry of Education, 1995)

Northern Regions Center, *Hoppoken Today: Toward a New International Community* (Sapporo: Northern Regions Center, 1982)

Norway

Andersen, Ole Johan, Arbo, Peter, Jussila, Heikki, Nilsson,P and Sanderson, Haken, *Høgskolene i Nord-Skandinavia – drivkrefterfor regional noeringsutvikling* (Refo, 1993)

Bie, Karen Nossum, *Creating a New University – The Establishment and Development of the University of Tromsø* (Norwegian Research Council for Science and Humanities, 1981)

Dahl, Jorunn and Stenskaer, Bjorn, *Fra modernitet til tradisjon? Styring og organisering av virksomheten ved Universitetet i Tromsø* (Norwegian Institute for Studies in Research and Higher Education, 1999)

Eskeland, Trond, 'How to Maintain a High Standard of Universities in the North – The University of Tromsø as a Case Study', pp. 52–4 in W. Morrison (ed.), *The Role of Circumplar Universities in Northern Development* (Thunder Bay: Lakehead University Centre for Northern Studies, 1991)

Fulsås, Narve. *Universitetet i Tromsø 25 ar* (Tromsø: University of Tromsø, 1993)

Saether, Bjørnar, Peter Arbo, Mønnesland, Jan, Onsager, Knut and Sørlie, Kjetil, *Hogskolenes regionale betyding* (Norwegian Institute for Urban and Regional Research, 2000)

Russia

Andreyev, V. S., 'The Role of Yakut State University in the Development of the National Economy of Yakutia', pp. 24–6 in W. Morrison (ed.), *The Role of Circumpolar Universities in Northern Development* (Thunder Bay: Lakehead University Centre for Northern Studies, 1991)

Bravina, Roalia, 'The Culture of the Aboriginal Peoples in the Higher Eduational System of the Sakha Republic', pp. 73–7 in S. McLarnon and D. Nord (eds), *Northern Parallels* (Prince George: UNBC Press, 1997)

Gurtov, Valery and Vasiliev, Victor, 'Education in the European North of the Russian Federation – Regional Features and Trends in Development', pp. 605–12 in H. Myrlund and L. Carlsson (eds), *Circumpolar Change* (Luleå: Luleå Technological University Press, 2000)

Heleniak, Timothy, 'Out-Migration and Depopulation in the Russian North During the 1990s', *Post-Soviet Geography and Economics* (1999), 155–205

Ivandaev, A. I., 'The Role of Tyumen University in the Development of the Northern Territories', pp. 5–8 in W. Morrison (ed.), *The Role of Circumpolar Universities in Northern Development* (Thunder Bay: Lakehead University Centre for Northern Studies, 1991)

Kauppala, Pekka, *The Russian North: The Rise, Evolution and Current Condition of State Settlement Policy* (Finnish Institute for Russian and Eastern European Studies, 1998)

Lausala, Tero and Valkonen, Lelia (eds.), *Economic Geography and Structure of the Russian Territories of the Barents Region* (Rovaniemi: Arctic Centre of the University of Lapland, 1999)

Luzin, Gennady, *The Northern Economic Region – Problems, Tendencies and Perspectives on Development* (NAUKA, 1992)

Roginsky, V. M., 'Contributions of One of the Most Northerly Universities in the World to the Development of the Norilsk Industrial Region', pp. 69–71 in W. Morrison (ed.), *The Role of Circumpolar Universitiies in Northern Development* (Thunder Bay: Lakehead University Centre for Northern Studies, 1991)

Tomsk Polytechnic University, *Principles of the Current Stage in Social, Economic, and Organisational Reform of the Higher Schools in the Russian Federation* (Tomsk: Tomsk University, 1997)

Zakharov, Y. A. and Ryabykh, S. M., 'Kemerovo University as an Educational, Scientific and Cultural Centre of Kuzbass', in N. K. Frolov, A. N. Silin, and A. B. Shabarov (eds), *The Role of Universities in Northern Development* (Tyumen: Tyumne University, 1992)

Sweden

Bergenda, B. and Carling, A., *Higher Education and Manpower Planning in Sweden* (National Board of Universities and Colleges, 1977)

Carlblom, T., *Høgskolelokaliseringen in Sverige 1950–1965* (Almquist and Wicksell, 1982)

Cullblom, E., 'Luleå University towards the Year 2000', in N. K. Frolov, A. N. Silin and A. B. Shabarov (eds) *The Role of Universities in Northern Development* (Tyumen: Tyumen University Press, 1992)

Dahllöf, U. and Selander, S. (eds), *Expanding Colleges and New Universities* (Uppsala Studies in Education, 1996)

Holm, E. and Wiberg, U. (eds), *Samhällseffekter av Umeå universitet* (Umeå: CERUM, 1995)

Lane, Jan-Erik, *Creating the University of Norrland – Goals, Structures and Outcomes* (C. W. K. Gleerup, 1983)

Larsson, L.-G. and Elgqvist-Saltzman, I., *Ett Universitet växer fram* (Norrlands universitetsforlag, 1995)

Lorendahl, B. and Persson, L.-O. (eds), *Utbildning för utkanter* (Högskolan i Östersund, 1992)

Lundgren, N.-G., *Högskolan i Luleå och Norbottens utveckling* (Luleå Universitet, 1992)

Svensson, Åke and Broadbent, Noel., 'Northern Studies at the University of Umea and its Influence on Northern Development', pp. 17–20 in W. Morrison (ed.), *The Role of Circumolar Universities in Northern Development* (Thunder Bay: Lakehead University Centre for Northern Studies, 1991)

Umeå Universitet, *Umeå universitet 25 ar* (Umeå Universitet, 1995)

Wiberg, Ulf (ed.), *Botnianätverket. En strategisk allians mellan nordliga kunskapsstäder* (Umeå: CERUM, 1993)

United States of America

Cole, T., *The Cornerstone on College Hill* (University of Alaska Press, 1994)

Gillespie, Judith, 'The Roles of Higher Educational Institutions in Educating Regions', pp. 293–99 in W. Morrison (ed.) *The Role of Circumpolar Universities in Northern Development* (Thunder Bay: Lakehead University Centre for Northern Studies, 1991)

Harcharek, Robert, 'Higher Education in Arctic Alaska: An Evaluation of Two Approaches', pp. 309–15 in W. Morrison (ed.), *The Role of Circumpolar Universities in Northern Development* (Thunder Bay: Lakehead University Centre for Northern Studies, 1991)

Kresge, D., Morehouse, T., and Rogers, G., *Issues in Alaskan Development* (University of Washington Press, 1997)

Lich, Glen, 'The Role of the University in Regional Development: Two Models – Wisconsin and Texas', pp. 91–5 in W. Morrison (ed.), *The Role of Circumpolar Universities in Northern Development* (Thunder Bay: Lakehead University Centre for Northern Studies, 1991)

O'Dowd, Donald, 'The University of Alaska: A Northern University', pp. 36–40 in W. Morrison (ed.), *The Role of Circumpolar Universities in Northern Development* (Thunder Bay: Lakehead University Centre for Northern Studies, 1991)

Wadlow, Joan, 'Current Issues of Higher Education in the Circumpolar North – The United States and Alaska', pp. 7–11 in S. McLarnon and D. Nord (eds), *Northern Parallels* (Prince George: UNBC Press, 1997)

Index